At Home
and At Sea

An American Navy Couple
During World War II

Royce A. Singleton, Jr.

At Home and At Sea
An American Navy Couple During World War II

Copyright © 2024 by Royce A. Singleton, Jr.

ISBNs:
979-8-9899101-0-6 (paperback)
979-8-9899101-2-0(hardcover)
979-8-9899101-1-3 (ebook)

For Becky and Royce

CONTENTS

PREFACE

MY FATHER, ROYCE, served as a Navy fighter pilot during World War II, but I knew very little about his or my mother Becky's experiences during the war until they were in their 70s. It was then that a member of Royce's squadron, John F. Smith, wrote a memoir, *Hellcats over the Philippine Deep*, chronicling his year in the Pacific War. From Smith's book, I learned for the first time about the battles in which Royce fought and how his tour of duty ended after 13 months at sea.

About the same time that Smith's book appeared, my parents passed down to their children over 200 letters they had written to one another during the war. What is special about this collection is that it contains both my father's letters from his time at sea and those from my mother on the home front. Due to space limitations, transfer, and combat conditions, letters from home often were destroyed and were much less likely to survive than those written by men in combat. Yet Royce managed to save Becky's letters, reading them again and again while at sea and then bringing them home for safekeeping. Through Becky's letters, I learned about her experience of building a life and sustaining a marriage in a time of war.

Reading my parents' letters inspired me to tell their story. I realized the larger significance of their experiences—what they revealed about young couples separated during the war—and the power of letters to deepen our understanding. As Lisa Grunwald and Stephen Adler stated in *Letters of the Century*, letters lend immediacy to a story: "Letters are what history sounds like when it is still part of everyday life." The loss of lives in Pacific War battles resonates more deeply by reading Royce's report to Becky that a member of the air group—and one of their closest friends—was shot down by antiaircraft fire. Letters also resonate with history because of their intimacy. By sharing their innermost thoughts and feelings, Becky and Royce gave a candid account of how they confronted the stress of the war years.

By the time Royce came home, Becky had written 140 letters, amounting to 450 pages in her small, elegant handwriting. Not only are her letters often quite long, reaching 5–10 pages, they also are repetitive at times and refer to over a hundred names of friends and relatives, whose connections to Becky and Royce are frequently unclear. In telling their story, I therefore have used mostly excerpts and abridgements, which I have integrated into the narrative. To further improve readability, I also made minor changes in punctuation and corrected a few misspellings. I made no changes, however, in the language or words in the letters. Their language reflects the times, even though certain word choices (e.g., "Japs") may be offensive to modern sensibilities.

As I pieced together this story, time and again I regretted that I had not asked my parents about their experiences during the war. Until I read John Smith's memoir and other accounts of Royce's time at sea, I did not know the location or meaning of the battles at Tarawa, Kwajalein, Eniwetok, Saipan, Guam, and Leyte Gulf. I could not tell the difference between a fleet carrier and an escort carrier, what kind of plane my father flew, or how his ship, air group, and squadron contributed to the westward advance across the Pacific.

Likewise, I had no idea what life was like for my mother during the war until I read her letters. I did not know that she worked at a full-time office job during her pregnancy until, in accord with the social norms of the time, she resigned several weeks before her due date. Nor did I comprehend the sacrifices wrought by rationing and other effects of war mobilization on the home front. Although as a social psychologist I understand the importance of social support, especially in times of stress, I knew very little about my mother's network of family and friends and how they supported her and other brides while their husbands faced the dangers of combat. During my young adult years, I rarely had friends who died. And so, I did not fathom the impact of losing so many friends and relatives—in the prime of their lives—or the anxiety evoked by these constant reminders that you or your husband was in peril.

Had I asked my parents about the war, I don't know what they might have told me. Thankfully, from their letters, I learned the inspiring story of this exceptional time in their lives.

-1-

INTRODUCTION

ROYCE WAS SERVING in the Pacific as a Navy fighter pilot aboard an escort carrier when he wrote to his wife Becky on October 11, 1944. He told her not to expect to receive mail "for some time after this letter," but not to worry. They were "ready to go" and "hope to get home after this." Censorship of letters home prevented him from revealing where he was. "This," as Becky eventually learned, turned out to be the Battle of Leyte Gulf. Two weeks later, she wrote:

> For the past couple of weeks, the news out there has been prominent in all the papers. We have read of the softening up of the Philippines by carrier planes . . . and of the successful landing on Leyte Island [by General Douglas MacArthur] and today we have listened all day to the reports of the engagement between our fleet and the Jap fleet. They say the Japs have suffered a crushing defeat. We lost our aircraft carrier, The Princeton, and suffered damage to other carriers and destroyers. I hope VF-60 [Royce's squadron] came out ok and that now you can come home.

My parents, Royce and Becky, were among the Greatest Generation. They came of age during World War II. Royce was 20 years old when he enlisted in the Navy in January 1942, one month after the Japanese attack on the U.S. naval base at Pearl Harbor. Becky was 21 when she and Royce were married in March 1943. Before the end of that year, Royce was aboard ship, taking part in the American offensive in the central Pacific. When he wrote Becky in October 1944, he was in his 12th month at sea, well beyond the time when pilots ordinarily returned to the States from combat duty. While he was away, Becky was living at home in Oklahoma City, pregnant, working, managing the finances, preparing for childbirth, then becoming a mother, all while planning for a future with her newlywed husband.

This book is Becky and Royce's story about living through the war. They would have celebrated their centennial birthdays if they were still alive today. Like their quickly vanishing generation, they are no longer here to tell us what it was like aboard ship, in combat, and on the home front. To tell their story, we also cannot rely on oral accounts of their experiences imparted to their children. When the children were growing up, Becky and Royce never, as far as anyone can recall, talked about the war years. In their youthful self-absorption, the children did not think to ask what it was like during World War II. And, both parents, especially Royce, may consciously have chosen to let the past remain in the past. Veterans of WWII and other wars, the evidence shows, often are reluctant to talk about their combat experiences.

Fortunately, Becky and Royce left a firsthand account of their untold story in the form of personal correspondence—nearly all the letters they wrote to one another during the war. Becky wrote to Royce about every 2–3 days. Her letters are filled with details of her daily life—preparing and eating meals, getting together with friends and family, seeing movies, shopping for gifts, visiting the doctor, caring for the baby—and reminiscences of their times together. Becky's letters also reveal differences between that period and the present day—differences that point to historical changes in women's work, marital egalitarianism, birthing, and postnatal care.

Royce wrote less often, especially in his first few months at sea, penning about half as many letters as Becky. Because of restrictions on what active-duty military men could write, his letters reveal very little about life aboard ship, let alone his combat experience, and rather more about his love and longing for Becky. Royce's letters also tended to be relatively short. His longest letters were in response to what Becky had written. Many of his missives were less than two full pages, some written hastily when he learned the mail was going out and wanted to let Becky know he was safe and sound.

From the time Royce's ship departed from San Diego on October 19, 1943, until it returned, the letters form the core of Becky's story on the home front. To describe Royce's combat experiences, I relied on flight logs, action reports, an oral history of his ship and air group, and especially two memoirs written by shipmates: Green Peyton's *5,000 Miles towards Tokyo* and John F. Smith's *Hellcats over the Philippine Deep*. Green Peyton Wertenbaker (whose pen name was Green Peyton) served as the air combat information officer of Royce's fighter squadron for eight months, from the summer of 1943 until he was transferred in February 1944. Fighter pilot John Smith joined the squadron in late December 1943. Wertenbaker roomed with Royce aboard ship; he and his wife became friends of Royce and Becky before the ship sailed. Smith flew with Royce as his wingman; Royce wrote the Foreword to Smith's book. Both books contain several accounts of Royce's activities aboard ship and in the air.

Becky and Royce's letters evoke a passionate love story of a couple in their first years of marriage, living apart and maintaining a relationship under the uncertainty and stress of the war. Their letters are deeply romantic—from reminiscences about their times together to eloquent expressions of endearment. As time passed, these expressions became longer and more frequent. Royce conveyed an extraordinary depth of feeling despite knowing that every letter he wrote was stamped and initialed by a censor, one of his fellow officers aboard the ship. On the other hand, having spent only six months together before they were separated, Becky and Royce were still adjusting to one another as marital partners, and their letters reveal areas of tension and conflict.

The Pacific War as Context

Royce and Becky's experiences are placed in social and historical context. A primary context is the Pacific War, which serves as the integrative narrative for the book. After Pearl Harbor, it took almost two years for the United States to build up the Pacific fleet and develop a mobile service force capable of keeping the fleet supplied with the food, fuel, ammunition, and countless other items necessary to wage war far from its home bases. The massive buildup made it possible to launch the Central Pacific offensive, aimed at securing bases in the Gilbert, Marshall, Caroline, and Mariana Islands. Royce's time at sea marks the course of this offensive, from the first amphibious landing at Tarawa to General Douglas MacArthur's return to the Philippines at Leyte Island. Whether from Royce's direct involvement or Becky following the news, these battles shaped their experiences of World War II. The letters suggest that for both of them—as for many other Americans—there were two wars: one in the Pacific and the other in Europe. Caught up in the Pacific battles, Becky and Royce seldom mentioned news about the European theater.

Most of the popular films and books on World War II are about the war in Europe. Even films that have been made about the Pacific War— about Pearl Harbor (December 1941), Midway (June 1942), Guadalcanal (August 1942–February 1943), and Iwo Jima (February 1945)—leave two years largely unaccounted for. This gap includes Royce's entire tour of duty and all the battles in the Central Pacific offensive that helped turn the tide of war overwhelmingly in favor of the Allies. Historian Evan Thomas described the culmination of this offensive—the Battle of Leyte Gulf, where U.S. and Japanese forces engaged in the largest naval battle ever fought—as the "death knell" for the Imperial Japanese Navy. Yet, he said, "most Americans do not know when the Battle . . . was fought, where Leyte Gulf is, or even how it's pronounced (lay-TEE)."[1]

In addition, with few exceptions, histories of the Pacific War have overlooked the escort carriers, invariably focusing on the exploits of the big, fast fleet carriers, whose pilots engaged in daring raids on Japanese strongholds and air combat with Japanese pilots. Condescendingly called "baby flattop" or "jeep" carriers, escort carriers, Samuel Eliot Morison wrote, "were regarded by many an old salt as interlopers in the Navy—something like reservists, to be tolerated during the war but not taken too seriously."[2] But while the fleet carriers won the glory, the "jeeps" played a vital role, supporting every amphibious landing and performing endless hours of antisubmarine and combat air patrols. This book is one of only a few that give the pilots who flew off the escort carriers the attention and credit they deserve.

Family as Context

While Royce was at sea, Becky was living in the home city of her parents and in-laws. Family connections were central to her experience and are mentioned repeatedly in her and Royce's letters. A brief profile of their respective families will introduce the parents and siblings and illuminate how their upbringing may have shaped their wartime experience.

Both Royce and Becky were born in Oklahoma in 1921. Consequently, their early childhood years were spent during a period of national promise and prosperity, but before they reached adolescence, the onset of the Great Depression had devastated the American economy. A third of the nation's banks failed; unemployment reached an all-time high of 25 percent; and severe deflation caused many farmers, businesses, and homeowners to default on mortgages. Almost everyone was affected. Oklahoma, famously portrayed in John Steinbeck's novel *The Grapes of Wrath,* was especially hard hit, as drought conditions compounded the harm of the financial collapse. Becky and Royce's worldviews, aspirations, and life choices were profoundly affected by the successes and struggles of their parents during these difficult times.

All four of Becky and Royce's parents migrated to Oklahoma in the first two decades of the 20th century. As the population grew rapidly after Oklahoma statehood in 1907, they became part of the middle-class white-collar workers, professionals, and small business entrepreneurs who established themselves in the burgeoning towns and cities.

Royce's father, Sandy Henry ("Buddy"), grew up on a tobacco farm in Brandenburg, Kentucky and graduated from Western Kentucky State Normal School (now known as Western Kentucky University) in 1917. He moved to Oklahoma in August 1918 after he was hired for a teaching job in Loco which he had learned about while visiting his sister in nearby Duncan. In Loco, Sandy met and married fellow teacher Gussie Reba Whitten.

Royce Alan Singleton was the second of Sandy and Gussie's four children. Born March 31, 1921, he was thirteen months younger than brother Robert (Bob), four years older than sister Mina, and seven years older than Sandy Hardin (affectionately known as Dump). Royce grew up mostly in Duncan, Oklahoma, located 81 miles southwest of Oklahoma City and 44 miles north of the Oklahoma-Texas State line. Despite their age difference, he and Bob were in the same grade throughout school, and both graduated from Duncan High School in 1938.

While teaching and beginning to raise a family, Sandy took correspondence courses in law. He was admitted to the Oklahoma Bar in June of 1924 and began to practice law, first in Loco and then in Duncan. As Sandy was earning his law degree and starting his practice, he took on extra jobs and he and Gussie ran the Loco post office to make ends meet. But as his law practice grew in the 1930s, the family prospered. That is not to say that they did not feel the effects of the Great Depression. Clients often could not pay cash, so Sandy sold his legal services for a cord of wood, a cow, a hog, or whatever people could afford.

In 1931, the family—now with four young children—traded their house in Duncan for a house, barn, and 20 acres of land two miles north of Duncan. Sandy installed a chicken house and planted fruit trees, alfalfa and hay, and a garden covering over an acre. The farm was a source of income; for example, Gussie had a weekly delivery route for eggs and butter. Most importantly, it made the family self-sufficient.

In 1932, Sandy was elected as a Democrat to the Oklahoma House of Representatives, where he served three consecutive terms, from 1933 to 1938. By the end of his third term, he decided not to seek reelection. He campaigned for Leon Phillips in his run for governor, and when Phillips won, he appointed Sandy Chairman of the State Highway Commission, a position he held from 1939 to 1942. Chairing the highway commission prompted a family move from Duncan to Oklahoma City.

Becky's father, Herbert Spencer (H.S.) Caldwell, was born in Pittsburgh and grew up in New Wilmington, Pennsylvania. His boyhood ambition was to be a doctor, but he followed in his father's footsteps in becoming a druggist. H.S. joined his father in the drug business in Pennsylvania; then, after his father's death, he moved to Oklahoma City. He opened a drugstore in the city in 1913 and married Beulah May Wakefield in 1917. Until she married, at the relatively late age of 28, Beulah worked as a stenographer and typist. Rebecca Rachel (Becky) Caldwell, the first of H.S. and Beulah's two children, was born in Oklahoma City on November 19, 1921. She was 2½ years older than sister Virginia May.

H.S. and Beulah were very civic-minded. H.S. was active in Republican politics. He served one term, from 1925 to 1927, in the Oklahoma House of Representatives and ran for U.S. Congress in 1944. He also frequently wrote newspaper articles and letters on political issues. He held leadership positions in local, state, and national druggist associations, including president of the National Association of Retail Druggists.

Beulah, for her part, was a Democrat and served as a precinct clerk or judge in more than one state election. She was an active volunteer in

women's civic organizations: She served as president of the women's auxil-
iaries of the local and state pharmaceutical organizations, belonged to the
Oklahoma Hospitality Club, and held various offices including president
in the United Daughters of the Confederacy's Oklahoma City chapter.[3]

By contrast to the Singletons, the Depression was hard on the Caldwells.
H.S. laid off staff and moved the store from its corner location in 1935, and
the family purchased a smaller home. He personally opened and closed
the store six days a week.

Royce and Becky both came from stable families: Through grade school,
they each lived in the same house in the same small town or neighborhood.
Their fathers were public figures to varying degrees, their mothers strong,
capable women. By virtue of their fathers' professions and political activity,
their families were well integrated into the community. Neither family was
very religious or spiritual. Although Sandy could cite many a Bible verse,
he never attended church; nor did H.S. Beulah and the girls occasionally
attended services at different Protestant churches. And for a while in the
1930s, Becky was a member of the First Christian Church.

Although representing different political parties, both Sandy and H.S.
were fiscal conservatives who valued economic self-sufficiency. During the
Great Depression, as banks were closing, businesses failing, and millions
were out of work, the Singletons and the Caldwells found ways to adapt
and thrive. Royce and Becky learned self-reliance and independence from
their parents' example; they developed a strong work ethic and grew into
resourceful, resilient young adults. Their parents also valued education.
All four finished high school and one graduated from college, which was
highly unusual in their time.[4] So, it is not surprising that Royce and Becky
were good students—smart, conscientious, and hardworking.

In high school, Royce demonstrated a high level of self-confidence
and the ability to meet challenges, qualities that would serve him well as
a fighter pilot. He loved to read and did well academically.[5] He was also a
member of the debate team and acted in school plays. Becky also did well

in a college preparatory curriculum at Central High School in Oklahoma City. Like Royce, she was well integrated into the high school culture. At Central, she was a member of the Red Skirts Pep Club. During her senior year, she was one of a select group in her sales class who were given part-time work as "salesgirls" at Brown's, at that time the premier upscale department store in Oklahoma City.

After graduating from high school in 1938, Royce and his brother Bob remained in lockstep in continuing their education. They both attended Duncan Junior College in the fall. Then, when the family moved to Oklahoma City in January 1939, they enrolled at Central State College (now the University of Central Oklahoma) in Edmond. While at CSC, Royce made the honor roll, was a class officer, and belonged to various student organizations. As in high school, he pursued an interest in drama, acting in several plays. There is no evidence, however, that he wanted to pursue a career in theater. Royce was set on going to law school.

After Becky graduated from high school in 1940, she attended Southwestern University in Georgetown, Texas, for one year. There, she completed courses in English, history, and math as well as two semesters of business administration and one semester each of Bible, speech, and education. She also had an active social life as a freshman cheerleader and member of Alpha Delta Pi sorority and other student organizations. During her year at Southwestern, Becky lived with the family of a friend. She relished everything about her first year of college and wished she could have continued, but she lacked the financial wherewithal to return the following year.

Royce and Becky met while they were both working for the Oklahoma Natural Gas (ONG) Company in Oklahoma City. Royce began working at ONG in the summer following his second year at Central State. He was employed there full-time from June 1941 to January 1942. Becky started working at ONG in June 1941. We know almost nothing about their courtship. Neither of them ever said it was "love at first sight," but it is easy to imagine a strong initial attraction when a handsome, gregarious young man meets an attractive, outgoing young woman. We do know that for seven months, Royce and Becky saw one another daily at work, and this developed into a romantic relationship.

-2-

GOING TO WAR:
December 1941–October 1943

AS ROYCE WAS finishing his third year in college and Becky her first, the United States was moving closer and closer toward war. Isolationism was the dominant American ideology during the 1920s and 1930s. Consequently, from the beginning of the war in Europe, the United States maintained an official policy of neutrality, and most Americans supported it. In May 1940, only 7 percent of respondents said "yes" to a Gallup poll asking whether the United States should declare war on Germany. Then came the fall of Belgium, Holland, and France and the bombing of Britain in the summer and fall of 1940. Public opinion quickly changed, as a majority of Americans said it was more important for the United States to help England win than to keep out of the war.[6]

Meanwhile, President Franklin D. Roosevelt and the U.S. Congress began to take actions that departed from neutrality and set the stage for American participation in World War II. In September 1940, Roosevelt brokered a deal that sent 50 old U.S. Navy destroyers to Britain, and Congress instituted the first peacetime draft in U.S. history. In March 1941, Congress passed the Lend-Lease policy, which allowed the United

States to send food, oil, and materiel to Britain and other Allied forces. In fall 1941, Roosevelt issued a "shoot-on-sight" order for U.S. ships and planes to attack any Italian or German submarines entering American waters. On the other side of the globe, as Japan became a growing threat to the United States, Roosevelt, with Congressional support, imposed embargoes on iron, steel, oil, and other exports to Japan, and then froze all Japanese assets in U.S. banks.

Like most Americans, especially those coming of age during these years, the Singletons were almost certainly aware of these developments. By summer of 1941, Bob had reached the age of 21, which made him eligible for the draft.[7] Anticipating that the United States would be drawn into the war and expecting to be drafted, he dropped out of school. Royce, one year short of earning his degree, with a major in history, also dropped out. The decision to defer his education that fall was prescient—for on December 7, 1941, the Japanese attacked the U.S. Naval base at Pearl Harbor in Hawaii, an event that would irrevocably alter the lives of an entire generation. A day later, after a speech in which President Roosevelt famously described the previous day as "a date which will live in infamy," Congress formally declared war against Japan. Three days later, Japan's allies Germany and Italy declared war on the United States, bringing the United States fully into World War II. Thousands of men enlisted in the military in the first few months after the Japanese attack. Bob decided to enlist in the Naval Air Corps, and Royce again followed suit. Both were inducted in January 1942.

When the United States suddenly entered the war, Royce and Becky were still exploring possible life directions. Each of them was living at home and, at least in part, dependent upon parental support. But the war disrupted their lives. Royce left home for good when he entered flight training. Becky continued to work full-time at ONG while living at home with her parents. Separated for nearly all of 1942, they were able to maintain their relationship, apparently through letters, phone calls, and visits.

Flight Training

Once inducted, Royce spent the next year undergoing naval aviation training. Flying aircraft in combat requires stamina, skill, and intelligence. To select men most likely to have the physical and mental ability to successfully pass flight training, the Navy limited candidates to those between 18 and 26 years old who had completed at least two years of college. They also had to be unmarried and to pass a physical examination. Key requirements included a minimum of 20/20 vision and normal color perception.

Training consisted of four stages: pre-flight, primary, intermediate, and advanced. Royce did his pre-flight training from February through April 1942 in Grand Prairie, Texas, just west of Dallas. During this stage, as Navy historian Barrett Tillman described, there was "no actual flying but intense preparation," including class work and "rigorous physical conditioning with constant emphasis on teamwork." Of particular importance for aviators was swimming ability: "those who failed to learn, failed to fly; it was literally sink or swim."[8]

After completing pre-flight school, Royce was sent to Corpus Christi, Texas, for six months of primary and intermediate flight training. The primary stage involved both ground- or classroom-based instruction and experience in the air. Ground school covered theoretical topics like the science of aerodynamics and how to think in three dimensions as well as practical aspects of flying: taxiing, takeoffs, climbs, turns, and so forth. Before flying solo, students in primary training flew in biplanes with tandem seating and open cockpits; the instructor sat up front and communicated with a student through a speaking tube. Students in the intermediate stage progressed to superior aircraft and more sophisticated flying such as radio instrument and night navigation. The attrition rate from the primary through the intermediate stage was about 30 percent.[9] Those who completed intermediate training won their wings and commission. On November 6, 1942, Royce was thus appointed an Ensign in the United States Naval Reserve (USNR) and designated a Naval aviator.

From Corpus Christi, Royce had a short leave before undergoing almost two months of advanced, or operational, training—five weeks at Miami Naval Air Station (NAS), followed by two weeks at the Carrier Qualification Training Unit (CQTU), NAS Glenview in Illinois, and another week at NAS Norfolk, Virginia. At this stage, pilots were assigned the fleet-type aircraft they ultimately would fly, such as fighter, dive-bomber, torpedo, or patrol planes. Fighters were more exciting, as they involved air-to-air combat and were the fastest and easiest planes to control and maneuver. Many pilots, including Royce, chose fighters, but not all pilots were assigned the type of aircraft they preferred. The most important skills carrier pilots learned in operational training were takeoffs and landings on an aircraft carrier, which took place at Glenview, a Chicago suburb on Lake Michigan. To make up for the shortage of carriers early in the war, the Navy acquired two Great Lakes excursion vessels and modified them with flight decks.[10] To become carrier-qualified, Royce, like all pilots, was required to complete a minimum of eight successful takeoffs and landings.

Throughout his flight training, Royce had very little time off, and it is doubtful that he saw much of Becky. She must have visited him at least once, because in a letter written while Royce was at sea, she mentioned becoming engaged: She and Kathleen Sims, the girlfriend of Royce's brother Bob, each received an engagement ring in Corpus Christi in August 1942. Royce's next stop was NAS Seattle, Washington, where he was assigned to a composite squadron comprised of fighter and bomber aircraft. He had almost a month of leave before reporting for duty in February, and he spent this time in Oklahoma City visiting with Becky and his family.

In late January 1943, Bob and Kathleen were married. A newspaper announcement mentioned that Becky was one of "only three guests," aside from the bride's and groom's parents.[11] Royce did not attend the wedding, as he was on his way to Seattle. Becky and Royce had not yet set a date for their own wedding. In ordinary times, they probably would not have waited long to marry, but the war gave them pause. When the marriage rate spiked following the United States' entry into the war, a national debate ensued, played out in the popular and scholarly press, about the advisability of marrying during wartime.[12] Some marriage experts, concerned about the rush to the altar and the youth of many newlyweds, believed that hasty wartime marriages threatened the sanctity of marriage; they warned of an inevitable postwar wave of divorces. Some claimed that marriages undermined the war effort because married soldiers would be more distracted and more hesitant to sacrifice their lives for their country than those who were single.[13] On the other side, experts favoring war marriages "argued that being married gave soldiers and their wives a meaningful stake in the war effort. Soldiers, in other words, would be fighting not for abstract ideals, but for a tangible better life for their wives and future children."[14]

Concerns about marrying in haste did not exactly apply to Becky and Royce, as they had been romantically involved for more than a year. Still, a May 1944 letter from Royce to Becky indicates that he had been inclined to wait until after he returned from the war to get married, perhaps because, like many servicemen, he didn't think it was fair to Becky.[15] They may have discussed the possibility of his coming back wounded or not coming back at all. But Becky convinced him. As Royce wrote, "you helped me [overcome] those spots where my knees were growing weak. I darn near weakened after I'd called you to come to Seattle. Of course, I'm profoundly thankful that I didn't." And so, a month after Royce reported for duty in Seattle, Becky traveled there at his invitation, and on March 9, 1943, they were married.

Like so many wartime weddings, theirs was a modest affair. Royce was in his uniform and Becky wore a gray suit with a Navy flight officer's pin on her breast pocket. None of the family was able to attend; an announcement in the *Daily Oklahoman* stated that Mrs. Stephen H. Reed attended the bride and Ensign John D. Shea Jr. (a member of Royce's squadron who served with him during the war) was best man.[16]

Wedding photo, March 9, 1943

As newlyweds, Royce and Becky moved into an apartment in Seattle. It was not for long, however, because in early May Royce was transferred to NAS Astoria, Oregon. Located in the northwest corner of Oregon at the mouth of the Columbia River, Astoria is about 120 miles from Seattle. Royce and Becky, along with other married members of the squadron, found quarters in the nearby tourist town of Seaside.[17] By all accounts, the weather there was miserable, fogbound or raining much of the time. Yet, as often happens, they held a special fondness for the place that was their home during the early months of their marriage. Later, during Royce's first month at sea, Becky wrote, "I've thought many times about Seaside and how I wish we could be there now . . . fog and all."

It was during their stay in Seaside that Becky became pregnant. Like wartime marriage, the desirability of bringing a child into the world during the war was widely debated. Sociologist and marriage counselor Paul Popenoe presented the two sides of the debate in a 1942 *Ladies' Home Journal* article, in which he anchored his observations with interviews of two recent war brides.[18] One bride proposed that a child would give the husband "more to live for and look forward to" and add "to the wife's happiness during their separation." "The nation needs babies," she said. "And after all, we have to face the fact that our husbands might not return. I'd at least have his child to comfort my future years." The other bride argued that "a child shouldn't be brought up by one parent," to which Popenoe added, there were more effective ways of "ensuring the future success of the marriage" than becoming pregnant. A 1944 letter from Royce suggests that he and Becky themselves had this debate. As with marriage, Royce was reluctant to start a family during the war. "I sort of wanted to wait until after the war for children," he wrote in his letter, "but I am glad you didn't want to."

At Astoria, Royce's squadron prepared for duty aboard an escort carrier. In mid-July, the squadron was re-designated as an air group consisting of Royce's fighter squadron VF-60, with 12 F6F Hellcats, and a composite squadron VC-60 of 9 TBM Avenger torpedo bombers and 9 SBD Dauntless scout dive bombers.[19] Prior to Astoria, the fighter pilots were flying the F4F Wildcat; in Astoria, they "learned the feel of their new planes," the F6F Hellcat.[20] The Hellcat was superior to the Wildcat in many ways; most importantly, it outclassed the Japanese fighter plane, the Zero. Whereas at the beginning of the war, the Zero was faster and more maneuverable than Allied fighter planes, the Hellcat was faster, better armed, and had far superior armor to withstand enemy attacks than the Zero. The Zero's "Achilles heel," wrote Evan Thomas, was that it "did not have self-sealing fuel tanks; they tended to burn or explode when hit by even a single .50 caliber round. The Japanese did not worry as much as Westerners about pilot safety."[21]

Grumman F6F Hellcat in flight from USS *Suwannee*
(Official U.S. Navy photograph in the National Archives)

Becky returned to Oklahoma City in August, when Royce was again transferred—to Holtville, in the California desert. At Holtville, the fighter and torpedo plane pilots in the air group underwent extensive night training with flights over the Salton Sea. While there, accidents took the lives of two VF-60 pilots: One "crashed during a night strafing exercise"; the other "crashed due to hypoxia during a night high-altitude flight."[22] These incidents underscore the dangers of flying, which were ever-present for Navy pilots, not only during wartime but also flight training. When the United States ramped up aircraft production in World War II, many planes were hurriedly designed and not properly tested. In addition, there was an enormous increase in pilot training. As a result, training accidents, often fatal, were all too common.[23] Aviation personnel fatalities in the Navy in World War II totaled an estimated 12,133. Of these, 3,618 were caused by enemy action, but almost as many, 3,257, were caused by plane crashes during training operations.[24]

After completing their training at Holtville in mid-September, Air Group 60 squadrons converged at NAS Los Alamitos, just south of Los

Angeles. There, for the next month, they prepared to board the carrier USS *Suwannee,* which was undergoing repairs at Alameda Works Shipyard, across the bay from San Francisco. As they awaited its arrival, pilots qualified in carrier landings on another carrier. Squadron member John Smith reported that there was ample spare time at Los Alamitos for "partying and interacting with females of the species,"[25] which may explain why Becky took the train to Los Angeles to rejoin Royce. For a few weeks, they lived in a tourist court in nearby Long Beach, where their neighbors were VF-60 pilot John Simpson and his wife Mary Edith and VF-60 air combat information officer Green Peyton Wertenbaker[26] and his wife Barclay. We don't know exactly when, but by this time, Becky and Royce knew that a baby was on the way.

The air group was notified on October 15 to prepare to leave. The next day, Becky and Royce said their goodbyes before the pilots flew down to meet the *Suwannee* in San Diego. The planes were hoisted aboard the carrier the following day, and all personnel and equipment were on board by October 18. Taking the train from Los Angeles, Becky arrived in Oklahoma City on Tuesday, the 19th, which turned out to be the same day Royce's ship set out from San Diego. Most Navy air groups spent about six months at sea.[27] But, given the exigencies of the war, there was no timetable for their return, and Becky and Royce did not know when they would see one another again.

The War in the Pacific

When the *Suwannee* set sail, nearly two years had passed since the Japanese attack at Pearl Harbor in Honolulu, where almost the entire U.S. Pacific fleet had been moored. The attack had devastated U.S. naval sea and air power, damaging or destroying 19 ships, including 8 battleships and over 300 aircraft, and killing 2,403 servicemen and civilians. But the losses did not end there. Before the sun set in the Far East on that infamous day, the Japanese also raided U.S. air bases in the Philippines. Within the next few days, they invaded two other U.S. territories, Guam and Wake Island, as well as British-controlled Hong Kong, Malaya, and Burma (present-day Myanmar). It was all part of a Japanese plan to conquer resource-rich Southeast Asia and to establish a defensive perimeter in the southwestern and central Pacific.

Japan's war plan was intended to resolve the conflict between its expansionism and its dependence on the United States and other nations for oil, scrap iron, and other raw materials to sustain its economy. By banning the export of strategic materials to Japan in July 1941, the United States hoped to deter Japan's expansion in China and its invasion of Indochina. When the British and Dutch followed with their own embargoes, Japan faced a dilemma: Withdraw from China and renounce its planned conquests or go to war with the United States, Great Britain, and the Netherlands to gain access to oil and other resources for further conquests.[28]

The Japanese assumed that the war in Europe would make Great Britain a negligible factor in the Far East and that the United States would be their primary adversary. Therefore, they sought to destroy much of the U.S. Pacific fleet at Pearl Harbor and to establish a line of military bases across the Pacific that would prevent the United States from mounting any noteworthy offensive in less than 18 months to 2 years.[29] An American counterattack would result in a murderous prolonged war; and in such a war, the Japanese further assumed, Americans would be unwilling to pay the price of total victory and would accept a political settlement.[30]

Due to the element of surprise and to strong, well-organized, and well-trained forces, the Japanese succeeded beyond expectations in all their initial offensives. But as history would show, the attack at Pearl Harbor erred tactically and politically. The destruction of warships was not nearly as crippling as it could have been. Salvage work began immediately. Only three of the eight torpedoed battleships were beyond repair; three battleships, three cruisers, and two destroyers were back in service by February. The attack did very little damage to the base's infrastructure. Indeed, the salvage operation was possible because the Japanese planes ignored the dry docks in the harbor as well as warehouses, machine shops, and oil storage depots. Fortuitously, all three American aircraft carriers stationed at Pearl Harbor were at sea on the day of the attack. Prior to World War II, navies were built for decisive long-range gun duels between giant battleships; however, the new war at sea would be fought predominantly by aircraft flying from aircraft carriers.

Finally, the attack united the American people. Polls in 1941 showed that Americans supported economic sanctions against Japan but were hesitant to provoke war.[31] In a Gallup poll conducted days after the attack on Pearl Harbor, 97 percent of respondents approved of Congress's declaration of war, even though they realistically foresaw a war against Japan as long and difficult.[32] Outraged "at what was perceived as a dastardly sneak attack," Americans were, contrary to Japanese expectations, "determined to defeat Japan at any cost." As naval historian Nathan Miller concluded, "This was the true importance of Pearl Harbor": The way in which the Japanese had begun the war forfeited their hope of a negotiated settlement after a series of deadly battles.[33]

Through April 1942, Japanese expansion continued as they gained control of the Western Pacific and established a defensive perimeter of island bases stretching on the southern edge from New Guinea to the Solomon Islands, and from there, on the eastern edge, through the Gilbert and Marshall Islands to Wake Island. The United States was incapable of launching a major counteroffensive; that would have to await the buildup of the Pacific fleet. The only practicable offensives were hit-and-run raids from aircraft carriers.

Of these early strikes, the boldest was a retaliatory raid on Tokyo made by 16 Army B-25 bombers on April 18. The planes were launched from a carrier, but the deck was too short for landing. So, the plan was to bomb Tokyo, 650 miles away, and then fly another 1100 miles to friendly airbases in China. All but one of the five-man aircrews bailed out or crash-landed in coastal China after running out of fuel, although 69 of the 80 crew members escaped capture or death and reached safety with the help of the Chinese.[34] Named after commanding officer Lieutenant Colonel James Doolittle, the Doolittle Raid did minor damage but was consequential in other ways. It boosted American morale at a low point in the war, and it led Japan to commit hundreds of planes for homeland defense.[35]

The Japanese overextended themselves in May and June 1942 when they attempted to expand their perimeter southeast to Port Moresby in New Guinea and northeast to Midway. Securing Port Moresby would put Japanese bombers within range of Australia and cutoff the Allied line of communications across the South Pacific. By attacking Midway, the Japanese hoped, no less, to lure the U.S. Pacific Fleet into a decisive battle that would hasten a negotiated peace. Instead, the two offensives resulted in strategic defeats for the Japanese that halted their advance and turned the tide of the war.

In the Battle of the Coral Sea (south of Port Moresby, New Guinea), May 4–8, 1942, the Japanese could claim a limited tactical victory in terms of ships sunk, which included a U.S. carrier. On the other hand, they lost a light carrier, suffered damage to one carrier and heavy plane losses to another, eliminating both from the Midway operation. Furthermore, they abandoned their prime objective when they had inadequate air cover for the Port Moresby invasion.

At Midway, the battle was "decisive," but not in Japan's favor. On June 4, U.S. dive bombers struck and sank three carriers as the Japanese were refueling and rearming their planes, and then returned to sink a fourth carrier. In addition to the carriers, the Japanese lost a cruiser, over 250 aircraft, and suffered 2,500 casualties, including 200 of their most experienced pilots. By comparison, the United States lost one carrier, a destroyer, 145 aircraft, and suffered 307 casualties.[36] Two days later, Japanese forces retreated.

The Pacific Theater

CHINA

JAPAN

RYUKYU ISLANDS

Okinawa

FORMOSA

China Sea

PHILIPPINE ISLANDS

BORNEO

DUTCH EAST INDIES

Philippine Sea

BONIN ISLANDS

Iwo Jima

PALAU ISLANDS

Peleliu

Halmahera

Hollandia

NEW GUINEA

Port Moresby

AUSTRALIA

MARIANA ISLANDS

Saipan

Guam

CAROLINE ISLANDS

Truk

ADMIRALTY ISLANDS

Manus

Rabaul

SOLOMON ISLANDS

Guadalcanal

Espiritu Santo

Coral Sea

NEW HEBRIDES

WAKE

Eniwetok

MARSHALL ISLANDS

Kwajalein

Majuro

GILBERT ISLANDS

Makin

Tarawa

MIDWAY

Pacific Ocean

HAWAIIAN ISLANDS

The Battle of Midway ended the "Japanese Offensive," the first of three phases in the Pacific War. For the first six months after Pearl Harbor, Japanese naval forces spread destruction and fear across the Pacific. At Midway, the United States derailed their advance and obtained near parity in naval air forces. As Barrett Tillman stated, the battle "had enormous strategic importance." Never again would the Japanese launch a major offensive in the Pacific. The United States had gained the strategic initiative.[37]

For the next 18 months, Allied operations were constrained by a lack of resources and a commitment to a "Europe First" strategy, aimed at defeating Germany before turning attention fully to Japan. The main objective of the Joint Chiefs of Staff was to hold Japan in check. Chief of Naval Operations Admiral Ernest J. King believed, however, that it was important to keep the Japanese off-balance with limited offensives that would prevent them from strengthening their defensive position. At first, this took the form of strikes such as the Doolittle Raid. But King was emboldened by Midway. The "rude shock" of the battle, he wrote later, provided a "good chance to get the enemy off balance and *keep* him off balance."[38] Therefore, in July, he gained approval for an operation that marked the beginning of the second phase of the War in the Pacific. The operation began at Guadalcanal in the Solomon Islands; the new phase constituted an "offensive-defensive" strategy.

On August 7, 1942, U.S. Marines landed at Guadalcanal, where the Japanese were building a new airfield. The Guadalcanal Campaign was part of a larger operation intended to move through the Solomon Islands to the Japanese stronghold at Rabaul. Bitterly contested, it became a six-month battle of attrition that entailed "seven major naval engagements, at least ten pitched land battles, and innumerable forays, bombardments and skirmishes."[39] By the time the Japanese evacuated the island in February 1943, both sides had suffered heavy losses. The losses on the material side were roughly even, with each side losing over 600 aircraft and 24 combatant ships. But the number of Japanese lives lost were far greater, as an estimated

24,000 Japanese compared to 1,600 American ground troops were killed in battle or died from disease.[40] During this period, the United States also lost two carriers, leaving them with only two fleet carriers in the Pacific, which largely explains their slow progress for the next several months.[41]

As the United States mobilized for the next phase of the war, limited offensives continued. Forces re-captured two islands in the Aleutians (jutting out from the Alaska Peninsula), which the Japanese had taken in 1942, and advanced in the Solomons from the Russell Islands to New Georgia to Vella Lavella to Bougainville. Finally, in late fall 1943—when Royce and his air group embarked on the *Suwannee* from San Diego—the Pacific Theater was supplied with "sufficient ships, planes, ground forces, and supporting equipment" to begin a thrust across the central Pacific to Japan's doorstep.[42]

-3-

GETTING UNDERWAY:
October–November 1943

A S THE *SUWANNEE* cast off from San Diego, it was joined
by two other carriers, the *Sangamon* and *Chenango,* and three
destroyers, whose main purpose was to protect the carriers against
submarine and air attack. Together, these ships made up Carrier Division
22 (CarDiv 22). The three escort carriers were commissioned in the first
year of the war, when there was an urgent need to replenish the U.S. fleet.
They were converted oilers, which could be built quickly; it took about six
months in 1942 to construct the *Suwannee* with the hull from a Standard
Oil tanker.

The U.S. Navy operated two other types of aircraft carriers: fleet carriers
and light carriers. Fleet carriers (designated "CV") sailed with the Navy's
main fleet; varying in length from about 800–888 feet and embarking
90–100 planes, they were the largest, fastest, and most heavily armed
carriers. Light carriers (designated "CVL") were converted cruisers that
had the speed of the fleet carriers but were smaller at around 600 feet and
embarked a third as many planes. They were less seaworthy than either
the fleet or escort carriers, and relatively few light carriers were launched
during the war.

Escort carriers (designated "CVE") were smaller and slower than the fleet carriers. Their thin skins and single engine rooms made them more vulnerable to torpedo attack, and they possessed inadequate antiaircraft armament. As a result, their crews sarcastically referred to their CVE classification as standing for "Combustible, Vulnerable, and Expendable." On the other hand, escort carriers were quite versatile, perhaps giving a less derogatory meaning to their "jeep carrier" nickname. First deployed in the Atlantic in 1943, CVEs were used primarily for antisubmarine defense against German U-boats. In the Pacific, they continued to provide antisubmarine protection, but also conducted combat air patrols, ferried aircraft from one location to another, and, most importantly, furnished air support for convoys and for amphibious landings.

USS *Suwannee*, tied to a mooring buoy in the New Hebrides. Her two elevators are lowered to her hangar deck. (Official U.S. Navy photograph. Posted at NavSource Online: Escort Carrier Photo Archive. URL: https://www.navsource.org/archives/03/027.htm.)

The escort carriers varied in size. The largest were converted oilers, known as the *Sangamon* class, which consisted of the three carriers in

CarDiv 22 plus a fourth carrier, the *Santee*, still operating in the Atlantic. Only slightly smaller than a CVL, the *Sangamons* had a flight deck of 503 feet by 105 feet and an overall length of 553 feet. They may have appeared small next to a fleet carrier. But they were not small ships: they carried a crew of 120 officers and 960 enlisted men. Being lower to the water, the *Sangamons* operated better under challenging sea conditions than other early-war escort carriers. And being larger in size, they could embark more planes (30 or so); were more apt to carry air groups consisting of fighters, bombers, and torpedo planes; and had decks long enough to permit the operation of F6F Hellcat fighters.[43] As ex-oilers, they also had the equipment to fuel other ships and a large fuel capacity capable of keeping the ship and its escorting destroyers operating for several weeks.[44]

Below the flight deck on the *Sangamon* carriers was the gallery deck, location of the combat information center and ready room where pilots gathered for pre-flight instructions; two decks lower was the hangar deck, where planes were parked when not in operation. On the starboard (right) side of the flight deck was an island superstructure; the ship was piloted from atop the island on the bridge. Two elevators brought planes back and forth between the hangar and flight decks. The forward elevator was abreast the island; the rear elevator was about two-thirds of the way back on the flight deck.

All aircraft carriers, regardless of type, had a dual organization: a regular crew and an air group. The regular crew ran the ship and supported the air group. The air group maintained and flew the planes. The air groups were designated with numbers. Air Group 60, consisting of two squadrons, VF-60 (a fighter squadron) and VC-60 (a composite squadron of torpedo bombers and dive bombers), flew from the *Suwannee*. With the same complement of planes, Air Group 37 was on the *Sangamon* and Air Group 35 on the *Chenango*.

When Air Group 60 left San Diego, they did not know exactly where they were going or what sort of action they would see. With few exceptions, pilots and crew members were never informed about their next mission until it was fast approaching. They assumed their first port would be Hawaii, but it quickly became clear that they were headed south, not west. In his first letter to Becky after the cruise began, on October 28, Royce wrote, "Now that I have talked to a member of the Censor Board, I think I can tell you this much. We are not going where we thought but a bit farther on." Writing again on November 2, he added, "I wish I could tell you where we are going but I can't. I don't know either as a matter of fact." Censorship of wartime letters prevented Royce from revealing where he was or anything else that might be of value to the enemy. Becky could only infer his location from newspaper and radio reports of Naval operations in the Pacific.

Throughout the voyage, pilots practiced carrier tactics and maneuvers and conducted air searches. Although the pilots had qualified in carrier landings a few weeks earlier, it was valuable to have additional time to work with deck crews and landing signal officers to perfect this technique. Takeoffs and landings on a carrier required precision. When taking off, planes were hooked to a compressed-air catapult that accelerated them to flight speed. When landing, they were rapidly decelerated when the plane's tail hook caught one of a series of arresting cables that ran across the flight deck and were raised five or six inches during landings. Beyond the arresting cables on the forward end of the flight deck were a series of three barriers.

Whereas Navy pilots today have technologically advanced instrument landing systems, during World War II pilots were dependent on signals from landing signal officers (LSOs) standing on the front of the deck. Using a pair of paddles, LSOs indicated whether a plane was too high, too low, too fast, and so forth. Accidents were not uncommon; in fact, operational losses exceeded combat losses in the Pacific. Before they reached their initial destination, CarDiv 22 "lost eleven planes overboard, from one cause or another." According to Green Peyton, "for a division of three carriers, with green squadrons aboard, operating daily in intensive preparation for battle, these were not excessive losses. A big carrier's losses would be as high, or higher." Air Group 60 lost two of those eleven planes, both Avengers (torpedo bombers) that operated with a crew of three. All six of the men forced down in the water were picked up by CarDiv 22's destroyers—"another kind of practice for the serious business ahead." VF-60 lost no planes, which Green Peyton was inclined to attribute to the pilots' unusually lengthy training period, as most of them "had been trained two or three times as long as the average carrier pilot when he first goes to sea."[45]

Given the constraints on what Royce could write about his activities and whereabouts, it is no surprise that his letters home often were brief. On October 23, he wrote: "I am rooming with Frog, Skin, and Simp." All pilots were known by their radio call names: "Frog" was Quinn La Fargue, "Skin" was Earl Helwig, and "Simp" was John Simpson. Royce was known as "Lip," which, Green Peyton said, was because of his sharp tongue. Of the four roommates, two would not make it back home. Royce went on to say, "I can truthfully say that more sleeping is done in this room than any other aboard ship. Someone is always in the 'sack.' I am enjoying the cruise very much – the ship is a smooth one and the food is good. If you were here, everything would be perfect."

Royce wrote again on November 2, this time describing more about life on the ship. He said the ship has its own newspaper, which carries world news and sports (obtained via radio communication); he has read a couple of books and especially enjoyed van Wyck Mason's *Stars on the Sea* (about the founding of the U.S. Navy during the American Revolution); has "played poker a few times but there isn't much money involved [as] the playing is mostly for small limits"; and has seen a couple of movies, which are shown every third or fourth night, although they are a bit dated.

Finally, after 19 days at sea, on November 7, having bypassed Pearl Harbor, crossed the Equator, and veered west, the ship dropped anchor at the island of Espiritu Santo in the New Hebrides. Colonized by the British and French in the 1800s, New Hebrides (present-day Vanuatu) is an island group in the South Pacific, northeast of Australia and southeast of the Solomon Islands. Espiritu Santo became an important supply and support base for the Allies during World War II. James Michener's Pulitzer Prize-winning collection of stories *Tales of the South Pacific* was based on his observations while stationed there during the war. It was a good place for the Fleet Post Office to catch up with the *Suwannee*, which received its first mail. Royce wrote to Becky on November 10, "I got four letters from you yesterday and I am the happiest man in the world. It was like a ray of sunshine."

By this time, Becky had written to Royce nine times. In her first letter, dated October 21 (a Thursday), Becky described her adventurous three-day train ride home from Los Angeles after seeing Royce off at Los Alamitos. She missed her connection in Amarillo when her train was five hours late and then got bug bites in the overnight pullman enroute to Oklahoma City. She would be living with her parents, and her father picked her up at the train station. The next day she stopped by the gas company on her way to visit Royce's parents, where she dropped off gifts and clothes brought back from California. She mentioned that Royce's folks had gotten a letter from Royce's brother Bob, who had seen action in the Pacific flying a PBY Catalina seaplane in a patrol bombing squadron. On Thursday, Becky entertained John Simpson's wife Mary Edith ("M.E."), executive officer Edward Dashiell's wife Charlotte, and the air group flight surgeon Philip Phillips' wife Tommie, who stopped in Oklahoma City on their way home to the east coast. Four months pregnant, she then assured Royce: "I'm feeling fine, honey. . . . I haven't gone to see the Naval doctor yet, but probably will next week." After that, she brought up the subject of work:

> *Miss Rice from Brown's [department store] . . . left a standing call*
> *for me just as soon as I got back. I haven't called her yet. Am going to*
> *see Mr. [Roy] Deal [personnel manager at Oklahoma Natural Gas*
> *ɪpany (ONG)] first. Bill F. said when I was home last time Mr.*
> *l wanted to know if I wanted to go to work.*

This leads to news about friends who worked at ONG, followed by a brief note that her sister Virginia, who was attending Oklahoma A&M College (now Oklahoma State University), is coming home today with her boyfriend Marvin.

Thus began several threads that ran through Becky's letters: Updates on family and friends, contacts with other Navy wives, her health and care as an expectant mother, and working. She continued the thread on work, which spills over into finances, when she wrote on October 29.

> *Guess what! I'm a working girl again – at the Gas Co. and I'm being re-instated at my old salary, $110 per mo. . . . I'll probably work for two or three months. That will help a lot and I can use it for Christmas, save enough for the hospital bill and have some to run on. I can save everything you send home. Mr. Deal even said I could work after the baby is born, but I'd rather stay home then and besides you should be home by the time I'd be ready to go back to work.*

Perhaps because they were children (or at least adolescents) of the Great Depression, Royce and Becky were constantly concerned about money. In her previous letter, Becky reported a balance of $109.57 in their bank account and revealed that they owed Royce's father Sandy $100, which they probably borrowed to finance Becky's trips to the coast. On November 10, Royce wrote, "I don't think you'll have to worry about the darn bank account anymore. I have sent you 392 dollars and will send you another 300 or so the first of December." These amounts vastly exceed the $225 allotment that Royce told Becky she would receive at the beginning of each month. The extra cash, as it turned out, came from gambling. Royce had written on November 6 that he cleaned up in a dice game. But much of the additional money probably came from poker. According to the Air Group Sixty Yearbook, which commemorated the Group's time together, "poker sessions staffed by Luke, Douche-Bag, Rex, Mis, Pitch, Joe, Lip and other standbys" were routine at sea. The yearbook also describes Lip as "a sharp, smart fighter pilot [who is] wicked in the air and worse around the blanket covered table."

Without much to say about his activities at sea, Royce mostly responded to Becky's letters when he wrote to her. On November 10, he wrote, "I don't think you ought to work. I won't tell you not to. If you feel like you can and want to, go ahead, but it isn't necessary at all." Royce's ambivalence about Becky working reflects prevailing attitudes. Prior to the war, there was strong opposition to married women working outside the home. Most women who took jobs were young and unmarried. World War II changed the pattern of women's employment. Mobilizing for war required a greatly expanded workforce: to fill new jobs in the industrial production of war goods and to replace the millions of young men inducted into the armed forces. As labor needs increased, it was essential to employ large numbers of women. Their expansion into the work force came "slowly and often grudgingly" at first but, with intensive recruitment, shot up after 1942. By July 1944, 19 million women were gainfully employed, almost 50 percent more than in March 1940. Married women accounted for 72.2 percent of this increase.[46] The most notable additions were women blue-collar workers in the defense industries, which Norman Rockwell memorialized in a *Saturday Evening Post* cover of "Rosie the Riveter." Office workers such as Becky also significantly increased.

Becky had written on October 23 that she liked a swing version of "Pistol Packing Mama," which she heard Frank Sinatra sing on the "Hit Parade." She remembered Royce and Crash (Green Peyton Wertenbaker) harmonizing on that tune, and she asked if Crash had gotten his guitar before they left. Royce answered: "Crash did not get his guitar. We have had a few sessions of singing but we have no instrumental accompaniment."

In another letter, Becky wrote: "By the way, you told me that you didn't have any twins on your side of the family; your mother said today that both Sandy's brothers had twins and I found out tonight that my great uncle had two sets of twins. So, maybe, you weren't kidding after all when you mentioned twins. Wouldn't that be something?" Royce replied that he "had forgotten all about the twins on my Dad's side of the family . . . What do you think about that?"

Becky also asked: "How are you doing with your flying?" Early in his November 10 letter Royce wrote: "I hurt an airplane yesterday for the first time in my career. I blew out a tire on landing. There was no wind and I was fortunate (as were we all) to do no further damage. I have been duly nominated to become a member of the honorable order of Dilbert, etc." Royce refers here to a cartoon character, Dilbert, created in 1942, that was used by the Navy to help eliminate pilot errors. Widely circulated posters of Dilbert showed "what not to do in an airplane."[47] Later in the letter he added, "I'm getting along fine with my flying. I flew the longest hop yesterday I have flown. My rear end was sore when I got done. It felt like I had had a spinal injection. It feels ok this morning . . . so I guess the damage wasn't permanent."

Royce's lengthy flight occurred during the squadron's preparation for warfare. For after three nights in Espiritu Santo, the ship moved to Efate, another island in the New Hebrides chain, where the air group practiced for an amphibious invasion. When the ship returned to Espiritu Santo, air combat information officer Green Peyton Wertenbaker was briefed by a member of the Admiral's staff about the exact objective and plan of the operation: They were going to support the Marine invasion of Tarawa in the Gilbert Islands.[48] Wertenbaker was forbidden, however, from giving the pilots any hint of the operation until after they left Espiritu Santo. So, it was not until the next day, November 14, when the ship set sail, that the pilots were convened and finally informed of their objective.[49]

The Central Pacific Offensive

The invasion of Tarawa was the beginning of the third phase of the Pacific War: the United States offensive. It would be the first step in a series

of amphibious landings across the central Pacific on islands held by the
Japanese, part of a two-pronged offensive toward Japan. One offensive,
under the command of General Douglas MacArthur, moved northwest
from the southwest Pacific via the Solomon Islands and New Guinea
to the Philippines; the other, under the command of Admiral Chester
Nimitz, moved westward across the central Pacific via the Gilbert, Marshall,
Caroline, and Mariana Islands. (See map of the Pacific Theater, page 23.)
To defeat Japan, the Allied forces sought to meet two objectives. Because
Japan depended on water transportation to obtain raw materials in the
Dutch East Indies (now Indonesia), Malaya, and Burma, one objective was
to cut off access to these resources. The other objective was to bomb home
industries, which could be done once the Allies captured strategic islands
within range of Japan. To meet these objectives, the United States had to
gain control of the sea by defeating the Japanese Navy and by capturing
Japanese-held bases throughout the Pacific.[50]

Before the island-hopping offensive in the central Pacific, Navy planners regarded the invasion of islands beyond the range of land-based
air power as very risky and logistically problematic. Carriers and troop
transport ships would be vulnerable to enemy land-based planes, and a
mobile service force would be required to keep the fleet "supplied with
food, fuel, ammunition and countless other items which fighting men
afloat must have in order to wage war."[51] Existing bases were too far to
maintain the fleet for the "massive and swift transpacific advance" that
was planned. The Gilbert Islands were 704 miles from the nearest Allied
airfield, at Funafuti, and were over a thousand miles from Espiritu Santo
and 2,100 miles from Pearl Harbor.[52]

By fall of 1943, the Central Pacific offensive became possible because
of the massive buildup of the Pacific Fleet and the development of a mobile
supply base that "acted as a logistic annex to Pearl Harbor for servicing
the fleet at sea."[53] The assault force engaged in the Gilbert Islands operation, codenamed Galvanic, was the largest ever assembled: It comprised

over 150 ships, including 19 carriers, 11 battleships, 8 heavy and 4 light cruisers, nearly 60 destroyers, and three dozen transport vessels.[54] These combat forces were accompanied by a large mobile service group of tankers, hospital ships, repair vessels, and store ships. By various routes, the fleet converging on the Gilberts carried "108,000 American soldiers, sailors, Marines, and aviators."[55]

For its operations, the Navy organized the fleet into task forces, which were subdivided into task groups, each with its own distinct mission. In the Gilberts, the Japanese had built an airfield on Tarawa and a seaplane base at Makin, 125 miles north of Tarawa. The primary objectives of Galvanic were to attack and gain control of these two atolls. The two main task forces, TF52 and TF53, corresponded to these objectives. Task Group 53.6, consisting of the three *Sangamon* escort carriers and five destroyers, would support the Marine landing on Betio Island in the Tarawa Atoll. Other task groups in TF 53 included a transport group carrying some 18,000 Marine troops (TG 53.1) and a fire support group of battleships, cruisers, and destroyers (TG 53.4).

D-day for Galvanic was November 20. As the *Suwannee* sailed toward the Gilbert Islands, the pilots conducted daily air combat and submarine patrols. To many it seemed highly probable that the Japanese would detect a force of their size before they reached the Gilberts. But for several days, there were no enemy sightings. On the 18th, the *Suwannee*'s task group was joined by two other escort carriers, the *Barnes* and *Nassau*, each carrying 22 Hellcats, which would form the garrison squadron on Tarawa, once the U.S. forces had secured it.

Then, on the morning of the 19th, about 250 miles from Tarawa, fighter planes from VF-60, led by the squadron executive officer Lieutenant Edward Dashiell, intercepted a four-engine Japanese Kawanishi aircraft. Their attack set the Kawanishi's outboard engine afire and hit a gas tank that sent the plane into a steep corkscrew dive. It all happened so quickly that the pilots believed there was not enough time for the enemy plane to send a message of the presence of U.S. planes. Nor did it seem likely that the enemy plane had detected the task force, as it was not within sight. Credited with Air Group 60's first "kill," Dashiell and his wingman Winston Gunnels were greeted as heroes when they returned aboard.[56]

Two days before D-day, as TG 53.6 was closing in on Tarawa, Royce wrote to Becky.

November 18, 1943

My Dearest Becky,

   Tomorrow is the nineteenth and your birthday. I had intended to write you a nice long letter then, but it looks like I may be busy. I know you will not mind my writing it today.

   During the past month you have been in my thoughts and heart constantly. I've thought of a thousand things to tell you, but – as you already well know – they leave my mind when I pick up paper and pen. Today, as best I can, I shall tell you some of them. I would tell them all, but I know I won't be able to bring them to mind.

   On board a carrier a pilot has a lot of time to think and reminisce. I've been remembering things that happened to me in the past – when I was a little boy – while I was with you. I must admit my life has been a very happy one. And you have made me happier than anyone or everyone else possibly could. Although you know I haven't been too decorous in my religious affairs lately – my darling, I have thanked God many times that I was able to acquire such a wonderful person as you for my wife. I think of the many times I could have been much nicer to you than I was. Although I have always done what I thought was right at the moment, I know there have been times when I was not fair.

   Many times, I have thought of your becoming a mother. I must admit that I have imagined us years hence – with kids in school, etc. I wondered just how I would go about bringing them up to be the kind of men or women that parents (we) – and everybody – would be proud of. Now I know why everyone has visions of his or her son growing up to be president. I don't see how ours could miss – personally.

I know this won't get to you for several weeks. When I get back to the States, I'll be able to tell you why. Until then, I hope you will not mind too much the infrequent intervals at which you receive mail. I am in the same predicament – having received only 6 letters since we left. The ones I get are really dear to me and I have read them all many times.

I'll be glad when we have put in a long-enough stay out here to be ordered home. I don't dislike what I am doing – I enjoy it very much. But compared to being with you – it stinks!

I must close this and go play volleyball. Treasure this letter, because you know it is very hard for me to write one like it. It is not that I mind – I want to very much – but it's just not my nature, I guess. I love you more each day – and I want you to know it very much. Take good care of yourself and let me know what you have heard from the doctor.

Yours always,
Royce

On the Home Front

It would be well over a month before Becky received her birthday letter. She had written on November 8: "I'm so anxious to hear from you. I don't expect to hear often or regularly, but it's been a long time since you left. Do hurry and write." When she finally got her first letter, on November 14, she wrote: "It's been a month now since I left Long Beach. That's one month to our credit, honey. Let's hope it won't be many more." A couple paragraphs later, she added:

*Say, Doc. What did you tell me before you left about what to write
to you and what not to write? You said in your letter that you missed
me, and whether you want to hear it or not I miss you like all get
out. I couldn't appreciate the time we had together, darling, as much
as I should, until we were separated. You can be sure that when you
come back, we'll make every minute count. I love you so very much,
Royce. I'll be glad when our baby comes so that I'll have something
that really is you until you come back home.*

The next day Becky received three more letters. Then, on November 17,
she received the letter Royce had written on November 10, when he first
heard from Becky. "I'm so glad you finally heard," she wrote. "I know . . .
how much better I felt when I [heard from you]. I knew everything was all
right, but, oh, what a letter can do for a person." About Royce's financial
windfall, Becky wrote:

*Honey, where did you get all that money? You surely didn't win it
all in a dice game, did you? I almost fainted when I found the M.O.'s
[money orders] and read your letter. Of course, I can't say a word
about "shooting craps" when you win like that, but you be careful,
young man, hear?? Anyway, darling, I was simply thrilled to death
that you sent it home. That was perfectly sweet of you. I'm going to
pay Sandy with one $100.$^{\underline{00}}$ and deposit the other $100.$^{\underline{00}}$. I deposited
your check today, so our little bank account is coming right along. I
don't want to worry you about finances, but if you would like to know
the bank balance each month, I'll let you know. . . . Anyway, darling,
with me working, we should be able to save everything you send home
as long as I work. I'll try to take care of Xmas and everything out
of my salary. By that time (when I stop working), I'll have most of
the baby's things and there won't be much expense except for hospital
bills and bare necessities.*

In the first month that Royce was at sea, Becky was leading a busy life at home. Less than two weeks after coming home, on Monday, November 1, she was back at work. The first day was little rough.

Well, dear old Gas Co. I'm ready to quit already. Mr. Deal put me in Contract and said I could sit down most of the time. You can imagine, of course, how much sitting down I do. . . . And to top that off, I started working one day and the very next day they put me in charge of the dept. Ruby, who has been running it, is on P Cs desk this week. Monday night I was exhausted. I started out at high speed like I used to and found out I couldn't take it. So today I sat at the desk most of the day doing that work and let the others answer the phones and get the bills. That's what I'm going to do this week, and next week when Ruby comes back, I'm hoping they will let me sandwich a little switchboard in with Cont. Also, Frances has a week's vacation coming and as far as I know I get to take the board all that week.

Becky followed this account with updates on several employees of the Gas Company—what she calls "Gas House News." Ten days later, she again complained about work: "They are running me to death in the Contract Dept. Don't know how long I'll last." But a couple days later, after once again being placed in charge of the Department, Becky wrote, "It's getting to be much easier now cause I'm getting used to it, I guess." On November 17, she finally concluded: "I thought the first week I wouldn't last, but now I'm used to it and like it fine. As a matter of fact, I think I'm much better off keeping busy. And does that $110.^{00} do wonders!"

Becky implies that she was motivated to work at least partly for financial reasons, albeit not by economic necessity. Here and elsewhere she also implies other motivations. When she received a letter from M.E., she wrote to Royce, "M.E. sounded like she was pretty low. Don't say anything to

John, but I'm afraid she's taking their separation pretty hard. She's not working and has too much time to think and worry, I believe. I'm sure glad I'm working." Work, as Becky says, kept her busy, which helped to cope with the loneliness and anxiety caused by having a husband overseas. Personal accounts from the PBS Series "The War" reveal the anxiety that women on the home front in World War II had to endure while waiting for their loved ones to come home:

> It's terrible to live in fear that you're going to lose the person you love so, and you have no control over it at all.

> Once the war started like that, you didn't know where they were, you didn't know if they were alive or dead. You didn't know if you were going to get a letter from them and then find out that they had died right after they had written the letter. So, it just kept building up inside of you.[57]

One means of treating such anxiety is the use of distraction.[58] Becky may well have been correct about the beneficial "distracting" effect of work, especially for married wives of servicemen at war, as focusing attention on the mental and physical demands of work can divert attention from worries.

Becky had other "distractions" to help her cope with her wartime separation from Royce. Most important was her large network of family and friends. In fact, she was rarely alone. She lived at home with her parents, she visited Royce's parents and siblings often, and having grown up in Oklahoma City, she had many friends whom she saw regularly. In her first month home, Becky visited Sandy and Gussie once or twice a week, staying overnight on a couple of occasions, and her letters indicate that she took great pleasure in these get togethers.

I went over to your house yesterday, stayed all night and today. Your Mother is making me a black maternity dress. That'll save me $3.^{00} or more from a dressmaker.

. . .

Dump is going to a dance tomorrow night and he's all excited about it. He shuts himself up in the breakfast room and talks to his girl on the phone. We all made candy last night and really had fun. Of course, Sandy got me up for breakfast this morning. I had one of my grandmother's gowns (flannel) on that's about a size 40. They sure got a kick out of it.

Because Beulah had gone back to work as a secretary at the state capitol when Virginia went away to college, Becky sometimes called on Gussie for transportation. Thus, on November 14 she again spent the night at the Singletons', and the next day, she and Gussie drove to Norman, about 20 miles south of Oklahoma City, for her first appointment with the Navy doctor. In 1942, the U.S. Navy had established an air station at Norman, which included a 400-bed hospital. Becky had first mentioned this appointment on November 4.

I have an appointment with the Navy doctor Nov. 15 at Norman. I found out you have to go to the Naval Hospital there for delivery and can't be sure of having the same doctor right through. I'm going down to see him and see if I like him. If I don't like the set-up, I'm going to a doctor here. Miss Attaway, your mother's nurse, has offered to go to the hospital with me. I think I'll have her do it – just until the baby is born. I'd get plenty of attention then, wouldn't I?

On November 8, she more stridently expressed her reservations about having the baby in Norman.

I don't know if I told you about having an appointment with the Navy doctor Nov. 15 or not. Mother and Daddy are having fits about me going down to Norman. They say it's certainly going to be hard going back and forth all winter when it's so cold and I have to go real often. If I go to the Navy doctor, I have to go to the hospital down there. If I don't like it, I'm going to Dr. Allen or Dr. Rodgers here. (Specialists) They say Dr. Gerald Rogers has St. Anthony practically sewed up and I could surely get in there. Will let you know the developments. I'm between the Devil and the deep blue sea. Some say the Navy, others say stay here. I'm beginning to wonder if I have a mind of my own.

Becky's dilemma was easily resolved, however, after her appointment.

They have a very nice hospital and Outpatient Dept. at the South base at Norman. You can't be assured of the same doctor each time, but there is an ambulance here that takes patients to Norman when the time comes and you get a nice private room and, it appears, excellent care. The doctor who examined me today says I have enough room for a baby and said the baby was doing fine. He listened to it.

Another consideration in Becky's decision about where to have the baby may have been gas rationing. She first mentioned rationing in her letter of October 26:

Yesterday I went to the rationing board to get Book #III, canning sugar (for your mother) and gasoline to drive to Norman to the doctor. I have to have a statement from the doctor stating how many trips I'll have to make etc., and they won't give me gas to go down there and get that information.

With U.S. entry into World War II, the military grew rapidly, creating a tremendous demand for basic materials such as food, shoes, clothes, rubber, and metal. Rationing enabled the government to meet this demand while providing a fair distribution to consumers on the home front. The first item rationed, a few weeks after Pearl Harbor, was rubber, most notably automobile tires. Japanese control of Malaya and the Dutch East Indies cut off 90 percent of the U.S. rubber supply, which the military needed for vehicle and aircraft tires, boots, and many other items. Car owners were not permitted to own more than five automobile tires; all other unmounted tires had to be given or sold to the government under the Idle Tire Protection Plan. To conserve on wear, the nationwide speed limit was 35 miles per hour.

In May 1942, every family was issued the first war ration books, which indicated how much of specified items a family could purchase. One of the first food items rationed was sugar; beginning in December 1942 gasoline was rationed. Eventually, rationed items included coffee, meat, cheese, canned milk, butter, firewood, coal, nylon, silk, typewriters, and many other commodities. As a result, everyone was affected. People had to conserve or share or give up material goods. Becky wrote on November 19 that the tires on their car "are so shot that we can't do any extra driving." When she left California, she brought home clothing that Royce wouldn't need while at sea. This included a pair of shoes, which she gave to Royce's father, Sandy. It may seem odd now to give a prosperous person a pair of shoes, but not so during World War II after shoe rationing went into effect in February 1943.

On the night of her 22nd birthday—November 19, 1943—Becky wrote: "Darling, I hope you're getting along fine. We're watching the papers closely and have an idea of what you're doing. Do be careful. But give those Japs hell."

-4-

OPERATION GALVANIC:
November 1943

THE DAY AFTER Becky's birthday, Air Group 60 was poised for the U.S. invasion of Tarawa in the Gilbert Islands. The Japanese had seized control of the Gilberts on December 10, 1941. But it was not until January and February of 1943 that American photographic intelligence revealed the enemy's airstrip on Tarawa and the seaplane base on Makin. Further reconnoitering in fall 1943 provided thorough intelligence of the coastline and defenses at Makin and Tarawa. It was found that Makin was defended by very few guns and a relatively small garrison (fewer than 800 men, as it turned out), but Betio Island in the Tarawa Atoll was well fortified. Naval scholar Nathan Miller summarized Betio's defenses:

Only about two and a half miles long and six hundred yards wide, it was . . . honeycombed with blockhouses, pillboxes, and artillery emplacements covered with concrete, sand, steel plates, and coconut logs, each one supporting another, and impervious to all but direct hits from heavy shells. Eight-inch coast-defense guns . . ., mortars, and machine guns had been sighted in on expected landing places. Betio was also ringed by a coral reef that formed a natural barrier to landing craft. To it, the Japanese had added mines, barbed wire, and underwater obstacles.[59]

In addition, the garrison at Tarawa had over 4500 men, many of them crack troops from Japan's Special Navy Landing Force.

Tarawa Atoll is a triangular shaped group of 38 islands surrounded by a coral reef, with a large lagoon within the triangle. The island of Betio, site of the airstrip, rests on the southwest side of the atoll (imagine the base of the triangle). U.S. strategists decided to land on the island's northern side, on the lagoon shore. To get there, Marines crawled down cargo nets from the transport ships into landing craft, which carried them three and a half miles from west of the atoll through a channel that afforded entry to the lagoon, and then another three miles south to the landing sites on Betio. The coral reef on that side of the island extended 800 to 1000 yards beyond the beaches.

D-day at Tarawa began at daybreak with a pre-invasion bombardment first by bombers from the fast carriers and then, for two and a half hours, by the battleships, cruisers, and destroyers in the TF 53 fire support group. The amphibious landing was to take place at three beaches. While the bombardment was underway, minesweepers swept a transport area through the entrance to the lagoon. Following the minesweepers, two destroyers entered the lagoon, where they engaged the enemy. Finally, for a brief period prior to the landing, aircraft from the escort carriers bombed and strafed the beaches, and the support ships resumed firing.[60]

Air Group 60 participated in this pre-invasion air warfare. At dawn, twelve Hellcats, one piloted by Royce, took off from the *Suwannee*. Their mission was "to patrol the air over the transports and landing craft,"[61] and then to request assignment of targets for strafing. According to the *Suwannee* Action Report, VF-60 was "ordered to strafe 'Red' beaches where the enemy still impeded landings by Marine troops." Although they strafed these beaches thoroughly, they were "covered with a heavy pall of smoke from previous bombardments," making it impossible to observe the effect of strafing.

> The Squadron was then told to attack an automatic gun emplacement in . . . the northwest tip of the Island, where enemy fire was making trouble for Marines on landing barges in the lagoon. They made three runs on this emplacement, also firing at buildings partly concealed under the trees. After the third run, the gun was silenced. The squadron then headed east along the Island, straffing (sic.) enemy installations all the way across, and returned to the *Suwannee*.[62]

Support ships and aircraft had bombed and strafed Betio from end to end before the Marines landed. Commanding officers had to believe that the island's defenses were demolished. By one estimate, 40 percent of the Japanese casualties were killed before the landing.[63] But despite these losses and the destruction of many of the enemy installations, the Marines discovered that the Japanese defense of the landing beaches was formidable.

Two types of landing craft carried the Marines from the transports to the beach: track-driven amphibious vehicles, known as amphtracs (short for amphibious tractors), which could move over the fringing coral reef; and Higgins and Mechanized boats, which required a depth of about 5 feet to cross over the reef. Only the first three waves of Marines, each with a different landing point, were carried by amphtracs. Two of the three waves made it ashore without serious losses; the third suffered heavy casualties before they reached the beach. Because of low tides, subsequent waves could not pass over the reef, so that the Marines were forced to disembark and wade hundreds of yards to shore through an enfilade of machine gun fire. Those who made it ashore were pinned down with very little maneuverability. As the situation became more and more critical, attempted landings slowed and by midafternoon, about 100 landing craft milled around in the lagoon awaiting orders.

Aircraft from the "escort carriers maintained combat air and antisubmarine patrol [CAP and ASP] over the area and supplied planes for strikes" almost continuously until sunset.[64] After completing its third CAP, the VF-60 squadron again was "ordered to attack automatic gun emplacements, including antiaircraft, [this time] in . . . the southwest tip of the Island." Two long runs on the area silenced all the gun batteries. This attack and aircraft bombardment on the east end of the island by bombers from fleet carrier *Essex* were the last two aircraft actions of the day.[65]

Throughout the night, the Japanese did not mount a massive counterattack as about 5,000 Marines maintained their positions. Navy medical corpsmen evacuated several hundred wounded. The next day, the first battalion of Marines going ashore suffered even greater losses than those of any of the battalions landing on D-day.[66] But soon afterward, the battle turned in the Marines' favor. As a high tide finally rolled in, reinforcements, guns, and tanks poured ashore, and the Marines began to systematically attack and eliminate enemy positions. Late on D-day+1, war correspondent Robert Sherrod declared "a sign of certain victory" when he saw two jeeps rolling along a beach pier, towing 37-mm guns.[67]

After two more days of fighting, Betio was declared secure on November 23. Royce's squadron continued to conduct air patrols during the battle. Then, while the Seabees (a Navy Construction Battalion) began to build facilities for a naval base and other ships dispersed to distant bases, their task group remained behind until December 7 to protect the Gilbert Islands. Regarding its first operation, Green Peyton concluded, "Air Group 60 had been either very lucky or very good." They had lost no planes or pilots to combat action. One Hellcat was wrecked when it went through the deck barrier in landing; one torpedo pilot was seriously injured and one of his crew members [Radioman Johnny Belo] died when the plane crashed just after takeoff.[68]

The Marines were not so "lucky." For them, the taking of Tarawa came at a high price: 980 Marines and 29 Navy medical corpsmen were killed and another 2,101 were wounded in action. The Japanese suffered an even greater loss. Indoctrinated to defend "to the last man," the entire garrison was wiped out, except for one officer, 16 enlisted men, and 129 Korean conscripted laborers who survived and were taken prisoner.

Meanwhile, north of Tarawa, 6,742 Army troops attacked the sea base on Butaritari Island in Makin Atoll. Despite outnumbering Japanese ground forces about 10 to 1, panicky green troops "firing at anything and everything" and poor ground and ground–air communication prolonged the battle, and Makin was not secured until November 23.[69] Compared to the Marines at Tarawa, the Army casualties at Makin were light: 64 killed and 150 wounded. But the slow advance proved costly to the Navy, whose ships remained in the area longer than planned. Early on November 24, a Japanese submarine torpedoed the escort carrier *Liscome Bay*. The hit detonated bombs on board, causing a huge explosion that tore the ship apart. Twenty-three minutes later, the carrier sank; 642 men went down with her; 272 were rescued.

On November 22, Becky wrote to Royce, "We have been watching the papers closely and believe we are following the battle right along." She enclosed newspaper clippings of two articles filed on November 21, from which she inferred the location of Royce's ship and air group. One article, an Associated Press release, reported "strong resistance at Tarawa," where "fighting continues." In the other article, war analyst John Hightower pointed out that although Tarawa is strongly defended, it is not "considered so powerfully held as several bases in the Marshalls.... To do the job which he has now undertaken Nimitz unquestionably has at his disposal the most powerful aggregation of American aircraft carriers, battleships, and other combatant vessels ever assembled."

In subsequent letters, Becky does not mention Tarawa again. Possibly, like many Americans on the home front, she was shocked by the heavy casualties reported in the days following Hightower's sanguine analysis. She also may have become aware of pundits who, critical of American tactics, considered Tarawa a horrible tragedy. Still, others such as *Time* correspondent Robert Sherrod, an eyewitness at Tarawa, were amazed at this kind of response. He called Tarawa "the finest victory U.S. troops had won in this war," pointing out that "for every Marine who was killed more than four Japs died—four of the best troops the emperor had." What Tarawa showed—and America had to come to grips with—was that "there is no easy way to win the war; there is no panacea which will prevent men from getting killed."[70]

To this day, Tarawa is still controversial,[71] but most historians seem to agree with Samuel Eliot Morison that Galvanic was "well planned and bravely executed" and "the lessons learned . . . were of inestimable value in the planning and executing of later operations."[72] To identify those lessons, an inquiry into the Navy and Marines' performance at Tarawa began within days of the battle. The inquiry disclosed several mistakes and flaws as well as remedies. Foremost, the combination of low tides and a shortage of amphtracs caused numerous casualties on the first day that could have been avoided. Thereafter, large battalions of armored amphtracs were assigned to all amphibious landings in the Pacific. Although massive, the pre-invasion bombardment of the island was not nearly enough, leaving dozens of pillboxes, bunkers, and emplacements undamaged. It should have been at least three times as great. There had been a 20–30-minute time lag between the last aerial bombardment and troop landing, which enabled the Japanese to regroup.

The analysts also found air support of the Marines at Betio lacking. Initial attacks, carried out by aircraft from the fast carriers, were poorly executed: Timing of the attacks was off; bombs often were off target; and strafing runs were made haphazardly.[73] To be effective, air operations required a high degree of coordination and control. However, for the VF-60 Hellcats, "coordination between ground and air units . . . attempted by a ship-based control station [resulted in a] considerable degree of confusion at times."[74] Plane strafing also was ineffective, as they would learn, because their .50-caliber bullets could not penetrate enemy emplacements.[75]

In his next letter to Becky, Royce wrote:

We have been in a little action – nobody got hurt! I was a little disappointed in it. It is hard to realize anyone is shooting back at you when you make an attack. Although you can see the enemy shooting at someone else you can never see him shooting at yourself. I can tell you nothing concerning what we did – I'll tell you when I get back.

It is hard to know exactly what Royce meant by being "disappointed." The squadron encountered very little antiaircraft fire, which made the mission less dangerous. He may have wished that they had been more involved in direct troop support rather than spending most of their time conducting combat air patrols. Or he might have been frustrated by the lack of coordination and confusion or by the inability to observe the effects of strafing or simply by the fact that air operations provided inadequate support for the ground forces.

-5-

Between Operations:
December 1943–January 1944

A S THE *SUWANNEE* sailed toward Pearl Harbor, Royce wrote two brief letters. He had not heard from Becky in a month. Besides reporting that the squadron had seen action, his only other news was about his enclosures of checks and money orders, the fruits of his gambling. The ship arrived at Pearl Harbor on December 14, where they spent one night, left their planes on shore as carrier replacements, and then unexpectedly sailed for San Diego. Perhaps anticipating that he would contact Becky when the ship arrived, Royce did not write again until after the New Year.

From late November through December, most of Becky's letters to Royce referred to her pregnancy in one way or another. She touched on shopping for the baby, Gussie sewing baby clothes and making her a maternity dress, the possibility of twins, naming the baby, purchasing a maternity girdle, trips to the doctor, when to stop working, gaining weight and dieting, the difficulty of finding clothes to wear, the baby kicking. In the fourth and fifth months of her pregnancy, as she began to "show," Becky became increasingly sensitive to her physical appearance.

I'm really showing now. Doc Wallace came right out and asked me
if I was pregnant. I really was surprised. Aunt Anne said years ago if
anyone said anything like that to you, you would be shocked to death.
She said it used to be a disgrace to be pregnant. I'm just the opposite.
I want to tell everybody, but it speaks pretty well for itself lately.

Clearly, Becky was not at all embarrassed by showing her pregnancy. In subsequent letters, however, she revealed reasons for concern. One of those reasons was work. Despite the increase of women in the U.S. labor force during the war, at its peak, fewer than one in four *married* women were gainfully employed. It was especially unusual for a middle-class married woman to be working outside the home. But it was exceedingly rare for a *pregnant* woman to be working. Once a woman became pregnant, she was expected to quit her job; and if she did not leave voluntarily, company policy often required that she leave.[76] Thus, Becky was probably not being flippant when, after seeing the doctor a few days later, she wrote, "If I keep getting larger at the rate I'm going now they'll fire me before Xmas." A week later, she reiterated this sentiment and added, "I just know that if they weren't desperate for help at the Gas Co. they would let me go."

Becky's hiring may have been due to the shortage of labor. Or, rather than an act of desperation, it may speak well for the Gas Company that they hired Becky and kept her until she voluntarily left. That they hired her soon after her return to Oklahoma City and then immediately put her in a supervisory position also suggests that she was a valued employee.

Becky's elevated self-awareness of her physical appearance also may have been due to concerns about the harmful effects of weight gain during pregnancy. In the 1940s, it was standard clinical practice to monitor and restrict weight gain in order to reduce the risk of toxemia and birth complications believed to occur because of larger babies.[77] After her first appointment with the doctor, she reported, "The doctor says I'm gaining weight too fast, so they've put me on a diet. I weigh 119½ lbs. and that only leaves me 10½ lbs. to gain by the time the baby is born. I've been gaining about a pound a week the past seven weeks and that's too much." A week later, she wrote that, assuming the scales are accurate, she "gained a couple more pounds last week." Then, a couple weeks later, she said she was up to 123 pounds.

Of course, changes in a woman's body are an inevitable part of being pregnant. Without her husband around to see these changes, Becky felt the need to convey them to him and imagine how he would react. As she told Royce, "You should see me now, or maybe, it's a good thing you can't, cause I'm sure getting large." In another letter, she said, "I told Mother it's sure a good thing you can't see me now – you would divorce me. I'm beginning to look like 'Mr. Five by Five.' Everybody says I look real good in the face. You got that 'in the face,' didn't you." And in still another letter, "More people have commented on how well I look – (in the face). Too bad I can't look like this all the time when my figure isn't so lopsided." Finally, she described a seemingly welcome change.

> *Say, doc, if you could only see me now. I really don't need those "glam-orizers" anymore. If I just didn't have this bay window, I'd be pretty streamlined. I'm anything "but" though. I'm really going to try to keep all this added attraction after March, but I'm afraid I'm going to deflate in the wrong places. I wonder if the censor can figure out all that double talk. Maybe you can, though.*

Two days before Thanksgiving, as Becky was painting an old bassinet for the baby, she listened to a radio broadcast of Bob Hope entertaining the troops at Los Alamitos Navy Base, where Royce had trained before shipping out. The show was an episode of Hope's popular radio program, *The Pepsodent Show*, which first aired for the U.S. Armed Forces in May 1941 at March Field in Riverside, California. During World War II, all but nine of the 144 episodes of the radio program were performed at a military training site.

Hope always opened the show with a monologue geared toward the troops. Recounting the show, Becky thought "Hope really got off some good ones." And, remarkably, she remembered and passed along to Royce several bits from his monologue.

He said most of the boys there would be on carriers – a carrier is the Burma Road with an anchor. He also said some of the boys there had had combat experience – the others couldn't get dates in Long Beach. He was speaking of eating Thanksgiving dinner there last year and said the fellows were certainly gentlemen and had good manners. When the food was set before them, they all dived in in perfect echelon . . . Speaking of turkey, he said the pilot got the breast, radioman, the back, bombardier, the wing. Just call me rear gunner, he said. When the turkey got to him it looked like the framework of a new Liberty ship. Here's one for the dive bombers. He said they were the fellows who six days a week dived from a high altitude at 500 mph and pulled out right above the ground, then on Sunday demanded their 10¢ back because they didn't get a thrill on the Ferris wheel.

During the war, Bob Hope became affiliated with the USO, or United Services Organization, formed at the request of President Roosevelt to boost the morale of the armed forces. A staple of the USO was its camp shows—live entertainment at military bases and camps. Hope became a headliner of many USO tours stateside and then overseas. After the war, he continued to entertain the troops, establishing a Christmas show that became a holiday tradition and made him an American icon.

Before Thanksgiving, Becky wrote, "There are still rumors that clothes will be rationed, so I'm going to start buying Christmas gifts right away." As she would demonstrate time and again, Becky was a thoughtful but practical gift giver. At Christmas time, she always made a gift list and kept mental track of how much she could spend. In 1943, that list included her new extended family. She told Royce, "Am thinking of getting your mother some lightweight wool for a dress, before they ration that. Mina loves cosmetics, etc., and I'll get Dump an identification bracelet like we planned. Don't know what to do about Sandy. What do you suggest?"

Becky reported that she went Christmas shopping all day on Saturday, December 4. "I didn't get all of it," she said, "but I've just about decided on everything. I'm going to finish up tomorrow [Monday] night if I can." She might have continued her shopping on Sunday, but unlike today, stores were closed on Sundays because of state blue laws, which restricted or banned many Sunday activities.

Later that week, Becky expressed some frustration with her Christmas shopping: "I've been trying to get all my shopping done and it's a problem. The stores are jammed, and merchandise goes as fast as they can unwrap it." She then showed her characteristic frugality.

I'm afraid we're going to have to disappoint Dump this Xmas, honey, as far as the identification bracelet is concerned. They are so expensive and it's already too late to get them initialed before Christmas. I thought I'd get him a nice sweater to wear to school and write him a note saying you would pick up an identification bracelet in San Diego's Ship Service on your way home. You could probably get a better one at half the price I'd have to pay. The cheapest I have found here that would do at all is $9.⁰⁰ or $10.⁰⁰ dollars and .10¢ per letter for the engraving – Sandy H. Singleton, Jr. is quite a long name and he needs a heavy chain since he is so large and has such big hands and wrists – don't you think so?

Two days later, on December 10, Becky's thriftiness again showed through:

I wrote you I wasn't getting Dump a bracelet, didn't I. Well, I went into Rothchilds B&M today to look for a sweater for him and mentioned

seeing a yellow one in the window I liked. They said they didn't have
anymore, except one that was brought back because of a little rip in
the seam under the arm and said if I thought I could fix it I could
have it for $2.$[50]. *It was a $5.$[95] *heavy 100% wool sweater. A beautiful*
thing, so I took it and your mother said she was sure we could fix it.
I'm going to get him some knit gloves for school, too, since he has a
birthday this month, too.

Becky finished up her shopping on Saturday, December 18. On that
day she itemized her purchases for Royce. The list was long; it included
every member of her and Royce's immediate family, Royce's Grandmother
Whitten and Aunt Letha, M.E., "four girls she went to school with and
their little kids," and a work colleague. "I think we did right well on Xmas,"
she concluded.

Almost Home for the Holidays
By this date, Becky had not heard from Royce in over a month and had
no idea where he was. A week earlier, she wrote, "I know you told me not
to be surprised if it was three or four weeks between letters, but it's so
hard not to keep looking and not be disappointed when I don't hear." On
December 18, she closed her letter with "Sweetheart . . . do promise never
to go this long again without writing. Please be careful. I love you very
much and plan all the time about what we'll do and the fun we'll have
when you come home."

Royce, too, must have been disappointed that he had not heard from
Becky. But he knew why: The Fleet Post Office had not caught up with
the ship since before the Battle of Tarawa. Even before they reached Pearl
Harbor, it was clear to the air group, let alone the Japanese, that the next
operation would be in the Marshall Islands. But it was not clear for a while
that the ship was headed back to the States, where they would pick up new
pilots, replace the planes left at Pearl Harbor, and prepare for the battle in

the Marshalls. The *Suwannee* arrived in San Diego on December 23; on that same day, Royce telephoned Becky. Just a few days before, Becky also had received Royce's birthday letter.

December 24, 1943

Dearest Royce,

Talking to you was wonderful – And I had been so afraid I wouldn't hear from you by Christmas. I feel that I've already had my Christmas now. That was by far the best Xmas present you could have given me. Just hearing your voice. Darling, I haven't calmed down yet. Jr. certainly protested at all the excitement. Nobody would believe at first you called me. I've stayed home every night since. Didn't even go to the Gas House Party, 'cause I didn't want to miss you if you called again. Hoping that you would get to come home was too much to ask for, I guess, but I couldn't help dreaming about it a little.

You must have spent the whole night getting your calls through. It must have meant quite a bit to you to talk to us. Darling, I wish I could tell you how much it meant to me. Getting your letters and then the call was almost too much for me. I was on the board next day with Francine helping to work the mail and I told her if anything else happened just to break it to me gently. I didn't think I could stand the shock of anything more.

Here it is Christmas Eve with you no telling where and me here with the baby. Actually, I wish the baby were here because it would be such a comfort. Things weren't meant to be this way – for you to be far away, but as long as the war goes on, we'll have to make the most of it. Maybe next year we can be together for our baby's first Xmas. Won't that be wonderful! I can just see what Santa Claus brought him. He won't understand then quite what it all is about 'cause he'll only be 9 mos. old, but he'll probably get everything imaginable.

Darling, my birthday letter was wonderful. I'll cherish that the longest day I live, because even though you don't break forth so often with sincere things in so many words, it was every word of it, "you." Royce I've thanked God, too, many times that you are my husband. I realize more everyday how very much I love you. Darling, when we get together again, I don't believe anything could ever come up we couldn't cope with. That bond between husband and wife does grow stronger day by day, doesn't it. And I think this separation will only strengthen it more.

I'm very tired from getting ready for Christmas, so I'm closing for tonight – I'll write again tomorrow. I'm spending most of the day at your house. Let me hear from you soon.

Yours always,
Becky and Sandy III

Uncertain of how long he would be in San Diego, Royce must have conveyed to Becky that he could be leaving soon. For on Christmas Day, after thanking Royce for the roses and card and describing her "very nice Christmas" with an abundance of gifts for Sandy III, she wrote, "Darling we've decided that you must have gone by now, but I'll never forget how wonderful your voice sounded." In reality, the air group knew they were not leaving San Diego right away, although they did not know when. According to Green Peyton, after going ashore, some of the men "whose wives were hurrying in" booked hotels in town, while others "spent Christmas waiting in telephone booths, the next day or two waiting in packed railway stations." But there "were to be no leaves, except for a few days at a time."[78]

Three days later, on December 28, Becky received another telephone call from Royce and wrote to him again. Given the uncertainty of his situation and no doubt concerned about Becky traveling "in her condition," Royce tried to convince her that she should not come to San Diego. But desperately wanting to see Royce, she sent the letter by special delivery in care of Barclay, who, she knew, was already there. "I really suppose it would be best if I didn't come," Becky told him, "but I know I could make the trip. Everybody treats me like I'm a baby and can't get around by myself, but I feel fine." She proposed to meet Royce, "like I said this morning, halfway," if he can get a leave. Then, having already called the railway, she described possible connections. Finally, Becky implored him: "Darling please try to get some time off. I want to see you so much. I'm just about to go crazy here with you out there and all the other wives going out to see their husbands – Let me know what you are able to do as soon as you can."

Royce would not leave San Diego, as it turned out, until January 14. It would be more than a week before he called Becky again. It's unlikely that he received her special-delivery letter before the New Year; however, much of their communication between the end of December and his date of departure—Becky by letter and Royce by telephone—revolved around Becky's wanting to see him.

Becky wrote twice before she heard from Royce again, each time showing a glimmer of hope that she would see him soon while trying to suppress this possibility. She felt keenly the unfairness of their separation. And, for one of the few times in her letter writing, she expressed resentment about the position she was in.

Forgive me for not writing – I didn't know that not getting to see you could get me down so. I was in bed Wed. – Been trying to do too much – the excitement and all – I guess. I haven't settled down yet – Feel like a caged lion. War is hell, isn't it. I'm getting hard as nails, I'm afraid. Every time I hear some "doting mother" so afraid her little boy is going to be drafted or doing her best to keep him on this side, I feel like letting her in on a few things. And those draft dodgers – how I hate them!! Sweet old Doug received his reclassification card and he was called up for his first physical the other day. Here he has a wife and three children, very devoted to them, but he wouldn't let

Mr. Deal do a thing to keep him at the Gas Co. He wants to go and wants to get in the Navy.

Later in the same letter, she wrote,

Figure that you have gone since I haven't heard from you, but I can't help but think you'll be back soon. You simply must come home, honey, if you get back to the States again. I'm losing my mind thinking about you on one side of the United States and me 1500 miles away and not able to do anything about it. Darling, I want to see you so much.

Two days later, on January 4, she repeated the same message: "Still can't believe you have gone back to the islands. Keep thinking you'll call again from San Diego and, perhaps, come home. That would be too good to be true." Then, she closed by saying, "I'm settling down a little, but still would love to see you. I don't dare think about it much – Too hard on my constitution."

The squadron was not idle during its stay in the States. On New Year's Day, they boarded the *Suwannee* for a three-day battle rehearsal off the coast of California. Green Peyton noted that the rehearsal was much bigger and "more involved than the hurried practice we had held in Efate on our way to Tarawa." In addition to the three carriers in CarDiv 22, there were "four cruisers, a couple of dozen destroyers and minesweepers, and some twenty transports." To test the tactical operation for the invasion, troops landed on San Clemente Island and land-based Navy planes worked with escort carrier planes, just as the fleet carrier forces would in the Marshalls.[79]

Royce called Becky a few days after returning from the squadron's rehearsal. When she wrote to him after their conversation, she once again complained about not being able to see him: "Honestly, Royce, I don't see why you can't come home. I'm so mad at the Navy. It's just awful sitting here with you out there, but it doesn't do any good to gripe about it and

I'm sure it doesn't make you feel any better." Then, Becky revealed her growing desperation to see Royce.

> *I wish you would tell them I'm in a bad way so you could come home*
> *– I really am but am not flat on my back. Now if this was March,*
> *I might fall down the stairs here at the Gas Co. so I could hurry Jr.*
> *along. The Navy might accept that for an emergency leave.*

On January 8, following another call from Royce the previous day, Becky finally calms down. Expressing a more reasonable tone, she began a letter with an amusing account of the scene when he called her at the Gas Company office.

> *I got bawled out by at least six different people for running, when*
> *Frances told me you were calling me. She called at almost closing*
> *time and said, "Now don't have a 'hissy' but Royce is calling you."*
> *And out of the office and up the stairs I streaked with half the office*
> *behind me. Ernie Robb told me that if I wasn't careful, I wasn't going*
> *to have my baby at Norman, but at the Gas Co. instead. I told them*
> *that if I kept on working, I was going to start bringing my suitcase*
> *to work, just in case.*

She went on to describe the snowstorm that hit Oklahoma the previous day, pointing out, "If you had gotten a furlough these last few days, I'm afraid you would have had a hard time getting home. All planes are grounded and some of the roads are impassable." Later, she told Royce, to "go out there and do your job and rest assured that your wife loves you and is waiting right here for you and soon there'll be somebody else waiting for you." Having learned that Royce (along with the nine other Hellcat pilots who had been with the squadron from the beginning) was promoted, Becky addressed the envelope to Lt(jg), rather than Ensign, Royce Alan Singleton.

Although the letter is missing, we know Royce wrote to Becky early in the New Year. This letter and a final phone call before he departed from San Diego convinced Becky that it was best not to try to see one another during Royce's brief return to the States.

I'm so glad you could call again before you left. I was kinda upset over the call a couple nights ago 'cause I feel I had quite disappointed you. Darling, I received your letter this evening when I got home and it's by far the sweetest you've ever written. I have no reason to be mad and I understand exactly. I'll try to be everything you want, darling. And I hope you won't have to mention any of this again. Unless it would be to get such a wonderful letter from you again even with the scolding.

I already feel like a different person. You just do wonders for me, darling. I love you so much. Never forget it for a minute. I want you to feel that you are doing your job, so that you can come home, and we can go ahead with the plans you've made. I'm waiting, honey, and saving our money so that we can go right ahead with our lives like this little lapse of time had never happened. But while you are gone, I'll do my best to be the kind of wife that you want and raise our baby for you to be proud of. I bet he'll be a sweet little 'feller.' And look like his daddy.

I'm going to be awfully happy to have him with me while you are gone. I only hope it won't be too long before you can see him.

Back at Sea

As the *Suwannee* was getting underway, on January 14, Royce wrote a short letter. "Here we go again," he said. "We're probably going where you think although I don't know . . . If my writing is very poor don't mind it. The ship is pitching and rolling so much my chair slides around and I have to continually hang on. I'm afraid some of our new boys may get a little sick." He told Becky that he "got the box from the Gas Co.

Some of the candy had become loose in the box and it was pretty messy. However, I salvaged most of it and am very happy to get it." Then, Royce mentioned two "surprises": he plans to let his hair grow so that he can comb it – "like the good old days"; and his taste for food is changing. "Bob would envy me at the moment. I ate about half a dozen fried oysters for lunch – something I've never done before. I even eat shrimp cocktail." He ended with,

I'm going to close this. I'm sliding around so derned much it's nearly impossible to write. I must say – I love you very much and am really looking forward to our next trip to the States. I'll get leave and get to come home to you. It will be wonderful.

The early stages of the voyage to the Marshall Islands were relatively uneventful. To conserve on fuel and limit wear on the airplanes, the fleet limited the number of CAP and ASPs. Each carrier was responsible for these duties every third day. At Hawaii, between the islands of Molokai and Maui, CarDiv 22 anchored for a couple days while they rendezvoused with other ships headed for the invasion in the Marshalls.[80] The size and number of air patrols increased after the fleet left Hawaii. Everything was going smoothly until the crew was jolted by two accidents midway between Hawaii and the Marshalls, on January 25 and 26. The first accident occurred aboard the *Sangamon*, within sight of the *Suwannee*. A plane landing went through two barriers and crashed into planes parked on the forward end of the flight deck. A serious fire broke out; seven men were killed, nine were injured, and five planes were destroyed.

A day later, the second accident, a mid-ocean collision, occurred. It was potentially very serious, but turned out, as Green Peyton described, "more like an elaborate practical joke."[81] Rather than travel in a straight line, it was standard practice for ships to maintain a zigzag pattern to hinder enemy submarine attacks. This pattern was coordinated with other ships in the fleet. For takeoffs and landings, ships turned into the wind to maximize airspeed over the deck, but this maneuver was carried out independently of the rest of the fleet. The collision occurred when "the *Suwannee* began a turn to the right to recover aircraft, while the *Sangamon* turned left in accordance with the zigzag plan."[82] Had the full weight of either ship—over 11,000 tons—impacted the other, the results would have been disastrous. Fortunately, the ships were moving slowly when they scraped one another; the damage was minimal and both ships were able to continue operating as usual. The *Suwannee* executive officer lost his "head" (i.e., toilet) when the *Sangamon* hit his quarters and dumped them into the sea. The *Suwannee*'s crew were convinced that the *Sangamon* was at fault. On a chart in the ready room that tracks the ship's location from day to day, a pilot marked a cross on 26 January with the note "Attacked by *Sangamon*."[83]

After Royce departed for the Marshalls, Becky prepared to quit working and undergo a change in lifestyle. The doctor told her on her first visit, in November, that it was all right to work, but she "should loaf the last six weeks." On her second visit, after being given a due date of March 25, Becky told Royce, "I'm going to work until Jan. 15 anyway, if Mr. Deal will let me, maybe longer." On January 14, when Deal told Becky he could really use her the following week, she was ambivalent, uncertain about whether to stay "at the Gas Co. awhile longer or go quietly nuts sitting at home all day – There's not even a good compromise in sight." Then, on January 24, Becky declared herself "a lady of leisure. Sure hated to quit work, but thought it was about time."

One change in her routine occurred on Friday, January 14. For the first time since Royce left in late October, Becky attended a movie, *No Time for Love* starring Claudette Colbert and Fred McMurray, with two of her girlfriends. "It was awfully cute," she wrote. "Guess I'll have to get back in the swing of going to shows." Like many Americans at that time, Becky and Royce enjoyed going to the movies. In 1944, 60 percent of the American public went to the cinema weekly, and they spent almost a quarter of their recreation dollar on films.[84] It was cheap entertainment; the average price of a ticket nationally was $0.32, the equivalent of $5.53 today. Further, you got more bang for your buck than you do today. In addition to double features, many films were preceded by shorts, newsreels, and cartoons. Becky conveyed this when she wrote about two more films she saw over the span of the next ten days.

Mother and Daddy and I just got home from the show. It's late, but I can't go to sleep without writing you a letter first. We saw "Destination Tokyo." It was really good. I'm sure glad I saw it. Did you see it in San Diego? I don't remember your saying. Super Mouse in "He Dood It Again" was the comedy. It was good. I always think of you, darling, when I see a cartoon. I think you enjoy them more than anyone I've ever seen.

A week later, Becky and her mother saw *True to Life* with Dick Powell, Mary Martin, and Franchot Tone. This show was accompanied, Becky described, by "a short on the progress of the Navy during 1941 and 1942," followed by news showing

a carrier's planes raiding the Marshalls with planes taking off before daylight. Do your fighter planes have all that fire shooting out from the motor? I remember watching some TBF's taking off at Astoria about dark and you could see sparks etc. coming from the exhausts . . . on either side of the cockpit. Are the fighters like that, too? I was wondering because these did that. It showed some coming in for a landing and the cables stopping them. One of them sure did bounce. I kept looking for you, but guess it wasn't your carrier. I like to see pictures like that, 'cause then I have an idea of your surroundings and can visualize what you are doing.

Movies were not just a source of entertainment. They kept people on the home front informed; "aside from newspaper photographs, newsreels shown at the cinema were often the only visual representation people had of the war."[85]

To help defray the costs of Becky's trips to the coast, Royce and Becky had sold Sandy their car. One of Becky's first moves when she stopped working was to get the car back from Sandy. Ever since her return to Oklahoma City in October, she had been dependent on her mother and mother-in-law for rides to work and elsewhere. Both of her parents worked, so without a car she was either stuck at home or dependent on public transportation. An early letter, however, suggested that selling the car to Sandy was a sore point: "I just wish we still had our car. Every time I have to ride the streetcar or when I think about going to Norman to the doctor and how I'll take the baby any place when it comes, I get mad all over. That was our first big mistake, I think."

So now Becky told Royce, "I talked to Sandy and he's going to let me have the car for what he paid for it $105.[00] . . . It needs a little work done on it that I'm going to have to do if I get it." Becky bought the car on Sunday, January 30; she took it to the garage on Tuesday. With money, as usual, an issue, she justified the costs.

I took the car to the garage today and am having a little bit of everything done to it. I had the Yow Brake Shop check the wheels and brakes and my bill was only 50¢. Then the Service Shop next door was supposed to fix the leak in the radiator pump and Daddy called a while ago and said that they had to put a new radiator pump on. They are going to check the starter, generator, and transmission. Then I'm going to have the filling station change the oil and check the battery. The garage, also, is going to try to fix the door lock and horn. It will be almost as good as new when all that is done, don't you think? If I wanted to sell it now, I think I could get $200.[00] for it . . . I need a *jalopy and can always get what I paid for it later on. Well, sounds like I'm trying to convince someone, doesn't it?*

When going over her expenditures and finances, Becky referred to the cost of Royce's telephone calls in a couple letters. The January 11 telephone bill did not contain the long-distance calls, she wrote, "so they won't come out until next month. That's going to be a whopper – But being able to talk to you was worth every cent of it." In 1944—as was true from the earliest days of telephone service until the introduction of area codes in the 1950s—a call from San Diego to Oklahoma City required far more effort and cost than it does today. Royce had to find an available public pay phone, contact a telephone operator, give her the telephone number he wanted to reach, and wait until the call went through and the person contacted agreed to accept the charges for the call. The cost of calls varied by distance; a 1,418-mile, 10-minute call, in 2023 dollars, was about $121 during the day and $91 at night.[86] Royce's calls to Becky ended up costing $92.65, the equivalent of $1,602.20 in 2023.

Given the cost of long-distance telephone calls, it is easy to understand how communication in the 1940s consisted mainly of letter writing. At one point, Becky told Royce, "I owe so many letters . . . I guess that's what I'll have to do first as soon as I quit work." Later, she says, "I'm trying to catch up on my correspondence in between letters to you. I don't think I ever will, though – I didn't know I knew so many people." That is no exaggeration; for in letter after letter to Royce, she writes about writing to, and receiving letters, from others. The list included Royce's brother Bob and his wife Kathleen; more distant relatives of both Becky and Royce; five wives of members of Air Group 60—Barclay, M.E., Charlotte, Tommie, and Beedie Barber; friends from Seaside, Oregon; friends from college; and still others. Royce, too, had a long list of correspondents, including Bob, Gussie, Sandy, and Becky's parents.

On January 18, Becky wrote, "I had a letter from Robert – a long one – four big pages." Then she engaged in some good-natured kidding.

Take heed, young man. He said he certainly was going to be one proud uncle – Said if it should be twins to save one for him and Kathleen, 'cause he'd be tripping over his long white beard before he got home. Said he was doing his own washing and that they always had that tattle-tale gray look. I told your mother you would throw yours over-board before you would wash them – you spoiled brat – Hm, I see the beginning of a new campaign when you come home, being I have the extra work of a child on my hands. Darling, I can hardly wait for the baby and for you to come home.

A few days after she quit working, Becky wrote,

I rather liked staying home today. It seemed sorta like when we were together – Fussing around – doing this and that – waiting for you to come home for dinner – the only catch today – you weren't coming home for dinner. Won't that be nice darling – having a home again – even if it is a couple rooms with a terrible rent? Me griping at you for throwing your clothes around when you come home at night, only the picture will be a little different this time. Instead of making yourself comfortable with a magazine or a deck of cards or even the evening paper, you'll have a youngster climbing all over you wanting you to romp and play. Or if he's not old enough for that yet, he'll still know you when you come home and expect you to hold him before his bed-time. By the way, darling, you might read-up on your bed-time stories in your spare time. That will come before you know it – I'm giving you the job, mister – official teller of bed-time stories. I think we'll like this family life, don't you? I'm really anxious to get started, so you get busy and clean up that mess out there, so that soon after you receive that cable about the newest Singleton, you can hurry home to us. We'll surely be looking forward to seeing you.

-6-

OPERATIONS FLINTLOCK AND CATCHPOLE:
February 1944

T HE NEXT TARGET in the central Pacific drive was the Marshall Islands, which the Japanese had occupied since World War I. Lying northwest of the Gilberts between Hawaii and the Philippines, the Marshalls consist of more than 1,000 islands and islets spread some 800 miles across two parallel chains of coral atolls. By 1943, the Japanese had established military bases on seven of the Marshalls' 29 atolls. The question was, where should the campaign strike first? The geographic center and Japanese communication and supply hub was Kwajalein Atoll. But Kwajalein was protected by airbases in the eastern Marshalls. If the Americans took the outlying atolls first, they could use them to launch an assault on Kwajalein. Yet, against the advice of his command staff, and to the surprise of the Japanese, Admiral Nimitz chose to strike directly at Kwajalein.[87] Codenamed Operation Flintlock, this was the first step in the Marshalls campaign.

Kwajalein Atoll is shaped "liked a boomerang, poised for throwing."[88] The main objectives of Operation Flintlock were the twin islands of Roi and Namur, on the northern end of the atoll where it turned west, and Kwajalein and Ebeye Islands, about 40 miles south on the southern tip of the atoll. In addition, the final plan targeted Majuro, a separate atoll 250 miles southeast of Kwajalein. It was known to be lightly defended, and it contained a large lagoon that could provide anchorage for the mobile supply system. Separate task forces were formed for each of these targets. CarDiv 22 was part of the Northern Task Force, given the mission of capturing Roi-Namur, site of the Japanese' principal air base.

The Gilbert operation proved to be significant strategically and tactically in preparing for Operational Flintlock.[89] Seizing the Gilberts was of great strategic value because it enabled the U.S. to restore the captured airfield at Betio and build additional airfields that put land-based aircraft within striking distance of Kwajalein. And tactically, the Gilberts had served as a testing ground for a large-scale amphibious assault. That operation had revealed various deficiencies and errors of execution, which needed to be corrected for a more successful invasion. Several of these deficiencies pertained to Naval support; most importantly, preliminary air and naval bombardment needed to be longer and heavier.

For seven weeks, beginning on December 8, 1943, land-based aircraft carried out photographic reconnaissance and repeatedly bombed five enemy bases, including Roi-Namur. Then, three days before Flintlock's D-day of January 31, 1944, aircraft from the fleet carriers joined the action. The result of these air operations "was the virtually complete destruction of enemy aircraft and shipping in the Marshalls, before the initial landings."[90] On D-day, the Northern Task Force first set up artillery at two islets adjacent to Roi-Namur, and then brought the fire support ships and transports into the lagoon, south of the landing site. So effective was the aerial and naval bombardment that the troops that landed on D-day+1 were able to go ashore standing up.[91] A large proportion of the defenders had been killed, and the twin islands were secured the next day.

Operation Flintlock's other two targets also were captured with relative ease. Photographic reconnaissance of Majuro had revealed nearly completed barracks and other structures, appearing to house three to four hundred

Japanese troops. But when the Marines began their assault on January 31, they discovered that the islands were abandoned. So, Majuro Atoll was secured without the loss of a man. Securing Kwajalein and Ebeye Islands took longer than Roi-Namur,[92] but was no less effective. By February 7, the Americans were in complete control of the entire Kwajalein Atoll. Neither the northern nor the southern battle in the atoll was bloodless; however, there were vastly fewer U.S. casualties than at Tarawa: 372 soldiers and Marines died, compared to 7,870 Japanese.[93]

During Operation Flintlock, planes from VF-60 went up early on January 31 and continued going off each day from dawn to dusk. For the fighter pilots, these flights consisted of "wearisome but necessary patrol missions," without the assignment of strafing runs to break the monotony of circling for hours over the sea.[94] The torpedo planes and dive bombers from VC-60 did see some action; however, one of these missions, on February 1, ended tragically when two SBD dive bombers from the *Suwannee* collided with another SBD from the *Chenango* as the planes were entering a dive. SBDs had a crew of two, a pilot and a radioman/gunner. Both VC-60 pilots, Lieutenant Byron Strong and Ensign William Sackrider, and one of the gunners, Radioman Philip Barton, were killed. For the most part, VF-60 and VC-60 pilots tended to fraternize within their own flight groups. But, according to Green Peyton, Sackrider often had spent his off-duty time with the Hellcat pilots. "Sack had always wanted to be a fighter pilot, but he had been put down for dive bombers at flight school . . . The ready room was not so carefree and full of fun without him."[95]

For several days after D-Day, the *Suwannee* was stationed off Kwajalein Atoll, putting up their usual air patrols. Then, on February 12, the ship cruised into the lagoon and dropped anchor to replenish its supplies. This required an overnight stay, but just after midnight, a general quarters alarm was sounded. Green Peyton described being shaken awake from a serene sleep by his roommate, Royce, hurriedly tossing on some clothes and weaving his way to the ready room. There, the assembled air group learned that Japanese bombers, about 20 minutes away, were coming in for a raid. There was no time for ships to leave the lagoon for open water where they could maneuver, and they did not want to draw attention to themselves. So, ships held their antiaircraft fire and made smoke to obscure their positions.[96] Soon, the Japanese planes flew over, dropped their bombs on Roi-Namur, and pulled away. The raid did considerable damage, but it could have been far worse if the ships in the lagoon had been bombed.

By this time, Royce had written to Becky three times since the ship left San Diego in January. Not having received any mail since their departure, he said, "it seems hard to write when nothing can be said of news." Trying to communicate news about the war front while following censorship rules, he referred to Operation Flintlock in two oblique references: "None of our fighter squadron has been hurt!" (and in his second letter, "All our fighter pilots are still ok."); and "Tell Mother to tell you what Gussie Lois's husband's first name is!!"

Becky responds in letters she wrote in February. About the first bit of news, she asked: "I noticed you said all fighter pilots were ok. Does that mean you've lost some SBD and TBF pilots? Anybody I know?" Royce cannot say if anyone is killed, let alone identify who that is. On March 4, he was able to say, "You were right in your guess at what I meant when I said all the fighter pilots were O.K. Strong and Sackrider."

About the second reference, Becky said, "I'm a little dense sometimes, but then it finally soaks in. I thought you meant that Roy Rector's first name was funny or something." When Beulah suggested that mentioning Gussie Lois and her husband's first name meant something, Becky "realized what," which led to this leap of inference:

> You haven't been land-based there have you? I thought of that as
> soon as I heard of the capture of Roi Island. I knew somebody would
> have to be left there and remembered your saying that if you were
> land based, there was no telling when you would get leave to come

*home. Just answer me "yes" or "no" as to whether you are still based
on the carrier.*

Fortunately, in short order, Becky received additional mail confirming
that Royce was still carrier-bound.

In his letter of February 6, Royce wrote, "I read a poem the other day
in an old, tattered magazine. I thought you would appreciate and enjoy it
as much as I did so I am enclosing it with this letter. Keep it, if you can, so
that we may read it together sometime."

For Life Worth While

By WILLIAM W. PRATT

Among the many things that please
A normal little girl are these:
Her dolls, so sweetly feminine,
A shiny cart to wheel them in,
A doll house filled with furnishings,
A jumping rope, a top that sings,
A bubble pipe, a set of jacks,
Some colored crayons made of wax,
A teatime tray of chinaware,
And yellow ribbons for her hair.

Among the things a boy should like
While he is still a little tyke
Are these: A drum that he can bang,
A book about a pirate gang,
A baseball mitt, a railroad train,
A rocking horse with flowing mane,
A scooter painted brilliant red,
A box of soldiers made of lead,
A water gun, a horn to toot,
And then, of course, a cowboy suit.

Among the things that girls and boys
Should have along with treasured toys
Are these: A home where hearts are gay,
A yard in which to romp and play,
A shelf where jams and jellies are,
An ever-loaded cooky jar,
A dad to join them in their fun,
A prayer to speak when day is done,
A mother's kiss with words unsaid
When they are fondly tucked in bed.

Poem Royce sent to Becky, February 6, 1944

On February 10, prior to the Japanese raid, Royce said, "Let me know how you are doing. Tell me everything concerning the expected heir. I'm beginning to wonder if I'll be home by the time he's born – there's a pretty good chance I will. If not then – shortly afterward – I hope." This was not the last time Royce told Becky that he might be coming home soon. Given the lack of information and that the next mission was never known until it was imminent, rumors frequently emerged about when they would be ordered home.

The day after the Japanese raid, CarDiv 22 moved south in the lagoon, anchoring off Kwajalein Island, where ships were gathering for another invasion. The next target was another atoll in the Marshalls, Eniwetok, located 326 miles northwest of Roi. This atoll would put U.S. forces within striking distance of Truk and other islands in the Carolines, located west of Eniwetok and north of New Guinea. Originally, the capture of Eniwetok was planned for a month or two following Operation Flintlock. But when Kwajalein fell surprisingly quickly, an expeditionary force, including CarDiv 22, was formed. The expedition, dubbed Operation Catchpole, sailed from Kwajalein lagoon on February 15.

D-Day at Eniwetok was February 17. To neutralize possible air interference in the invasion, U.S. forces attacked two bases at Panope and Truk. It had been determined that the Japanese bombing raid on February 12 came from Panope; so, bombers from Tarawa struck this site first. A massive air and sea attack on Truk, carried out by three of the four fast carrier groups, coincided with the first assault on Eniwetok. After these attacks, nary a Japanese plane was seen during Operation Catchpole. But the significance of the two-day strike on Truk went well beyond this narrow mission. Truk was Japan's main base in the south Pacific; many strategists believed it was impregnable to an amphibious assault. By destroying 250–275 Japanese planes and several ships, the attack did irreparable damage. After February 18, it was unnecessary for U.S. forces to occupy Truk, because it was effectively isolated and no longer useful to the Japanese as a naval base.[97]

A circular atoll, Eniwetok had three main islands: Engebi, the only island with an airfield, in the north; and Eniwetok and Parry, in the south. The plan of attack was similar to that at Kwajalein. Engebi was assaulted first; U.S. forces entered the lagoon on D-day, established artillery on two adjacent islets, and then pounded Engebi from the sea, air, and land. After landing on D-day+1, the Marines secured the island before sunset. The assaults on Eniwetok and Parry began the next day but took longer than expected. U.S. forces had underestimated the size of the Japanese garrisons, naval bombardment at Eniwetok Island was lighter and less effective than at Engebi, and Parry was honeycombed with well-camouflaged gun emplacements and underground hideouts. It took until February 22 to secure these two southern islands.

As at Kwajalein, Air Group 60 planes were deployed throughout Operation Catchpole. Over a period of six days, VC-60 bomber pilots bombed areas on all three islands. Most of VF-60's missions were combat air patrols; however, on February 21 and 22, the fighter pilots were ordered to strafe personnel and ground targets defending Parry Island. Royce was involved in the first of these two runs. Although limited, this action was more successful than the pilots' strafing runs at Tarawa. New methods of ground-to-air communication, which gave pilots greater control of target assignments, led to better results.[98]

For a few days after Eniwetok Atoll was taken, CarDiv 22 remained in the area conducting air patrols. Then, on February 26, the unit was released with orders to return to Pearl Harbor. Royce wrote to Becky as soon as he learned of their destination. "At last," he said, "we are heading for a place where we can get some mail." He now realized, however, that his return to the States would be later than he had estimated in his last letter.

Do you realize it has been nearly five months (when you receive this) since we left? I[t] shouldn't be any more than this much longer 'til we get back to the States for a stay. I think we won't come back before then because we should keep pounding the Japs now that things are going our way. We are whipping them so soundly and with so little personal danger that it is as safe here as in the States. Don't be too surprised if some of our group gets decorated. If we go on another operation or so I think we will all get something or other in the way of a citation. However, as they told us when we first came aboard – it is 98% flying and 2% fighting. That is the way it goes – Lots of work and not much fun. We are all becoming pretty proficient at carrier operations.

Enough of this hangar flying – Now I'll say what's on my mind – I love you more every day – more than anything in the world. I miss you terribly and I don't mind admitting it. The day when we can be together again won't come too soon for me. I am ready for it at any time.

In the four months since first leaving San Diego, Air Group 60 had supported forces that conquered two powerful groups of Japanese Island bases and moved U.S. outposts in the Pacific 2,400 miles closer to Japan. Regarding the performance of the air group, Green Peyton's observations resonated with Royce's own assessment:

[They] had yet to meet a Jap fighter in the air, had sighted just one enemy plane of any sort and shot it down. They had lost two bomber pilots and had one torpedo pilot seriously hurt in accidental crashes. No fighter pilots had been lost or harmed. It was a remarkable record for efficient carrier operations . . . As for a combat record to match their operational achievements, they would have to wait a while longer for that.[99]

FIRST WEDDING ANNIVERSARY:
February–March 1944

BECKY AND ROYCE often shared news that friends or husbands of friends had become war fatalities. For Becky and other wives of servicemen, these deaths were constant reminders that their loved ones might not return home safely. Simply receiving letters from Royce was therefore reassuring. Becky sometimes openly expressed her anxiety and fear after getting the latest war news. Yet, she almost always followed this by reassuring Royce (and herself) that everything would turn out all right.

Your three letters arrived last Wednesday [January 26], and I was really glad to hear – Surprised, too, because I didn't expect them so soon. From the newspapers I can understand why you said I wouldn't hear from you for quite some time, for according to them things are really popping in the Marshalls. You won't get this until that's over with, probably, but I hope it won't be too long. If I shouldn't hear from you before the baby comes, I won't worry, darling, 'cause I just know everything's going to be all right and I don't want you to worry over me, hear? The baby and I are going to be ok, too.

At one point, Becky mistakenly assumed that Royce's squadron was involved in the raid on Truk. When she didn't get further news on this battle, she said, "naturally I'm anxious." Then she added, "I'm not worrying, though, dear, and don't you. Everything is going to be all right for both of us. I just feel it – It's woman's intuition, you know!"

Mail deliveries became more erratic in the ensuing months. Becky received several additional letters from Royce in February, but Royce did not hear from Becky until the *Suwannee* reached Pearl Harbor in early March. After receiving Royce's February 6 letter, Becky wrote:

> *I love you so much, honey. The poem you sent was so sweet – I'll certainly save it. Do you remember before we were married and you were home on leave, reading poetry to me one evening? I was thinking about that not long ago and wondering why we never spent an evening that way after we were married. . . . You know what I think an ideal evening would be? Good records of the Strauss Waltzes or the like playing softly and you reading poetry. Doesn't that sound relaxing and wonderful? You know I've never felt since you left, Royce, that wonderful enjoyment of a quiet evening at home, just we two, where we usually went to bed early and read or played cards. Funny how things we did together that used to be such fun aren't any more. I need you, darling and, honey, you will have someone depending on you and sticking right with you you'll never be able to get rid of when you get home.*

Becky's letters during the month of February indicate that she was not at a loss for things to do. Cooking, cleaning house, shopping, sewing, visiting the doctor, and writing letters took up much of her daytime hours. And in the evenings, she led a very active social life, going to the movies with family or friends at least once a week and hosting or visiting her girlfriends for card games and "hen" parties, as Becky called them.

Related to these activities, an important change occurred in Becky's social circles. Whereas her social life in her first three months back in Oklahoma City was generally limited to family and fellow workers at the Gas Company, it later expanded to include a core group of girlfriends from high school—Margaret, Mary, and Verla—whose husbands were in the military. For the next several months, Becky mentions this group frequently. Royce either had not met or did not know any one of them well. Margaret's husband was with the 4th Marine Division that took part in the Kwajalein operation. Mary's husband was at various Army training sites, and Verla's husband was a soldier in the European theater. Becky was fortunate to have the support of a large network of relatives while Royce was at war; however, these war wives as well as wives of men in VF-60 with whom she regularly communicated had a special emotional bond based on their common life situation and shared experiences.

Becky had not learned to cook before she was married. But now, living at home with both parents working, she often cooked for herself and her mother. More than once, she proudly referred to her cooking.

Honey, I'm getting better at cooking every day. And every time I fix a meal, I think about you and wish you were here to share it . . . Tonight I fixed a roast and cooked potatoes, carrots, and onions around it. Also had spinach, jello salad and chocolate pudding and coffee. That isn't fair to talk about food, is it, darling.

Wanting to send a photograph of herself to Royce, Becky made a few trips to a photography studio. She fancied a photographic portrait rather than a simple snapshot. But aside from that, it was common in the 1940s to have personal photographs taken in a studio. Unlike cameras today, cameras then were fully manual, without any kind of battery or power source; focusing was not automatic and usually done by estimation; and getting results required the time and expense of developing film. Becky's first trip to the studio, however, was unpleasant.

I want you to know that Mr. Pace, the photographer I went to, showed me an awful snapshot that he had. He's a regular old reprobate and I can't stand him, but he does do good work. It was sent by a fellow in the South Pacific showing how he was doing his duty. He had each arm around a black mama with a breast in each hand. I should have slapped him, but I just laughed and told him I wasn't worried about my husband. I guess he judges everybody by how he himself would act and his filthy mind.

A few days later, Becky wrote, "My proofs are terrible, I think. Mother likes a couple of them, but I don't like any . . . Mother wonders what I want. I guess something that doesn't look like me."

On February 14, Becky mentioned a few purchases:

I bought an unfinished chest of drawers for the baby today. I'm going to stain it a light oak and put a couple of coats of varnish over that. I don't have enough drawer space for the baby things, and this isn't going to be enough if I keep getting more things. You should see the bassinet now. I told you about re-painting the one Virginia and I used. Well, it's really dolled up in pink and blue satin. I keep it all made up, ready for Junior.

I bought your mother a crepe dress today to go with her new red coat for making all these baby things. You should see the plans she's making for my shower next week.

I also bought a \$100.$\underline{^{00}}$ War Bond on this 4th War Loan Drive today. I hesitated at first, because you are really doing your share in this War and we're saving for your education, but buying bonds is saving money, too, and I thought the bonds we have can go toward the children's education. We'll have enough for you to go to school on, too. I asked Sandy about it and he said to go ahead if I wanted to. He bought 3 \$100 ones the other day.

Money to finance the government's massive buildup of the military during the war came mainly from taxation and borrowing. Congress raised individual and corporate income taxes and imposed a 5 percent "Victory" tax on all incomes over $624. In addition, to accelerate tax payments, for the first time taxes were withheld from every paycheck. But taxation accounted for less than half of the war's cost. A major source of income was War Bonds—essentially a loan to the federal government. They sold for less than face value (e.g., Becky paid $75 for her $100 Bond), and after a period of time, buyers received the full face value plus interest.

A lengthy letter written on February 23 focuses on social engagements, in particular a baby shower hosted by two of Becky's girlfriends. She began by saying that her dinner party for the girls a few days ago "sure went off swell . . . They really thought everything was goody." On Saturday night, February 19, she continued,

> *Daddy brought three young couples from O.U. [Oklahoma University] and a case of beer out to the house. We really had a swell time. They had been coming to the store [her father's drugstore, which had a soda fountain] on Saturday nights and singing. They all had good voices and harmonized real well. They were about our ages. One of the girls was from Ada. She said she used to go up to Duncan quite a bit. One of the other girls had had a couple of dates with Bob at one time. Small world, isn't it?*

Sunday afternoon, Becky and two girlfriends went to see the movie *The Heat's On* with Mae West. "Now for the big news."

> *Probably won't thrill you as much as it did me, but Verla and Mary gave me a baby shower last night [Tuesday] and you should see every-thing I got. You'll never believe it unless you saw them all. Verla and her mother gave me a bathinette. Just what I wanted . . . It's*

just beautiful. I have all the things out on the dining room table so everybody that comes can see them.

In the next five pages, Becky described in exquisite detail every gift she received.

Becky pointed out that three of her friends were going to social events sponsored by the USO on Wednesday nights. "I don't want you to think for a minute that I'm getting dissatisfied or anything like that," she said, but

I thought I'd like to do that too, after the baby comes. You are to act as a hostess there and just talk to the fellows, play cards and games (ping pong is about the extent of it) and serve refreshments. A lot of the girls who go are married and I thought it would be something to do when I'm able to be out more. Especially since I'll be pretty busy during the day. What do you think about it? Just anybody can't go. You have to give them references and be accepted before one can become a hostess. Please let me know what you think and if you don't want me to, please don't be hurt because I asked you. I really didn't think you would mind, though, or I wouldn't have asked.

Less than a week after the baby shower, Becky told Royce that Margaret and her "bunko party went off well last night." She mentioned that many of the girls had never met Royce or seen his picture. "You should have heard them," she went on.

I was so proud. They thought you were the sweetest and best looking thing and I readily agreed. I had all your pictures out – even the one in your flight gear with "Lip" on your life jacket. They said that was a perfect match for me – Can't understand what they meant. Can you??

Royce in the cockpit of Hellcat, circa September 1944

Becky and Royce were both strong-willed; they spoke their minds; more than once, their letters refer to their marital spats, usually as something they hope will never happen again. Becky's account of a trip to the doctor exemplifies her assertive, determined nature. When she, Beulah, and Gussie went to Norman for her appointment, she related,

> *I waited about three hours to see the doctor. Then they almost sent us home because they are short of doctors, and they were all busy. I raised such cain about coming so far and only having so much gasoline etc. that they didn't send me home and I finally got to see the doctor between [baby] deliveries.*

Royce and Becky's squabbles often concerned finances, which would explain why Becky felt compelled to keep Royce abreast of her expenses and her attempts to economize. In early February, she told him,

I'm paying my way here [at her parents' house] now. I don't remember telling you. Sandy made the remark one day he thought I should pay room and board. I had given Mother money [all] along for groceries, but now I'm paying the Gas Bill and give Mother five dollars a week for groceries. I haven't received the phone bill yet, but they will get around to it I have no doubt.

On February 27, Becky tells Royce that she received the money orders he sent.

Thanks, our bank account needs that. If it's all the same to you let's wait until you get home to go over our bank account, because I'm afraid you'll never be able to understand where all of it goes. I told you I was paying an average of $20.^{00} per mo. here at home. And this last mo. it seemed like everything fell due – Car, $110.82, work on car $20.^{00}, bond $75.^{00}, tele-bill $65.^{00}, my insurance, baby chest of drawers, then I've bought several pieces of material to make up [dresses] for myself when the baby comes for Spring and Summer. If you still want our balance each month, I'll tell you all checks written and what for so you'll understand. I don't think I'm extravagant, but I'm not skimping either. I have a lot of things for the baby and they all cost money. Darling, please don't worry over financial matters. We'll have a nice bank account when you get home.

With their first wedding anniversary approaching (March 9), Royce wrote to Becky.

Our "plan of the Day" for yesterday included a calendar. I see by intent study of same that in one week you will no longer be considered a bride – the honeymoon will be over – in short and according to the rules of society in which we live – you will have become in one day an old married woman. I think you may have noticed several times in the past that I care not a damn what people say should or should not be. The honeymoon for me has not as yet even well begun. As J. P. Jones said, "I have not yet begun to fight" or Farragut "Damn the torpedoes – full speed ahead!" or as I say when I think of you, "To _ _ _ _ with the Japs – full speed astern." I miss you more and more as the time slowly drags by. After fifty-one weeks of being married to you my only statement is that I hope I shall be blessed with your company forever. Right now my heart feels like an old chunk of lead within me. I guess I am feeling a few nostalgic pains, but I suppose everyone does on his wedding anniversary – especially if he is as much in love with his wife as I am with mine. . . Darling, I wish I could spend our anniversary with you but I cannot. Remember that I shall be thinking of you especially upon that day. I think you'll probably not get this letter until about the 15th, but you will then know that I have not forgotten you upon our anniversary nor will I ever.

Before she received this letter, Becky reflected on their anniversary.

March 8, 1944

My Dearest Husband,

Tomorrow is our first wedding anniversary. Married one year – It has been the happiest and fullest year of my life. And, though, I didn't think it possible a year ago, I love you even more now than I did when we were married.

You have made me very happy, darling. I want you to know that truly loving and being loved is the most wonderful thing in the world. I can't imagine what life would be without it now.

Our first year may have been cut short, but we did a good job of those seven months. And I don't doubt but that we'll make up for our separation in the years to come.

I was hoping the baby would be born on the 9th but I'm afraid it won't be. Anyway, it won't be long now. Then you'll have two of us to come home to at this address instead of only one.

I love you with all my heart Royce, and think you are the best husband a girl could want. Take good care of yourself, dear, and hurry home. We will be right here waiting for you.

Your loving wife,
Becky

Respite in Pearl Harbor

The *Suwannee* docked at Pearl Harbor from March 3–15. There, CarDiv 22 was joined by the *Sangamon* carriers' sister ship, the *Santee*, which had been serving in the Atlantic. While the pilots and crew got some much-needed R & R, the air groups on all four carriers underwent a major reorganization.

All air groups in CarDiv 22 initially had three types of aircraft: F6F Hellcat fighters, TBM Avenger torpedo bombers, and SBD Dauntless dive bombers. Fighters are the lightest and fastest of these aircraft; armed with machine guns, their primary role, as the name implies, is to attack and destroy enemy planes. Torpedo bombers carry torpedoes designed for air launch against enemy ships, including submarines, although they also can bomb ground targets. Dive bombers can drop large bombs with great accuracy from steep dives aimed directly at the target, which makes them ideal for attacking enemy surface ships.

For a combination of reasons, the admiral in command of CarDiv 22 decided to replace the dive bombers with F6F Hellcats. The dive bombers were seldom called upon to attack shore batteries in support of amphibious landings. In addition to strafing enemy troops and installations, Hellcats could carry a bomb under their belly and be used in a dive-bombing role, if necessary. And, together, the Hellcats and Avengers could perform the other missions of the escort carriers: to provide combat air and antisubmarine patrols.[100] So, ten Hellcats replaced nine dive bombers on each of the *Sangamons*, VC-60 became torpedo squadron 60 (VT-60), the dive bomber pilots were ordered stateside for reassignment, and additional pilots, all young ensigns without combat experience, were added to VF-60.[101]

The addition of pilots led to changes in VF-60's divisional structure. Fighter squadrons fly in standard formations during flight operations. The basic "finger-four" formation of four planes, called a "division," consisted of two "elements," each with two planes. When viewed from above, the positions of the planes resemble the tips of four fingers of a human right hand. At the front of the formation (imagine the middle finger) is the flight leader of the lead element; to his left and behind him is his "wingman." On the other side of the formation is the second element, with the element leader in front and his wingman to his right and behind him. The leaders in this formation have offensive roles, opening fire first on the enemy; the wingmen have a defensive role, covering the rears of their leaders.[102] But the major advantage of the division structure was mutual protection.

During VF-60's early campaigns, Royce was an element leader and Paul "Eggbert" Barber was his wingman. After the reorganization of the squadron, Royce became a division or flight leader, with Barber leading his second element. John Smith, who joined the squadron in late December and would eventually become Royce's wingman, flew wing on John Simpson in another division. Besides these changes in the air, aboard ship John D. "Rabbi" Shea became Royce's roommate when Crash (Green Peyton Wertenbaker) was transferred.

Some Disagreements

While in Pearl Harbor, Royce received his first mail since the ship left San Diego in mid-January. Aside from fervent and heartfelt messages on the eve of their first anniversary, a few letters in early March reveal recurring disagreements.

One thing he and Becky agreed on, however, was their preference for the sex of the baby—something that, until the late 20th century, was unknown until a child was born. Many expectant mothers didn't even know if they were carrying twins. When Royce departed in October, he and Becky assumed, or at least hoped, that their first child would be a boy. Before one of her February doctor's appointments, Becky wrote,

> *I'm just dying to find out what the doctor thinks it's going to be. Everybody says a girl. They say I carry it just like it was a girl, so I'm about to decide that's what it is. If I made up my mind for a girl, I won't be disappointed if it is and if it should be a boy then I'll be pleasantly surprised – Good idea, no? You would just as soon have a little daughter, wouldn't you, sweetheart? Either way will be sweet.*

Many myths existed for "predicting" a baby's sex; for example, if a woman carries a baby low, it's going to be a boy; if she carries it high, it's a girl. A month later, Becky implored Royce not to "place any more bets on a boy. $30.^{00} is enough to lose – Now, who's being pessimistic? Just about everybody thinks it will be a girl."

The preference for a male child has a long history. The Gallup polling organization has asked about Americans' preference for the sex of their children 11 times since 1941.[103] With slight changes in question wording, Americans have preferred boys to girls in every poll. The margin in 1941 was 38 percent to 24 percent, with the remainder saying it "doesn't matter" or having no opinion. The respondents' gender was not asked in 1941, but subsequent polls show that the overall preference for a boy was due largely to the attitudes of men, while women showed no preference.

Becky and Royce also agreed that their son would be named Sandy, after Royce's father. Becky signed her second letter "Becky and Sandy III," which is how she ended every letter until the end of 1943. She also referred to the baby as "Sandy" in her letters, as in "Robert says he won't be home for 4 or

5 mos. after Sandy is born." And "I wrote to M.E. yesterday and told her I was going to the doctor the 15th and I'd let her know whether to count on a Sandy, Virginia or 'both.'" The only issue was the middle name. In November, Becky wrote, "Honey, I've changed my mind about the name again. Instead of Sandy Paul, how would you like Sandy James Singleton III? After Jimmy Walker – and that's, also, my grandfather's name. Let me know. Want your approval." Later, when Royce failed to respond to this query, Becky asked again, then said, "If it should be twin boys there is going to be a Royce Alan, Jr."

Beginning in the New Year, however, Becky signs only her name to her letters. And, she no longer refers to the baby as "Sandy." On February 16, she made explicit her reservations about the name.

Honey, just once more I'd like to ask you, "wouldn't you like to have your son named after you?" I really tried, darling, to get used to the name "Sandy" but so help me I can't imagine calling a tiny baby Sandy. Every time I say the name I'd think of Buddy, and I want our baby named after his Daddy. I promised you I'd call him Sandy and if you still insist I will. Think it over again, please.

This request was in one of a batch of letters Royce received on March 4. Despite Becky's strong feelings about the baby's name, his reply was curt: "I, too, can hardly wait for the baby to be born. It doesn't make any difference whether it's a boy or a girl, either. But I still insist on Sandy if it's a boy." A couple paragraphs later, he added: "Don't worry – there'll be a Royce Jr. one day. At least I intend to work on it!!!!!!"

The reply is part of an atypical letter Royce wrote. He began with, "I'll have to glance at your letters as I write so that I can answer what questions you have asked." Then, he went on for eleven pages.

In one of your letters you spent a paragraph or two letting me [know] about expenses and such. It sounded like you may have splurged a *little. If – by the time you receive this – you have 1100 dollars saved, I'll be very happy. I have sent you 1325 – and there was a little in the bank when I sent it. I had sorta figured on about 1400 but it isn't too important. I don't want you to lack anything at this time. Let me know how we're doing all along, though. If I don't get back until fall, I think we'll have over 2000 dollars saved at the very least. You know that I don't want you to skimp – but I do want you to try to save – don't waste it. And don't be angry because I want to know. In the past you've flown off the handle every time I've brought anything like this up. It wasn't long ago that <u>you</u> suggested a statement to me each month. I am not worried about finances, though.*

. . .

I suppose you know that a pregnant woman should not ride too much – so stay out of that damned car as much as you can. I don't intend to get another unless I can pick up a bargain. Furthermore, don't spend any more on that Plymouth than necessary. Don't let anyone talk you into anything approaching an overhaul job. I don't imagine you can go too far or wear out too much on what gas you can get though.

I think this life may be doing it. I guess I sound pretty Puritanic, but I don't like to hear off-color stories from you. Every time you tell me one (and I know you are just trying to make me feel better) It nearly makes me sick. As for that photographer who was evil enough so show you that foul picture, I'd like to beat him up. Don't ever go back there again if you never get to send me a picture.

. . .

If you want to do something for the USO, go ahead. I don't know why you asked me though. If anyone ever treats you badly – insults you or makes a pass at you – quit. If you don't, I shall certainly be disappointed, not in the USO but in you. I don't mean to be an old fogey, darling, but I <u>know</u> what you can hear at a USO Center. If a *person associates too long with something which disgusts them, it isn't long until it is a part of the person, even though he may not realize it.*

. . .

By the way, what gave you the idea that I'm not eating well? Every time you are talking about what good food you've had, you end up with "That's not fair," etc. etc. The worst that has happened to me so far is that the steak has been a little tough once or twice. We dine better aboard ship than I ever did at Corpus – etc. Of course, I'd still ditch it in a minute for some of your cooking. I told Bob that you were a good cook. I also told him you were a wonderful wife and that I loved you very much. I hope you don't mind my letting these little secrets out.

I just read the letter again which had your measurements in it. Please don't ever shock me like that again. My nerves just won't stand it. What if I should casually write you and say, "Remember the right arm that I used to hug you with now and then – well, it's gone!" The results would be appalling, I'm sure. I really didn't realize that you had gotten that big. I'll bet you'd look wonderful to me though and I'd give the world (if it were mine) to see you. It won't be long 'till you'll be back to your fighting weight again – and we'll have a family besides.

. . .

Becky I love you so much that I practically hurt all over right now. I am so glad you liked the poem, but I just knew you would. Nothing would please me more than to read poetry with or to you in the evenings while listening to some beautiful music. Hell – I'd even enjoy a good fight if it could be with you. I've a hunch we aren't going to be doing much fighting when I get home though.

. . . No! I don't like you to be finicky about an orderly house. I'd much rather have you slovenly, dirty, disorderly, etc. etc. I guess I can stand it if you want to keep the house clean though as long as you'll

not expect me to turn a hand. If they keep me away from you another
five months though, you're going to have an unmade bed for a week.
I suppose that's kinda bad talking like that, but I miss you physically
just as I do otherwise. After all I am young and healthy. What I'd
like most is to see you – so I'd know you're all right – and so I could
tell you over and over that I love you.

Concerning having the baby. I want you to be well before and after
the ordeal. That is all that matters to me. Don't you think I'd be just
as proud to have a daughter as a son. The fact that you are being the
mother of my children brings tears of joy to my eyes. Don't worry about
anything but taking the best care of yourself that you possibly can. . . .

. . .

Say I just came to that letter again about the bank balance. I
don't care how much you spend. I just want to know how our bank
account is getting along, that's all. I'll bet you've got more saved than
I expected because I only expected 1400 – and I'd deduct what I
spent from that – and the telephone bills – and the 100 dollars you
paid Buddy – and I know you haven't spent too much. If you have
over 1100 you're doing o.k. by me. I know it costs like the devil to
have a baby. I'd suggest that you take a couple of hundred dollars
and replenish your own wardrobe after the baby is born. I'll try to
save 200 (I don't have to have any money aboard ship) and send it
to you – as a little gift – I want it spent too – on clothes.

Becky must have been surprised by the tone of Royce's letter, which
deviated from his usual words of support, understanding, and love. As her
reply on March 11 shows, the letter was vexing, but she handled it with a
good deal of humor.

I received four letters from you on our anniversary and another one
today. Wasn't that lucky, my getting your sweet anniversary letter on

that very day! I guess I am just an old married woman now, but that title won't be for long, 'cause soon it's going to be "mama" instead. How do you like that, "Daddy"?

    . . .

To get down to your letter today. I still am trying to decide if I'm married to a preacher or a wolf. You were either "down in the dumps" or my letter didn't read very well to you or something. Really darling, I'm only kidding, but you did put a few things rather strongly. I try not to write letters when I'm not feeling "up to snuff" and I guess things do sound different on paper sometimes than you would think. Then, too, I'm not always too good at expressing my opinions and feelings anyway. So, darling, try not to worry over things I say! I certainly don't intend to 'cause you any consternation, but I know I have.

    . . .

Who told you pregnant women shouldn't ride in cars? They told me in Norman it was perfectly all right. Some people may not be able to – like June – who has been having trouble ever since she became pregnant and, besides, she's carrying her baby real low. Heck, fire, if I thought riding in a car would hurry this little job up any, I think I'd take a little trip – what about the 25 miles I have to go when I start having pains, doc?? Listen, I'm not paying any attention to all this stuff about what you can and can't do unless the doctor says it. My gosh, I'd be sitting around twiddling my thumbs if I did. I haven't had any trouble carrying it and if I can be as fortunate having it, we'll have that family of at least four you were talking about, but, say, let's slow down on that big family idea until we see how I get along with the first one – Ok??

I'm not planning on selling the Plymouth until you get home. Then you can take care of those details . . .

Ok, I won't tell anymore off-color stories. . . . Forget about the photographer. He's nothing but an old fool. I should have never mentioned the incident.

Here we go again. (I guess you can tell I'm reading your letter as I write this.) OK, so you are eating good. That's swell. Guess I've heard so much from Bob about what he has to eat that I thought it went for all the Pacific forces – "Dod-Oh-Dod" What did I do to deserve all this? Every other paragraph in your letter starts with "I don't ever want you to do so and so" or "I suppose you know etc.," "By the way," "And another thing." All in all, it really was a sweet letter, darling. A little rugged in places, you wolf. And you talk about me and my off-color stories. I think I've been a darn nice girl since you've been gone. Wonder how I'll feel when I get rid of this excess baggage. Wolfish, too, maybe.

I thought you'd be interested in my measurements. Really, honey, you don't know what you are missing. Not seeing me this way. I still don't think I look as bad as some I've seen.

We'll call the boy Sandy, Royce. But I hope it's a girl now. I've dreamed several times it was a girl and Mina did too.

I had my picture made again the other day at a place that absolutely is the worst looking place I ever saw on Grand Ave., but they specialize in baby pictures and some of the girls had their children's pictures made there that were just precious. It's a man, his wife, and his sister-in-law who do all the work and because of that and their low overhead they are much cheaper than other studios here. They made eight different poses and they are pretty good so I'm having some made up right away and will send them to you. They, also, take pictures of tiny babies and I really am glad because now I can have the baby's pictures made soon after it's been born and send it to you. They have pictures of babies, three, seven, and ten weeks old on display.

Well, darling, you can rest easy. Our bank account when I made the last deposit was a little over $1300.00. But three or four checks have been written since then. I received a bill from the Gas Co. yesterday for the last long distance call you made. It was charged to them – $28.38.

How do you like that? I was afraid the bill we got here last mo. didn't include all of those calls and sure enough. That made our telephone bill here almost $100.⁰⁰. I forget what your folks bill was, but Mrs. Singleton said your Sandy could settle that when you come home, when I offered to write a check for it. If you don't get home until fall, we should have $2000.⁰⁰ easy. But I don't like to have "my flying off the handle about expenses" thrown up to me. My dear, you should read some of your letters over where you said you realized that you weren't always fair. Honey, I don't want to discourage you. But I hope you are not building up any illusions about your wife. I'm still the "hell cat" you left in Long Beach.

. . .

Well, darling, have been all afternoon writing this. I really did enjoy your letter – Well, most of it anyway. You are just getting out of hand. The Navy had better not keep you much longer. I don't know what I'll do with you if they do.

-8-

To the Palaus and Back:
March 1944

BY MARCH 1944, the Central Pacific campaign was well along. General MacArthur was positioned to move westward along the northern side of New Guinea, and Admiral Nimitz, having secured the Gilberts and Marshalls, was ready to attack Japanese bases in the Marianas, a 425-mile-long crescent-shaped island group lying north of the Carolines and New Guinea, east of the Philippines and southeast of Japan. As early as January 1943, several high-ranking Naval officers had viewed the Marianas as the key to the American strategy. They

were convinced that relentless pressure by sea power could defeat Japan short of invasion. They looked on the Marianas as the logical point for an attack on the inner perimeter of Japanese defenses, and also as forward bases for long-range bombing, refueling submarines, and replenishing surface ships. They anticipated that American control of the Western Pacific, exercised from these bases, could destroy Japan's capacity to wage war by depriving her of oil, rubber, rice and other essential commodities.[104]

This objective was approved by the Joint Chiefs of Staff in August 1943; however, General MacArthur was strongly opposed. In December 1943, he argued for a single line of advance northward from New Guinea, under his command, that would abandon a separate Central Pacific offensive. According to Samuel Eliot Morison, the top strategists kept "war plans flexible, subject to change as the situation developed." So, MacArthur might have gotten his way. But "the balance was tipped the other way" by two factors. One was the quick conquest of the Gilberts and Marshalls by Nimitz's powerful fast carrier and amphibious forces; the other was the arrival of the new B-29 Superfortress, capable of carrying 10,000 pounds of bombs over a distance of 1,500 nautical miles.[105] Thus the Joint Chiefs decided to go directly from the Marshalls to the Marianas. Finalized in March 1944, the plan called for the occupation of Hollandia in New Guinea by General MacArthur's forces in April and the occupation of Saipan, Tinian, and Guam in the southern Marianas by Admiral Nimitz beginning in June. These operations would engage CarDiv 22 for the next four months.

Like the invasions in the Gilberts and Marshalls, CarDiv 22 was part of the task force for the invasion of Hollandia on the northwest coast of New Guinea. Before this operation, however, the *Suwannee*'s carrier group joined an armada assembled for an air strike in the Palaus, the westernmost island group in the Carolines. The Japanese had a naval base as well as an airfield there within reach of Hollandia. The purpose of the Palaus strike was to destroy aircraft and shipping that might interfere with the Hollandia landing.

CarDiv 22 left Pearl Harbor in mid-March. For the next five weeks, the ships spent much of their time cruising to and from CVE operations. The Palau Islands were roughly 5,000 statute miles from Pearl Harbor. The *Suwannee* could cover about 510 statute miles in a 24-hour period; however, the zigzag pattern used by the ships reduced the distance covered to 300–350 statute miles, which meant it took about two weeks to reach their destination.[106] This also meant that the officers and crew had a lot of downtime for relaxing or stimulating activities. Occasionally, a volleyball net was set up on the hangar deck so the pilots could get some exercise. Various board and card games were popular, including "acey-deucy" (a form of backgammon), Monopoly, and poker.[107] Royce described these occasions on March 20, as the ship sailed to the Palaus.

> *You should see this bunch now. We've been having the wildest monopoly games you ever saw. There's generally more kibitzers than players – and everyone talking as loudly and furiously as possible. I have repeatedly accused John Simpson of having no business ethics whatsoever. It is a good thing we don't have any knives or pistols around or someone might get hurt. We have some of the other fellows in the part of the ship where we play ask if we furnished cotton for the ears of those in the near vicinity who were not in the game. Anyway, we sure have lots of fun.*

The fun continued March 21, when the *Suwannee* crossed both the equator and the international dateline at the hour of the Vernal Equinox. As a consequence of this rare, awesome intersection, the sun was directly overhead, "90 degrees above the horizon in any direction one looked."[108] During Royce's time at sea, the *Suwannee* crossed the equator over 50 times. Crossing the equator was an occasion for a ritual known as the "Order of Neptune," which has been performed by seafarers for over 400 years. This ritual is an initiation for those aboard ship who have never made the crossing, called "Pollywogs," by those who have made it, called "Shellbacks." To be initiated, Pollywogs on the *Suwannee* endured a hazing ritual, passing through a "'slop chute,' followed by a much needed wash-off" performed by Shellbacks wielding high-pressure hoses.[109] Once inducted as members of the Royal Order of the Purple Porpoises, Pollywogs became Shellbacks. Royce had gained this status on October 27, 1943, his ninth day at sea after shipping out from San Diego.

Soon CarDiv 22 approached the Palaus and prepared for combat. The operation took place on March 30-31 and involved nearly the entire central Pacific fleet. The raid was highly effective: Avenger torpedo bombers mined two passages to the main harbor, trapping vessels within; 36 Japanese ships were sunk or badly damaged; numerous installations were demolished; and an estimated 150 Japanese aircraft were destroyed on the ground or in the air. Twenty-five American planes were lost, but 26 of the 44 men on board were rescued.[110] After learning about the Palau operation, Becky wrote, "The news sounds good." But she mistakenly thought the *Suwannee* squadrons were part of the carrier plane attacks and losses: "I take it you were in the bunch that did so much damage to the Japs not far from the Philippines. The report here was a loss of 25 American planes, but only eighteen pilots. That 'only' sounds rather ironic, doesn't it? Nobody I know, I hope??"

As squadrons in the slowest carriers in the fleet, Air Group 60 "drew the short straw" and provided air cover for the fleet supply groups while aircraft from the fast carriers made the strikes on the islands. Protecting the surface ships was a necessary role. Still, "the CVE pilots envied the fast carrier pilots the chance to make the quick hit-and-run strikes [that ran] up their scores in aerial combat."[111]

On the Home Front

Meanwhile, after a very active social life in February, Becky began to curtail her activities as the baby's due date drew near. And so, her letters contained fewer descriptions of hen parties, visits to friends and family, and other outings. When she did go out, Becky's sister Virginia often accompanied her. Virginia was now living at home after dropping out of school due to a prolonged illness. As Becky told Royce, "I hate to see her quit school, but we think her health is more important than anything else. She'll be a big help when I come home from the hospital." On March 21, Becky reported that she and Virginia were going to a skating show at the Municipal Auditorium. "A friend of Mother's," she said, "has a son who is home on furlough . . . He's a lieutenant in the army and they are trying to get him and Virginia together." The matchmakers were successful: Virginia began dating the son, Robert Parnell, and their relationship, according to Becky, quickly became "serious."

Becky continued to feel the effects of the war effort on the home front. "Our gasoline allotment is being cut to two gallons a week [on March 22]," she said. "That will hardly be enough to take the baby to the doctor every so often. Let alone over to your [parents'] house now and then." To alleviate some shortages, whenever Becky visited the doctor in Norman, she stocked up at the naval base commissary.

They have everything. You can get Kleenex there or have you heard of the shortage? There is also a shortage of soap. So, I get Kleenex (2 boxes per customer) and soap each time I go for the baby. You really use a lot of Kleenex and have to wash every day. I've given some Kleenex to Mina.

With so much food being shipped to the military overseas, civilian food shortages increased. To compensate, Americans were encouraged to plant their own fruits and vegetables "on any spare patch of land they had."[112] First introduced during World War I, these plots, known as Victory Gardens, were expressions of patriotism. In spring 1944, Becky's father H.S. was one of an estimated 20 million Americans[113] to plant his own Victory Garden.

A visit to the Gas Company on February 29 revealed that the company was facing a labor shortage. "I think Mr. Deal is getting worried," Becky wrote, pointing out that several employees from the Service Department are 1-A now, two others have received deferments, and another employee is on the limited-service list. The Selective Service, operating through local draft boards, determined who would be eligible for the military draft and who would be deferred. Those fit for military service were classified as 1-A, but there were more than a dozen other classifications, including exemptions for conscientious objectors, men with family economically dependent on them, and those employed in an essential occupation such as farming.

To classify each registrant and simultaneously meet induction quotas, local boards followed national policy but also represented local interests. It was not unusual for local business owners to appear before the board to request job deferments for their employees.[114] In an earlier letter, Becky mentioned that one employee "wouldn't let Mr. Deal do a thing to keep him at the Gas Co." As the war progressed, criteria for deferment changed to meet the pressing need for military personnel while still providing an adequate supply of labor for industrial and agricultural production critical to the war effort. For example, the draft age was lowered, and fathers began to lose their deferments. At the time of Becky's visit, the Selective Service had just finished reclassifying 2,000,000 men as 1-A after President Roosevelt called for a re-evaluation of those deferred.[115]

In mid-March, Becky wrote consecutive letters that paralleled her exchange of correspondence with Royce earlier in the month: first gushing about her feelings and then expressing her discontent about Royce's grilling her over finances. Becky opened the first letter by saying that she had received six letters in one week.

> *Darling, it's wonderful, you are wonderful, everything's wonderful when I hear from you. Did I ever tell you that you write the best letter[s] I've ever read? Honey, if I could only tell you how much you mean to me and put it as well as you can. But I hope it means just as much to you for me to say, "I love you with all my heart." Because I do and that love grows stronger and deeper every day. I can only think how dull life would be if you weren't constantly in my mind and a part of me.*

A day later, Becky's second letter begins:

I love the way you put things – "What you expect of me." You don't
want me to take offense, but, confidentially, what you said in your
long letter on the subject was enough. However, if you are going to
worry about it, I decided, as best I can to let you know what we have
and what the rest [of the money] went for.

Becky then described in detail her expenditures, beginning November
15 and ending March 15. The two-page letter is accompanied by three lists:
a "financial report" of all checks and deposits, items purchased by check
at various department stores, and clothes and other items purchased for
the baby. By her reckoning, they had $1,100–$1,200 in the bank. She
asked Royce to save the lists, and she promised hereafter to keep a better
account of things.

I'm sorry you had to let someone else read that letter [a reference
to Royce's long letter of March 4] – who is E.H. [the initials of the
censor that appeared on the envelope]? He's going to think you are
pretty tight unless he knows we're saving for your education or that
I'm an awful spendthrift who keeps you worried. Oh well, it doesn't
really matter, but you'll receive a bank statement each month. And
I hope these explanations suffice. . . I'm not mad, dear. And I love
you very much.

Great Expectations

Throughout March, almost every one of Becky's letters mentioned her
anticipation of the birth of their first child. Even though she knew that the
due date, March 25, was only an estimated time of arrival, like expectant
mothers from time immemorial she found herself counting the days, hoping
for an early delivery, and repeatedly experiencing false signs that the baby
would arrive soon. She first expressed her eager anticipation on February

8: "I'm getting awfully anxious, aren't you darling? It really feels like it's not far off." A week later, she wrote:

I haven't been sleeping too well the last couple nights and I think it's because the baby has dropped. It seems to be much lower now. Of course, it may not have dropped enough to really matter much, but when it does get in position, it won't be long then.

The following week, Becky reported,

Bet you figured something had happened in these few days since you received my last letter, but no such luck. A lot has happened in a way, but "it" isn't here yet. . . . [The doctor] said the baby's head was still floating, but it was in the correct position. I said, "You mean it won't be here early," and he said "No." He said the baby was about the right size for eight months. And everything seemed to be all right.

Despite the doctor's prediction and a due date still more than a month away, Becky continued to think she'll be in labor "any day now." As she wrote on February 29, for example, "Just three more weeks. But I'm a-thinkin' it can be any day." When nothing happens, her letters increasingly revealed her frustration and disappointment.

I'm at the hospital, but not for what you think. I came for a check-up and they decided I should see the doctor . . . when I come I usually just see the nurse for a check-up – blood pressure, weight, etc., but since I had a little trouble last night they thought I had better see the doctor – it may not be long now, honey – I had cramps and backache last night and am real sore today. . . . Well, I saw the doctor – False alarm. He said the head hadn't settled yet. He also said there is only one baby. So, it looks like it will either be on time or late. Won't be early, darn it, unless he hurries up and drops. (March 6)

You still are not a "papa" as yet, but you will be before long. My trip to the doctor Monday proved to be a little more encouraging. I saw the doctor again and he said the baby's head had settled. So that means any time now. . . . I packed my suitcase tonight. I'm already to go, when?? (March 14)

I think I'm going to have the baby tonight and tomorrow. You may think I'm crazy, but there is a way of telling. Have you ever heard of the "show"? It's a trace of blood and it showed up tonight. Margaret said she noticed hers two days ahead of time. And Mother only a few hours before. So, I'm going to quit working on this [letter] and get everything ready. I hope it's true. (March 18)

You are still not a "papa." And I'm beginning to wonder if you ever will be now. Grandma says it will be tomorrow when the moon changes. I hope she's right. But I don't put much faith in such things. It will come when it gets good and ready, I guess, and not before.

. . . I went with Virginia to see Dr. Dersch today and he said one sure way to get it started was to get an old beat-up Ford and drive it down the railroad tracks. That will do it every time, he says.

. . . Tell the boys in the squadron you might make it home for your heir's arrival yet. Tell Frog the "cake in the oven" is doing all right, but it's certainly taking a long time to get well done. (March 22)

Not yet. Mabel Haywood declares she believes it's a tumor. Isn't that awful? . . . Virginia and I went to see Mickey Rooney and Judy Garland in "Girl Crazy" last Monday night. It was cute. I had funny pains all through it, but they turned out to be another false alarm. . . .

I haven't been able to wear my [engagement and wedding] rings for almost two weeks. My hands are swollen. I'm wearing a ring of Virginia's. I have to wear something in public. I'd feel awfully silly without any rings. Be glad when I can wear mine again. (March 25)

No, it still hasn't happened. We're still not parents. [Saw the doctor yesterday.] He said the baby's head was real low and for me to wait about a week and everything would come out all right. Darn it. I wish since it's this late, it would come on your birthday. I'll die if it happens on April 1st. An April Fool's baby – wouldn't that be terrible? It wouldn't really, but poor child, it sure would be teased a lot. (March 28)

I'll be two weeks over Wednesday. We certainly must have miscalculated. You don't suppose that I really didn't get pregnant until after we started being careless, do you? That would really be funny. Good joke on us. . . . Well, honey, I suppose we'll have a child someday, but I don't know when. One trait I know this baby has before it even gets here is stubbornness. And don't say it takes after it's Mother!! (April 4)

Jr is getting too large and heavy for me to lug around much longer. I'm beginning to think he's unspeakably lazy. I'll probably eat those words, though, when he does get started. It's going to take dynamite to get him started, it looks like. Aren't I the most cheerful wife? I'll bet you're wondering just what you're coming home to, but don't worry, honey, I'm sure everything will be all right when "the child" makes its appearance. Then "mama" can settle down.

. . .

P.S. I'll bet those letters you received while in P.H. [Pearl Harbor] saying "it won't be long now," really sound funny, don't they? This is something I'll never try to predict again. (April 8)

Fittingly, the "P.S." was the end of this thread as the baby was born on Tuesday, April 11, 1944. It would be a while before Royce got the word.

By the time the baby was born, Becky had received no further communication from Royce concerning the baby's name. However, toward the end of March, she once again broached the subject in a lengthy expression of her view extending over two days.

I don't suppose it will do any good to go into this again, but I found out that you can't tack a "III" on a child's name unless the grandfather, father, and the child all have the same name. Dump should be the one to carry on the name Sandy. Then it would have some distinction – Sandy III – otherwise it will just be another Sandy Singleton and you certainly don't want two grandchildren named Sandy. Dump is going to want to name his son that – after himself and his father. What about it? If you don't want to name it Royce Jr., I'll compromise with you. I'd be afraid it would be called Jr. anyway and I can't stand that, but neither can I stand Sandy James, the more I think about it. To me it's embarrassing to have someone ask me what Sandy stands for as if it is a nickname. If it's a boy, I think I'll just mark the announcements "boy" and not put a name until I hear from you. I know I promised you I'd call the boy Sandy. But I still think it's rather unfair for you to insist on a certain name, not caring how I feel about it. I'm willing to compromise. I think parents should both like the names they give their children. After all, they both have to call them that as long as they live. Royce, I hate to keep bothering you with this. But darn it, it's important to me. If Virginia Ruth didn't satisfy you for a name for the girl, I'd be willing to compromise with you. Look, marriage is supposed to be 50-50. The naming of the boy is 100% Royce and Becky has nothing to say about it, except supplying a middle name, which is damn hard to do. See if you can think up anything that sounds really good with Sandy.

So much for that. It doesn't do for me to get started on that subject or I get upset. I still would like to add "I love you very much" – although I don't imagine you are much in the mood for that after reading this letter. Anyway, darling, I do love you and miss you too.

She followed this the next day by saying:

I didn't mail this letter until I had slept on what I wrote about the name. Perhaps I put it a little strongly and I know you have enough on your mind without my worrying you more. But, Royce, I feel that this is important and that I can't and wouldn't do anything without consulting you.

You know that I have never from the very beginning said I liked the name Sandy. And truly I have tried the past nine months to get used to the idea. But I simply can't. It has worried me so lately that I've laid awake nights thinking about it. Look, Royce, if you absolutely didn't like a name, I wouldn't think of insisting. I'm perfectly willing to start all over and get a name that has no connection whatsoever with anybody we know. Sentimentality can be carried too far. You say you know what a boy would like. Sandy sounds just like Johnny, Tommy, or Jimmy. I've never seen many men yet who wouldn't rather be called John, Tom, or Jim when he got older. If we name the boy Sandy, he'll have a horrible nickname like Dump. It won't be called Sandy. Especially if we live here.

Well, I've had my say. Think seriously about what I said about Dump carrying on the name. It is rightfully his place. His wife would probably like the name, because it was her husband's, too. I can't see why you wouldn't want a son to carry on your name. If this should be a boy, what makes you think there will be another boy. You never know.

Then, less than a week later, she seemingly had her final say:

March 30, 1944

Dearest Royce,

My letters to you lately haven't been good, have they? I let my feelings show too much in everything I do. I hope the letters haven't worried you. I think when the baby comes everything will be all right. I guess I don't have too much patience.

Royce, I keep thinking of the letter I wrote you several days ago about naming the baby. It has been on my mind constantly. I carried it around with me for days before mailing it – trying to be sure it was the best explanation I could write. I'm not very good about putting my thoughts and feelings in words or on paper, so you'll have to read between the lines, darling.

I meant what I said in that letter, Royce, and yet I didn't want to hurt you. I never want to do anything that would really hurt you or make you love me less. I love you with all my heart and I couldn't stand it if you didn't love me.

But, please, Royce, try to understand my side. I know you love your father and you would be proud to have your son named after him. I think the world of your father, too, but I still have the same dislike for the name Sandy that has nothing to do with your father or brother. You may think it will break your heart for the boy not to be named Sandy, but it will also break mine if he is. Isn't there some way out for both of us?

I'll be a good Mother to the baby when it arrives even though I can't help feeling restless and impatient now. We'll be waiting only for you to come home to us, darling. I love you very much. Please try to understand about the name. I can't imagine a boy not proud of being name[d] after his father, especially if his father is you.

Tomorrow will be your birthday. We're hoping against hope the baby will arrive then. How would you like that for a birthday present? Happy Birthday, darling. I'll be thinking of you.

Remember Margaret O'Brien in "Journey for Margaret"? I saw her last night in "Lost Angel" and it was wonderful. We'll have to see it together when you come home. You'll enjoy it, I know.

Well, Katie Deal beat me. She had a 7½ lb. boy yesterday. Only a day late. Wouldn't you know that would happen when I was so sure ours would be early. Lynette said this afternoon she guessed that I'd just go on being pregnant the rest of my life. Horrible thought? Never lose this bay window.

Hope it won't be too long – don't you? We're concentrating on tomorrow. I love you.

Yours always,
Becky

-9-

OPERATIONS RECKLESS AND PERSECUTION: April 1944

O N APRIL 2, CarDiv 22 sailed eastward for Espiritu Santo, the Naval base where they had spent time briefly in November before their first operation. They arrived on April 7 and remained there until April 11, when they began moving westward to rendezvous with the rest of the task force for an April 22 invasion at Hollandia. Before the invasion, Royce wrote to Becky three times. The first letter has a conciliatory tone, perhaps an implicit expression of regret for the chiding letter he had written in early March.

> *I guess I'm pretty much of a damned blind fool, but I have just lately learned something that I'd have given anything to have known ten months ago. You may thank John Simpson for my finding out. It concerns the many times you have done something which should have been especially pleasing to me. Often, I was pleased but never made it evident. Most of the time I'd make some kidding remark that hurt you (and often caused a slight squabble). I didn't intentionally do it but that doesn't alleviate the fact that I did it. I'll try to restrain myself from the kidding henceforth and show proper appreciation.*

I'll certainly be glad when I get back to you to give it a whirl. I hope you'll just forget these things I've done (or rather, failed to do), but chew me out good if I do it again.

A week later, Royce wrote that he hadn't received any mail for nearly a month, "so I still haven't gotten the 'word'." With few exceptions, mail came in and went out only when the ship was in port. Two days later, on April 14, the ship was anchored in the Solomon Islands on their way to New Guinea. Knowing that it would be a few weeks before they returned to port, Royce wrote again.

This will probably be the last letter you get from me until after Mother's Day, so I am taking this opportunity to let you know that I will be thinking of you then. For the first time in my life, I, who have never been worried, am anxious about you. We have received no mail for a month and now our mail has been sent to the wrong port. It looks like there is no way of finding out how you are and how the baby is for another month at least.

We are all well. The whole squadron is "sweating out" this blessed event. Someone is always asking me whether I'm going to be a father (of a boy) or a mother (of a girl). I can take their teasing though. I'd just like to find out how you are getting along.

I suppose you never thought a year ago that this Mother's Day would find you a mother. It is a great task we have undertaken and there is no other I'd care to assume it with. I know we'll have so much happiness around when we are together again that it will practically be felt in the air around us. I am more in love with you than ever before and am very certain that it will always be thus. In six months of absence from you I have thought of you alone – and if I should be gone years, I could never bring myself to touch anyone else. I am yours alone and shall be happy to remain so until death do us part.

A "Relatively Easy Time"

To this point in the war, General MacArthur had relied on land-based air support for his troop invasions. Initially, the plan was to strike first at Wewak, the largest Japanese airbase on New Guinea, which was within range of land-based aircraft. However, this plan was revised in favor of leap-frogging Wewak, 400 miles up the coast, for westerly bases in Hollandia, which had the best natural harbor on that part of the coast. The value of this bold strategy, Green Peyton explained, was that the Japanese bases along the coast of New Guinea are like islands: "They are cut off on one side by the sea, on the other by jungle and immense, rugged mountains, which are virtually impassable."[116] Islands can be bypassed. Once the enemy was bypassed and U.S. forces set up bases in the rear, they could isolate the enemy by cutting his supply lines. To execute this plan, MacArthur needed the assistance of carrier aircraft.

Ultimately, to provide protection from western movement by the Japanese, it was decided to seize a forward airfield, at Aitape, at the same time as the attack at Hollandia. So, the advance in New Guinea involved two operations: one, codenamed Persecution, was the seizure of Aitape; the other, codenamed Reckless, was landings 125 miles to the west of Aitape at Tanahmerah and Humboldt Bays in Hollandia. The assault forces for these operations rendezvoused on April 20 at Seeadler Harbor in the Admiralties. CarDiv 22 and one other division of escort carriers provided CAP and ASP for the attack force enroute to New Guinea, then close air support for the landings at Aitape.

As pilot John Smith described, the battles in New Guinea were a "relatively easy time."[117] Heavy bombings of Wewak by U.S. forces in early April suggested to the Japanese that this was the objective; consequently, the landings at Aitape and Hollandia took them by surprise. On April 22, a small contingent of Avengers from VT-60 bombed Japanese-fortified islands near Aitape and enemy installations on the shore. They were followed by 16 Hellcats from VF-60—including Royce—which strafed buildings and beaches. But by the time the Hellcats attacked, there was little sign of life. Intelligence had overestimated enemy strength. There were only about 1,000 Japanese, most of them service troops who fled into the jungle when the assault began. Within two days, the airstrip at Aitape was secured and readied for 27 Army P-40 Warhawks, and the *Suwannee* moved down the coast to perform CAP in support of the Hollandia operation.

Writing to Becky on April 24, Royce reported, "We have taken another crack at the Japs since I last wrote. As usual we had a lot of fun and came thru fine." Despite the relatively easy time, a mishap occurred during Operation Persecution that became part of the air group's lore. A flight of Avengers directed to bomb an offshore island hit the wrong island. The fliers were congratulated when they returned to the ship for having "qualified as Army pilots."[118]

Baby Boy on Board

Two days after the baby was born, Becky broke the news.

April 13, 1944

My Dearest Royce,

We have a son, darling, and he looks like you. He was born April 11, at 17:44 o'clock. He had black hair when he was born, but it was blond yesterday morning when they brought him in. And, honey, he has practically as much hair now as Merrilee had at 18 mos. I'm not kidding. It comes down over his ears and is long on the back of his neck. Also, it's curly on top. Grows just like yours does. He's really pretty. Has the bluest eyes, but, of course, they may change color later – a little pug nose and a beautiful mouth. But you should see his hands and feet. They're huge. His fingers are long and slender. Look like they might be musician's hands. I'll bet he makes a big man. He looks every bit of two weeks old. That can be understood since he was 20 days late. Mother said he lifted his head off the bed when she was watching him through the nursery window. I hope you're happy over a boy, honey. I had made up my mind on a girl. Because everyone was so certain it would be. Two nurses who listened to the heartbeat said they thought it would be a girl. I really couldn't believe it was a boy, but I'm glad it is.

I'm ok. Sore in every joint. I was in labor sixteen hours. I'll tell you all about it when you get home. No use going into that now. I'll be here at the hospital for eight more days, then I'm taking Junior home. They won't let anyone in the room when I'm nursing him, so I'm anxious to get him home so everyone can see him real good.

Mother and your mother stayed with me the whole time. I came down for a regular checkup Monday and when I told the doctor about the pains I'd been having, he made an examination and decided I had better stay. Mother stayed with me that afternoon and evening and finally went home since it looked like nothing was going to happen. But the fireworks started about 2:00 A.M. Tuesday. They called Mother about four A.M. and she, your mother and Sandy came down. Sandy went on to Shawnee and Hugo on business. Your mother went down to Loco Wednesday A.M. to see your grandmother. Mother, Virginia and Daddy came down yesterday afternoon and brought me some flowers etc. Virginia came this afternoon, too. . . .

Well, at last, we're Mama and Papa. How does it feel? By the way, let's buy the baby's crib with the $30.$^{\underline{00}}$ you won. Ok? I hope it isn't too long before you hear about your heir. I know you've been anxious. I'm certainly glad it's over and I'll write often, honey. I can't sit up yet, so I'm lying on my side writing. Hope you can read this. I have a lot more to write about the baby but will save it for other letters. We'll take some snaps of him the day we take him home if it's pretty.

I love you darling more than anything else in the world. I can hardly wait until you see our son.

Yours for always,
Becky

From this point on, all of Becky's letters are about her *and* the baby. Of the eight letters she wrote between the 13th and the end of the month, all but one begins with information about the baby—his appearance, behavior, development, and care. She described in detail what parents talk about as they watch their children grow, with her letters taking the place of conversations she and Royce surely would have had if he were home. As she wrote, "Say, do you like hearing all these homely facts? I imagine you do since you can't be here to witness all these wonders that seem so important, homely as they are." Thus, she began subsequent letters as follows:

Your son is just doing fine, but he's sure got his mother's temper I'm finding out. He gets so mad that he turns red, doubles up his little fists and screams bloody murder. Of course, I can't blame him too much. Because the first couple days I didn't have any milk and they told me to let him nurse just five minutes to get him and me used to it. When I'd take it away from him, he'd have a breakdown. But my milk finally has come and he's getting plenty to eat now, only he doesn't keep it down very well. I suppose it agrees with him, but he just isn't used to it yet. I wish you could see him, darling. He's really old for his age, because he can lift his head up off the bed. (April 15)

The baby was just in. He really was hungry tonight. Just ate and ate and then dropped off to sleep. He's the sweetest and cutest thing, honey. All the nurses are crazy about him, He and the little girl in the basket next to his, who was born a few hours after he was, are said to be the prettiest babies in the nursery now. He seems so smart. Of course, I'd think so, but he is. He doesn't act like a helpless newborn baby. I forgot to tell you that he isn't a bit red-faced like most new babies. He sure looks like his daddy, except the nose. It's definitely pug, and he has a beautiful mouth. Don't know where he got that. I think he's going to have large eyes. They are a real deep blue. (April 16)

This son of ours is quite the thing. And I do believe he's going to be a redhead. His hair is getting redder every day. What do you think about that?

He was just in here. He was really greedy tonight and consequently lost some of his dinner in spite of my burping him. You should see him. Seems to me like he's developing so fast. Just squirms and kicks all over the place and when I make him quit eating long enough to burp him, he just frowns and starts to holler if he thinks he hasn't had enough to eat. He's really cute. He just grins in his sleep and makes all kinds of faces. Even looks cross-eyed. But they say all babies do that.

. . . I just talk to him about his Daddy and he just looks at me wide-eyed and then starts opening that mouth and looking for something to eat. He really can't see anything much yet. All newborn babies are near-sighted and can't focus their eyes at first. That's why he's always getting them crossed. But he sure gazes around like he was taking everything in. (April 20)

For a couple weeks, nearly every letter described the conditions of Becky's hospital stay as well as the stream of visitors eager to see the baby and congratulate the new mother. These accounts reveal much about postpartum maternal and childcare at that time. Becky did not leave the hospital until Friday afternoon, April 21, 10 days after the baby was born. Her length of stay was not unusual in 1944. The 1940s were a transitional period in childbirth practices and postpartum care. Before the 20th century, nearly all births occurred at home; midwives commonly delivered babies, and postpartum women and infants were cared for in their homes. But many physicians became convinced that home delivery put a woman and fetus at risk and that labor and birth were best managed medically, in a hospital. Giving birth in a hospital began gaining popularity in the 1920s. By 1935, 36 percent of births were in hospitals; ten years later, the hospital rate was 79 percent; by 1960 it was 96 percent. As hospitalizations became more common, extended postpartum stays were the norm. At many hospitals, the standard practice in the early 1940s was 10 to 14 days after a vaginal birth.[119]

Lengthy postpartum hospital stays were considered crucial for a safe recovery. Following the typical medical protocol, Becky was bedridden until day 7, when, she reported, "I sat up and dangled my feet over the edge of the bed." On day 8, she said, "I sat in a chair for a while. . . . It just thrilled me to death." Then, on day 9, April 20,

> *I got up and walked around today. I can go to the "head" now and not have to use the stinkin' bed pan. I'll bet you are surprised at the way I talk. But you certainly lose all the modesty you ever had when you have a baby. Nothing could ever bother me now, I don't believe. It really was swell to be up and about, but I'm pretty shaky. And when I put my weight on my feet, I feel like I'm on pins and needles. I'll walk some more tomorrow and then your mother and Mother are coming down to take me home Friday afternoon.*

Becky's recovery experience was regulated not only in terms of when she could get out of bed but also how much contact she had with the baby. The baby was kept in a newborn nursery and was brought to Becky every four hours, when it was time for feeding. This arrangement served to give mothers as much rest as possible to facilitate their recovery. Perhaps as important, it was consistent with prevailing theories of child development, which advocated rigid scheduling and limited parental affection toward their children as the best means of fostering independent children and adults.[120] Becky was clearly influenced by these ideas, as shown in a letter written after she left the hospital.

> *Our young son is yelling his head off. He seems to think all the time is feeding time. We had company all day yesterday – just constantly – and I think that's what's been wrong with him today. Too much*

excitement and his schedule all upset. He's going to be rotten if I
don't put my foot down. He already knows he will be picked up if he
cries. I want to do it and it's all I can do to keep everyone else from
petting him. They told me at the hospital to just remember that he's
a human being and that he could stand almost anything, except a
draft and too much handling.

Since Becky's time, challenges to postpartum care have brought about many changes. During the war and post-war baby boom, staffing problems forced many hospitals to send women home 3–5 days after birth. This experience and systematic evidence of the benefits of early ambulation led to a reduction in maternity stays of less than a week for an uncomplicated pregnancy in the 1950s, which further declined to 4 days by 1970. Today it is 24 to 48 hours.[121] In addition, research showing the positive effects of early maternal–infant bonding[122] and newer child development theories that supported more immediate response to infant needs led to rooming-in programs that keep mother and baby together all the time.[123]

Four days after the birth of the baby, Becky received two letters from Royce, the last dated April 4, which Virginia delivered to her from home. She tells Royce it was "really good to hear" from him, "especially at this time . . . I guess you'll really be surprised when you find out when the baby finally came." She thanks him for sending a check for her to buy a suit. Then, she mentions John Simpson's advice to Royce to engage in less kidding and show more appreciation for Becky. "Whatever John told you about," she said,

I don't want you to worry about it another minute. Honey, I've never
been anything but happy with you and proud of you as my husband.
Darling, I love you more than anything in this world. I always have
and always will. I'm afraid I didn't understand what you were talking
about, but it can't be very important, because I wouldn't have you any

different for anything in the world. I loved the man I married and if there's any changing I want us to do it together as we grow older. Just stay as sweet as you are and keep on loving me. I'll always love you, darling. And I'm so proud of you. We both are.

On April 16, Becky writes,

I wrote Bob this afternoon and enclosed an announcement. How do you like them? Nice, aren't they? And appropriate?? I'm sending out over a 100 to yours and my relatives and friends. Of course, I think just about everybody in the country knows about it. I know both families have called everybody they ever knew.

Later, after Becky finally disclosed the baby's name, she asked Royce, "Did you receive your announcement, honey? Dorothy Williams at the Gas Co. said she thought Baby Boy Singleton was an awfully cute name, but she couldn't decide whether to call him Baby or Boy." Over two weeks had passed between the birth and the naming of the baby. During this period, Becky refers only to the "baby" in her letters, which she signs "Mama and the baby," "Becky and the baby," or "Mama and Jr."

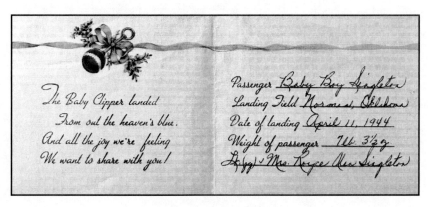

Birth announcement

Finally, on April 23, the day before taking the baby to a pediatrician in Oklahoma City, she wrote,

I discussed the name with your family and tried to explain to them how I felt – That there wasn't anything personal about my not wanting the baby named Sandy – That I just wanted to name him after his Daddy. Your Mother said she didn't blame me and for me to go ahead and name him Royce Alan Singleton II if I wanted to. Grandma said, "after all you had him." I told them, though, that I didn't want to name him without your consent. I don't want the responsibility. Dump said he didn't care what I named it, just so I named him pretty soon. So, darling, don't feel that you would be <u>giving in to me</u> by naming the baby after you. You would be giving him a name to be proud of and I can't understand you not being proud to have your son named for you. He looks like you, darling. So much more reason. Please, honey, understand. I love you with all my heart and we can hardly wait for you to come home.

Two days later, she continued,

Dr. Levy just gave me "hail Columbia" yesterday for not having named the baby so his birth certificate could be registered. She said the birth certificate could easily be lost lying around at the hospital until I made up my mind on a name. Also, I can't get a ration book until the baby is named. So, I'm up a tree. It looks like I'm going to be forced to name him. Royce Alan Singleton II sounds good to me. How about you, honey? Your Mother said yesterday she thought the oldest should be named for his Daddy. She said she thought Sandy was sorry they didn't name Robert – Sandy. Also, Sandy said for me to go ahead and name the baby Royce. You can't object too much, darling, having your own son named for you. He looks so much like you; he can't be anything else but Royce. He likes the name, too, honey. He just looks at me when I call him Royce Alan.

Finally, on April 28, Becky referred to the baby by his "official" name:

Royce Alan Singleton II is growing so that I can't keep up with him. Every morning he looks different. His face is filling out and getting so chubby and his little arms are getting so fat. I'm just dying to find out what he's gained this week. Honey, he's just precious. He's got the cutest grin. His eyes are just about set. You would swear he could see the way he looks at you. If you talk to him, he'll just stare a hole through you. Everybody who comes to see him raves about how cute and pretty he is. We really have something, darling. You'll be so proud of him.

. . .

Honey, I love you a whole bunch. Royce Alan loves his Daddy, too. He says to tell you to hurry home, so he can look you over. "Mama's" kinda anxious to see you, too. I can hardly wait, darling until we're together again. Wonderful thought, isn't it?

Love and kisses,
Becky and Royce Alan

With that said, Becky caught Royce up on the latest family news. Earlier, she had reported how arrangements had been made for Bob Parnell and her sister Virginia to get together when he was home on leave.

Virginia and Bob started dating frequently and it wasn't long until it was every night. Bob got an extension on his leave and things really looked serious. Well, he's reported back to Louisiana now, but he seems to be very much in love and wants Virginia to marry him and she really likes him, but she's not sure she wants to get married. Virginia writes to a half dozen fellows. There isn't a day goes by without her hearing from someone and there are several of the fellows I really like. Swell guys, but don't think if she looked from now on that she'd find anyone any finer or who would be any better to her than Bob. He's just wonderful. He has certainly been well reared. Has beautiful manners. How things will turn out only time will tell. I really don't think Virginia is ready to settle down. She thinks so much of you and she wants to do as well as she thinks I did when she gets married.

When letters started arriving in response to the birth announcements, Becky mentioned several of the notes she received, including those from VF-60 squadron wives M.E. Simpson and Beedie Barber.

ME wrote and told me about her job and what she's been doing. Sounds like my program – Hen parties and shows. She wants a baby so bad. Said she and John weren't going to lose any time getting their family started when he got home. . . . Beedie wrote me while I was in the hospital and then again the other day after she had received the announcement. I got so tickled at her. She wrote about the fellows kidding you about being a father or a mother. She said to read Paul's letter you would think that you and Paul were the one's having the kids. The doctor told her that she might have her baby early. I hope she doesn't, because the baby will be a lot better off to go the full nine months. It needn't wait as long as ours did, though. She seems to be having a pretty hard time carrying it. I'll be glad when it's over with for her sake.

-10-

GETTING THE WORD BETWEEN OPERATIONS:
May 1944

THE *SUWANNEE* REMAINED in Hollandia through the first few days of May, with VF-60 providing combat air patrol as the area was secured. These flights could become monotonous as the flyers endlessly orbited on station, and they sometimes would break the monotony by doing aerobatic flying. VF-60 pilot John Smith described a "snake dance" performed when "12 fighters were flying combat air patrol over a destroyer that was . . . doing radar and sonar surveillance" while also acting as "the fighter-director station in control of the fighters." The snake dance "consists of getting all of the planes into a column and following whatever maneuver the lead plane initiates. Each plane chases the tail of the plane in front of him, and the result looks like a long snake writhing its way through the sky." According to Smith, the planes "had been cavorting for 10 or 15 minutes when the flight-director station came on the radio: 'Emerald leader, this is Freddie. You're looking good up there. Keep it up!'"[124]

Once the airstrip at Hollandia became operational and Army planes began to arrive continuously, CarDiv 22 was relieved and headed back to Espiritu Santo. This was the beginning of a long break from combat, which would be followed by the most intense action that the *Suwannee* had seen.

The first stop, on May 5, was at Seeadler Harbor, off Manus Island in the Admiralties, just north of New Guinea, where the ship picked up its first mail in almost two months. Royce received four letters from Becky, written between March 26 and April 4. As he told Becky after receipt of the mail, "I have about ten weeks of back mail somewhere." He said that he received the birthday card and one of the three pictures Becky had sent.

> *The picture was lovely! You probably didn't realize it, but I didn't have any pictures of you with me other than that one we had made at Seaside. It was the one I didn't like – remember! When I got this one today, I was amazed. I hadn't realized just how lovely you are. I suppose that I have looked at the picture a hundred times today. Motherhood certainly seems to be agreeing with you. I only wish that I could be with you during such times as these.*

Photograph that Becky sent to Royce, April 4, 1944

"You should have seen this bunch 'sweating out' my letters," Royce wrote. "Eggbert [Paul Barber] was opening them and I was glancing madly over them for the 'word,' but there was no news. I guess I can hold out for a while longer." A short note also appeared at the end: "P.S. The old man is surely worried." It was signed by "Chief" (Robert Nesbitt), the VF-60 pilot who served as the censor on this letter.

Getting the Word

Departing from Manus on May 6, the pilots on the *Suwannee* had a lot of down time as they traveled to Espiritu Santo. Perhaps because of this or, not having gotten the "word," which magnified his concern about Becky, Royce self-consciously decided to write more often. "It is hard to find a lot to write about when we are receiving no mail," he said, "but I've made up mind to write more concerning my feelings and less concerning news. I hope you don't mind a little sentiment now and then." And so, from this point until early June, a period of 37 days, Royce wrote 23 letters, as many as he wrote in his first six and a half months at sea. And many of these letters contain effusive expressions of his feelings. In one letter, he says, "If you don't mind my quoting from a book, I am going to use this method to tell you just what you mean to me. I would tell you in my own words, but I think the author does it as well as can be."

"When I am worried, the sight of you refreshes me. When I lose sight of you through the trees, I have no need to see you in order to find you again. Something of you, I know not how, remains for me in the air thru which you have passed – on the grass where you have been seated.

"When I come near you, you delight all my senses. The azure of the sky is less enchanting than the blue of your eyes, and the song of the bird less soft than the sound or your voice. If I only touch you with the tip of my finger, my whole frame trembles with pleasure."

The boy in this book was very young and in love. He hadn't been blessed with this young lady as a wife, so he could not add other things which I would like to have had added. You mean more to me each day that passes, and it seems to be growing worse. Sometimes when I think of you, I am told that I look like a lovesick calf. I just retort, "Hell, I feel like a lovesick calf." There are times when I'd give all I possess just to have you near – many times. I'll say no more on this subject tonight, but don't be surprised if I am a little more sentimental in letters hereafter.

One night on the way to Espiritu Santo, Royce had the midnight to 4 a.m. security watch. Although he "must spend most of the time making the rounds – flight deck – hangar deck – paravane deck – bridge," he says he'll try to write a letter during his off moments. The letter revealed something about conditions aboard ship.

We have a phonograph (automatic record-changing) in the wardroom and the ready room. In case you don't understand just what each is, I'll explain. The wardroom is the officer's dining room – very large. We eat all our meals there and we can also get sandwiches, coffee, fruit, etc. at any time. The ready room is an air-conditioned waiting room for the flyers – where we spend most of our time. "Cactus" Garner of Crockett, Texas, Ralph Kalal, and I have just been singing accompaniment to that old Bob Willis number "The Convict and the Rose." We have also been singing "Barnacle Bill the Sailor." We also have a lot of Strauss music and Victor Herbert, etc., which receives some attention. Must go now.

I'm back. As usual I've been thinking of you a great deal. I have shown everyone the picture (#2). Of course, everyone wants to know what I am doing with a lovely thing like you. Sometimes I am amazed myself. As a matter of fact, I don't believe I tried too hard in my courting. That just goes to show that we are all blessed with the best of life's happiness without too much effort on our part. It seems that the woman has to uphold more than her half in this bearing of children.

On May 10, Royce conveyed his longing for Becky.

. . . Sometimes it seems that I can't stand to be away from you another day – but I stand it. I guess you feel the same way sometimes. All I can say for consolation is that the next meeting will be the nearest thing to heaven. I must say that I am eagerly awaiting that day when we can be together again. I must confess that I love you more than anything on earth. This separation has really made me realize just how much you are a part of me – a very essential part. I find that I don't really <u>live</u> when we're not together. I suppose you may laugh up your sleeve a little at my saying that, but I guess it just takes me a long time to realize a fact –and a longer time to admit it.

Please write me often about you and the baby. Even though our mail comes neither regularly nor in proper order as to date, I certainly enjoy every letter I get – most of all the ones from you! I guess it's because the letters are a part of you in a way. I read all of them over and over and I always feel exhilarated by doing so. I must confess that I steal a look at your picture (#2) many times each day. Sometimes I'm caught and the boys exclaim, "Aint that grand." I just retort, "You're damned right!!"

I miss you very much – as usual. (I hope you feel the same.) You really can't imagine how joyfully I anticipate our being together again. It's really hard to realize sometimes that I have <u>so much</u> to come home to. It isn't every man that is blessed with so many joys as I. I think I have the most wonderful wife in the world. This could not be true without your being obviously destined to be a wonderful mother also.

Oh, darling, I am so full of happiness sometimes that I can't write what I want to say – just read between the lines.

When the *Suwannee* reached Espiritu Santo on May 12, the mail finally caught up with them. As Royce said, "We hit the jackpot today . . . I have mail written in Jan. and March and to climax it all, just a few minutes ago I got the late April mail and the 'word.' . . . I am [the] happiest man in the world."

I've just got to tell you what happened about getting the word. I had a letter from Mother written April 10 (No word). After supper (about 1900), I went down to the post office and asked if there was any squadron mail. He handed me an arm load and on top of one stack was a letter to me from you. I told him to open it for me (my arms were full). I rushed to the ready room – tore the letter from the envelope and got the word on the first line. I immediately shouted, "It's a boy! Get out 40 bucks." Everyone started shaking my hand and congratulating me. I still haven't settled down.

"We have a son." I guess those are about the most wonderful words I've ever heard. I don't know how to even start to tell you how happy you have made me. I love you so much I wouldn't believe it in anyone else. It's really hard to write what I want to say. I'm practically wild to get home now! And I aint kiddin'!

Included in the mail, Royce said, were

those letters in which you urged me to change my mind on the name. When I read them, I was worried. I thought you might have put off naming the baby until you heard. Of course, it won't make any difference to me whether it's Sandy or not. I had not realized how set you were against the name, that's all. I received your letter of April

28 too, so I got the word on it being Royce Alan Singleton II. Good girl!! Who wouldn't be proud to have a son named after him? My primary concern was that you and my son were ok. Never forget that! Your welfare comes first – petty disagreements second!!

. . .

I must close now. I'll write as often as I can. I love you more than life itself. I am looking forward to our being together by the second anniversary of our engagement. Some of the guys don't think we'll get home that soon, but I do. Take care of yourself and write me often. I love you.

Yours always,
Royce (senior)

Two days after getting the word, Royce finally received the rest of his mail. He replied by telling Becky that they'd be going ashore for a while, by which he meant they would be flying to Henderson Field on Guadalcanal, the principal island of the Solomon archipelago, for a week of special training. Although it had been decided that the Hellcats would replace the dive bombers left in Pearl Harbor, the fighter pilots had yet to carry bombs and operate as fighter-bombers. On Guadalcanal, they would intensively practice "a whole new combat technique: the difficult art of dropping bombs squarely on land targets and on ships at sea."[125]

Because mail must go out from the ship, Royce would not write nor receive any further mail until the ship made it to Guadalcanal and they flew back aboard on May 24.

On the Home Front

Becky continued to describe the growth and development of the baby. Like many a proud first-time parent, she often used superlatives: The baby is the "prettiest," "the sweetest thing living," has the "cutest grin you ever saw," and so on. Early in May, she reported that Royce II was "growing like a weed and getting heavy to carry." When she took him to the doctor at almost five weeks old, he weighed in at 10 lbs., 6 oz. This showed, according to the doctor, that "he's gaining weight twice as fast as most babies." Of course, the reality is, as Becky said, "he's just getting along fine."

Among the baby's talents—"his favorite sport," according to Becky—is "spraying everybody and everything when his diaper is being changed." She described one episode in which after being undressed and placed on the bathinette, he wet all over everything just as she was ready to start bathing him. Then, when she grabbed a mop to clean that up, he relieved himself the "other way (#2)." On another occasion, her aunt, who was visiting, was watching Becky bathe the baby while standing at the foot of the bathinette. With the baby pointed in her direction, she got showered when he suddenly relieved himself.

Becky's descriptions of caring for the baby reveal further differences between practices in the 1940s and the present day. One area of difference is dietary. On May 16, Becky said,

> *Today . . . I started giving him orange juice. He didn't like it much at first, so I sweetened it a little bit and he took it right away and wanted more. I give him 1 teaspoon of orange juice to an ounce of water and increase the orange juice every day until he's taking so much. . . . I give him 5 drops of cod liver oil and he takes it real good now – poor child. Also, I've been giving him a little prune juice when he needed it. It's a good laxative and he just laps it up.*

It is safe to say that Becky was following either professional guidance or conventional wisdom regarding the baby's diet. Today, however, the American Academy of Pediatrics recommends against giving fruit juices of any kind to children under the age of 1, because they have no nutritional value for this age group. Cod liver oil for infants has a long history, and the evidence shows that it has many benefits. It was regularly recommended and given to infants in Becky's day, but it is seldom used today.

In another letter, Becky outlines the work she does in tending to the baby's needs.

> *His bottles (I have 10 8-oz. ones and 2 4-oz. ones) have to be washed and scalded after each use and then boiled 10 min. to sterilize them. All the water that he drinks or that goes into his formula and orange juice has to be boiled 10 min. I also have 4 doz. diapers besides all his other clothes, towels, wash cloths, and blankets to wash every other day. I do what family washing there might be along with it. Then he has to be fed every four hours, bathed once a day . . . and changed about sixty jillion times.*

Modern inventions such as electric dishwashers and disposable diapers have lessened this burden. Fortunately, Becky had a strong social support system to ease her workload and give her breaks from the long daily routine. Living at home, she got a great deal of help from her sister and parents. And given that Royce II was the first grandchild on both sides of the family, two sets of grandparents were willing and eager caretakers.

Less than three weeks after the birth, Becky enjoyed her first excursion away from the baby. Once or twice a week thereafter, she would go out with her sister or girlfriends to see movies in the evening, and one afternoon she went shopping with Virginia, all while leaving the baby with Beulah or Gussie. One night, she attended a USO dance at Fort Reno with Virginia and two girlfriends. Including chartered bus travel to and from El Reno, about 30 miles from Oklahoma City, it was a long night.

> *We met at the U.S.O. Center here at 7:15 and it took us until after 10:00 to get there and we arrived back in the city after 2:30 A.M. I danced with one fellow from Spokane, Wash. . . . The Norman*

Naval Base band played, and the music was swell. The fellow I
danced with was awfully nice. I told him about you, and he told me
he went with a girl for four years, had a letter from her every day he
was in the Aleutians for 14 months and then she ups and marries
a sailor (I'll bet he likes the Navy). One of the fellows Margaret
danced with . . . told her that when he came to Oklahoma, he bought
a house in Midwest City and the day after they moved in, his wife
died. (Margaret and Mother both said they saw it in the paper.) It
seemed as though she was asphyxiated, but they didn't know if it
was accidental or suicide. Margaret said after dancing with him
she could say for sure it was suicide. What an evening. I'll take my
entertainment with you, darling.

Another time, she left the baby with Gussie while she and Virginia
attended a dinner party given by the Parnells to announce Virginia's engagement to their son Bob. Becky told Royce that they hadn't set a date, but if
Beulah had her way, they would have a formal church wedding.

Although Becky's days were filled with motherly responsibilities and
she was able, with family support, to resume an active social life, Royce
must have been constantly on her mind. The baby was an ever-present
reminder, as were activities she was accustomed to sharing with him. When
people danced after the Parnells' dinner party, Becky joined in. "I enjoyed
the music and dancing for a while" she said, "and then I was ready to come
home. I got to thinking about the baby and missing you."

From April well into May, Becky's thoughts about Royce were concerning. Aside from the two letters she received in April, the last dated
April 4, she didn't hear from him again until May 7, when she learned that
as of April 24, he still hadn't gotten the news about the baby. Not hearing
from Royce in itself must have been worrying, but it was further upsetting
to learn that he was unaware of his son's arrival. Finally, as happened for
Royce in early May, the mail began to come through for Becky. She received

eight letters between May 15 and 20, although none indicated that Royce had gotten the "word."

With Father's Day approaching, Becky had photographs made of the baby (at four weeks old) to send to Royce. She sent five poses, numbered each photo, and sent them a couple at a time, hoping that Royce would get some of them and tell her which ones he received. On the back of each photo, she also recorded her thoughts when she looked at the picture, and she asked Royce to tell her his thoughts, "so we can discuss our child so to speak even if we are miles apart." "How do you like your son, honey?" she said, "Not bad, is he?" Mailing the photos over the next couple days, Becky included a picture of the baby crying and a cute, clever letter she composed from Royce Alan II.

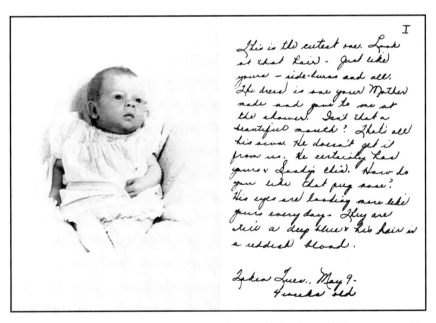

Photograph of baby with Becky's thoughts on the back, mailed May 20, 1944

May 20, 1944

Dear Daddy,

Ma-Ma say you don't know bout me, so i tell you.

It sure gets tiresome around here with just women Why don't you come home?

I send you a picture of me for Fathers Day. They would make one of me bawling. That's me showing who's boss.

Daddy hurry home.
I love you,

Your son,
Royce Alan II

Letter from Royce II as contrived by Becky, mailed May 20, 1944

Guadalcanal and Beyond

The flight on May 16 from Espiritu Santo to Henderson Field was long and dull. It took over four hours to cover a distance between 500 and 600 nautical miles, because of "time wasted in getting all air groups rendezvoused" and having to cruise at the slower speed of the TBM torpedo bombers. Although the flight was uneventful, the landing was not. VF-60 had an excellent operational record, with no barrier crashes or other accidents in well over a thousand carrier landings. But, according to the flight log daily reports, Royce landed at Henderson Field "with his wheels up." After checking with the head censor, Royce told Becky what he could about the accident.

I crashed my first airplane purely because (as the saying goes) I had my head up my ____. I got out of the damned thing and the commander of the field immediately wanted to know if I was hurt. I told him that nothing was scratched except my pride, which was really torn wide open. The airplane was really a wreck. As Vincent said, "Replace everything between the inboard guns." The skipper was very nice about it. He was a little disappointed in me (no more than I was), but he didn't ground me. I was flying the next morning.

The mission on Guadalcanal was to practice "for a landing invasion on unspecified islands of larger land mass than the atolls" in the Gilberts and Marshalls.[126] By this time, VF-60 had undergone another reorganization, with John Smith becoming Royce's wingman. Four days after Royce's near-disastrous landing, Smith described how, in one practice run, an observer could see the wheels of their planes retract synchronously, and then, "later, over the target during the bombing run, both bombs fell away from our planes at the same instant." On the way back to Henderson, however, Royce had to call a "Mayday (emergency) on the radio" when he lost oil pressure. According to Smith,

Lip handled the situation calmly and properly. He maintained a high power setting to overcome the friction of improper lubrication and plenty of altitude to optimize his choice of emergency landing sites should one be necessary. Fortunately, the engine kept running long enough for him to make the field and complete his landing, but the engine froze during the roll-out after the throttle was retarded. The plane stopped on the runway and had to be towed off.[127]

Royce's flying experience must have made him happy to leave Guadalcanal. More than that, Guadalcanal, as Smith described it, "was a hot, humid, thoroughly miserable place." The air group stayed in Quonset huts "located where no breeze blew. Heavily chlorinated drinking water was supplied in large canvas bags." And outdoor showers "were fed with salt water that was pumped from the ocean so that after a shower, when you dried, you were grimy with salt residue and felt just as dirty and uncomfortable as before."[128] In addition, Royce reported, "the trip ashore was costly. Dash [Executive Officer Ed Dashiell] turned over in a jeep and broke his leg. It's not so bad, but it knocked him out of the squadron." No wonder he told Becky, "At last, we are back aboard ship and we are all very, very glad of it."

A week after Royce was back aboard, he received another batch of mail, so that by June 1, both he and Becky had gotten all letters postmarked up to a week to 10 days earlier. Becky was thrilled when she learned on May 23, almost a month and a half after the baby's birth, that Royce finally knew about the birth of his son.

> *I was never so happy in all my life as when I received two letters from you today saying you had received the "word." I was pacing the floor right along with you until you heard. Now I start sweating out your getting the pictures Royce II sent you for Father's Day. How does it feel to celebrate that day for the first time? I felt pretty important on Mother's Day. My, we have a lot to talk over about our son when you get home. I can hardly wait.*
>
> *Now I don't know why I worried so over the name after reading what you said. You were so positive about naming the baby Sandy that I even imagined some pretty drastic reactions that I won't even mention. I can tell you now that I spent many a sleepless night and cried myself to sleep besides over naming the baby. I really didn't intend to name him until I heard from you, but when the doctor raised such a fuss about deciding on a name for the birth certificate and having to have a ration book, I went ahead and named him. Honey, he looks so much like you that I can't image him being called*

anything else. Thanks for being so wonderful about it all. I realize now each day what a wonderful husband I do have.

At the end of May, in advance of Father's Day, Royce received Royce II's letter and his first photos of his son.

I certainly agree with you that we have something. I thought I had about everything my heart desired when I had you, but this just makes my happiness more complete. I love you so much. I know that it isn't necessary to tell you just how much I want to come home. That was indeed a wonderful Father's Day gift my son sent me.

I don't know what to say about the picture. I think they are all ok, but I think the picture of him bawling is so cute. The others are very good, too, but I like that best. Anyway, I'm just about thrilled to death.

. . .

John Simpson just said to tell you "hello," so "hello." He also said to tell you he thought R.A. Jr. was cute as a bug. All the fellows think he's quite the thing. Eggbert can hardly wait until his baby gets here. I'm telling you, these fathers "sweat it out" too!

As usual, Royce and Becky responded to what the other had written. An exchange of letters suggests that the arrival of the baby had tempered some disagreements. Replying to Becky's contentious letter about their finances, written in mid-March, Royce said,

I think you misunderstood me in my letter. All I wanted to know was how we were coming along ever so often. There is no other way of my knowing except thru you. After all, do you think it odd that I want to know how much reserve cash we have? I want to know that you have a little in case anything might happen to me (now don't worry). That's the reason I send everything home to you. I'm about the only guy in the squadron who doesn't have a lot of money on the books. Just don't worry about it. I'll send you 130 dollars as soon as I can – 100 for you, 30 for the baby's crib(?).

Royce also attempted to make amends for those letters that "irritated" Becky. "I think I know what was wrong," he said. "I believe you misunderstood me" when "I was just kidding ... I know I don't always make myself clear – maybe I should put haha! in parentheses when I'm joking – huh? ... I believe my trying to make jokes has caused most of the friction."

When Becky received these letters, she responded in kind.

I'm sorry about writing you that letter on finances. There was really no excuse for it. I was just taking my discomfort at the last few weeks and impatience to have it all over with out on you. You were sweet about that . . . dear. Really, darling, you are so much more understanding than I ever realized, but, of course, seven months isn't long enough to find out everything about a person even when they were as close as we were. We're finding out so much about each other even now when we're apart.

Honey, you mentioned some letters I wrote you where I was irritated. I hope you didn't pay too much attention to them. A pregnant woman is usually pretty emotional and easily upset and that included me, I guess. I wrote things I'm sure I wouldn't have under ordinary circumstances. I'm not trying to excuse myself, however, 'cause the letters were really uncalled for. I just want you to understand, darling. I'm sorry I was cross. . . . The only thing I objected to was the way you started the letter on finances – about letting me know what you expected of me. It kinda hurt my pride, but that's not important, darling. The most important thing is for you to do your job, but to be careful and hurry home to us.

Honey, I don't want you to change. You said in your letter that you trying to make jokes 'caused most of the friction between us. I like for you to kid me. I know I fly off every once in a while. I still say that the reason I wrote some of the letters I did after you kidded me in some letters was due to the fact I was pregnant and so on edge to have it all over with. It wouldn't bother me a bit now and more than likely I'd get a kick out of you joking.

In several letters earlier in May, Royce expressed the belief that he would be home in time for him and Becky to celebrate the second anniversary of their engagement (in August). "Of course," he hedged, "we won't know when we are coming back until we are on our way." But now he seemed more certain.

I feel sure that we'll be coming home after one more "push." Read your papers and "if" and "when" another "push" comes off, start preparing for me. I'd suggest you get an apartment the first of August. We might have it longer than we actually need it, but I want to be by ourselves when I come home. I think you feel the same way.

From the moment Royce mentioned the possibility of his coming home in August, Becky embraced the thought, often closing her letters with it.

I'm certainly looking forward to August. Darling, keep your fingers crossed. You just have to come home by then.

I'm going to start looking for an apartment right away, because I'm afraid to wait until August. They are so hard to find and when you do find a desirable one, they won't take children. . . .

Honey, the thought of you coming home in August thrills me so I can hardly wait, but I try not to think about it and plan too much for fear I'll be disappointed. You must come, though. You just gotta!

-11-

OPERATION FORAGER AND BATTLE OF THE PHILIPPINE SEA: June 1944

IN EARLY JUNE, CarDiv 22 moved north to Kwajalein, where they joined the fleet that would participate in the Marianas operation. The Marianas comprise the summits of 15 dormant volcanic mountains, and all but the four largest and southernmost islands—Saipan, Tinian, Rota, and Guam—were largely uninhabited in 1944 and remain so today. Before U.S. entry in the war, Guam was a U.S. territory, having been ceded to the United States by Spain in 1898 as a result of the Spanish-American War. The rest of the Marianas were under the control of Japan following Germany's defeat in World War I. Two days after Pearl Harbor, Japan captured Guam, giving them complete control of the island chain.

As Morison pointed out, the Mariana Islands presented "new problems in amphibious warfare." The Gilberts and Marshalls "had been a story of coral atolls composed of islets only a few hundred yards wide, whence it had been comparatively easy to blast the enemy, once we had learned how at Tarawa."[129] By contrast, Saipan and Tinian, separated by a three-mile-wide channel, are 14 and 10.5 miles long, respectively, by 5 miles at the widest point; Guam, 100 miles south, is 30 miles in length by 8.5 miles at the widest point; and Saipan and Guam have mountain ridges with elevations that rise, respectively, to 1,545 feet and 1,334 feet. The mountains afforded numerous well-concealed mortar and artillery positions to bombard the beaches and difficult terrain with many limestone caves for hiding. Saipan and Tinian also had sizeable civilian populations that were loyal to Japan.

For the Marianas operation, codenamed Forager, a joint expeditionary force was divided into a Northern Attack Force for the invasion of Saipan and Tinian and a Southern Attack Force for Guam. Altogether these forces were vast in scope. According to Morison, no operation of this size, "with a final thousand-mile 'hop,' had ever before been planned."[130] The 535-ship fleet, almost four times as many as at Tarawa, carried or escorted 127,000 troops. Ships began arriving in the Marshalls, at Eniwetok and Kwajalein, on June 7. CarDiv 22 was part of the Southern Attack Force, which departed Kwajalein on June 12.

As the expeditionary force was beginning to form in the Marshall Islands, another operation on the other side of the globe, codenamed Overlord, was launched on June 6: the invasion of Normandy in northern France. On that day at Eniwetok, journalist Robert Sherrod was attending a movie, shown on an outdoor screen. Before the movie began, a lieutenant mounted a platform in front of the screen and quieted the crowd. "Here is a piece of news that has just come in," he said, "the invasion of Europe has just been announced." As Sherrod recalled, "The 400-odd sailors and Marines stood up and let out one great cheer. To them the beginning of the end of one war meant a step forward in winning their own particular war, half an earth away."[131] The European invasion was very much on the public mind at home. Yet, so focused were they on the Pacific War, Royce never mentioned it in his letters to Becky, and Becky's only mention, on June 9, was to say that Verla's husband was in the invasion. "He drives a tank. I do hope the invasion has no effect on your coming home in August."

Operation Forager followed the formula for amphibious operations that was set at Tarawa. Prior to troop landings, planes from the fast carriers struck Japanese airstrips, destroying planes and bombing runways to prevent the enemy from bringing in aircraft from other islands. Naval vessels bombarded the target, and planes from the escort carriers supported troop landings. The escort carriers remained in the area to provide combat air patrols until the airfields were prepared and land-based aircraft moved in.

Initially, D-day for the invasion of Saipan was June 15, with the Guam landing scheduled to begin three days later. Planes from the fast carriers blasted airfields and other targets on Saipan, Tinian, and Guam, beginning on June 11. While American planes moved north to bomb airfields on Iwo Jima and Chichi Jima, battleships and destroyers began the pre-invasion shelling of Saipan on June 13. One day later, a new element in amphibious warfare—the Underwater Demolition Team (UDT)—made final preparations. "Among the many lessons learned at Tarawa was the need for close pre-landing reconnaissance of beaches and their approaches, since no photographic process yet invented could indicate depth of water."[132] And so, under the arc of the naval bombardment, the UDT explored the reefs, charted the best paths and landing sites, and planted explosives to demolish obstacles.

The landings on D-day took place on the southwestern end of Saipan on a front almost four miles long. The first-day objective was about a mile behind the beach, at the contour of the foothills. It was hoped that armored amphtracs would climb over the barrier reef, splash through the lagoon, and rumble inland. But heavy enemy fire forced "most of them to disgorge their troops near the water's edge."[133] Pre-assault bombardments missed many gun emplacements. The positions of enemy artillery, deployed on high ground and reverse slopes over a large area, were difficult to detect, and many camouflaged "mortars and machine gun nests between the artillery and the beaches" were still intact.[134]

Besides these hazards, the number of Japanese troops—over 31,000—was nearly double intelligence estimates. About 20,000 Marines landed on D-day, but it became clear that the seizure of Saipan would be a prolonged, difficult task. It took three days to reach the first-day objective and three weeks to secure Saipan amid brutal fighting, as the Japanese retreated north to nearly impregnable defensive positions in the island highlands.

Battle of the Philippine Sea

During the early phases of Operation Forager, a major naval battle ensued west of the Marianas in the Philippine Sea. There the Japanese attempted to counteract the Saipan invasion by engaging the American fleet in what they envisioned as a decisive battle.[135] On June 15, as the Japanese fleet began to rendezvous in the western part of the Philippine Sea, their movement was spotted by a U.S. submarine and reported to fleet commander Admiral Raymond Spruance. Knowing that Japanese carrier forces were headed in the direction of the Pacific Fleet, Spruance prepared for battle. He postponed the June 18 invasion of Guam until July 21. Then he carefully monitored the location of the Japanese fleet as he maneuvered the American fleet into position west of Saipan toward the Philippine Sea. He placed a task group of battleships and cruisers, with deadly antiaircraft guns, in front of his four fast-carrier task groups, and when the time was right, he launched Hellcats to intercept the Japanese planes intent on attacking his carriers.

Japanese planes attacked on the morning of June 19 in four successive waves. When American radar picked up the first wave about 150 miles to the west of the fleet, the fast carriers launched every available Hellcat to intercept the incoming enemy planes. The forces collided about 60 miles west of the American fleet. From an altitude above 20,000 feet, the Hellcats nosed down to open fire, with devastating results for the Japanese. Of the 69 enemy planes sent in the first raid, 42 were shot down, most by Hellcats but some by antiaircraft fire from U.S. ships. And so it went throughout the remainder of the attack. In raids 2–4, the Japanese lost another 178 carrier planes. For the day, U.S. losses among aircraft involved in the interception and search mission were 15 planes and 14 pilots due to enemy fire.

During the air battle, U.S. submarines joined in, sinking two aircraft carriers. After the fourth raid, U.S. air forces turned their attention to Guam. Earlier that day, 33 Hellcats from the fast carriers were sent to Guam, where 36 enemy planes were shot down or destroyed on the ground. Now bombers and fighters returned to strike the Guam airfields and destroy or shoot down enemy planes from the last raid which sought refuge there.

The battle continued the following day, when the Japanese fleet was sighted in the afternoon 275 miles from the fast carrier task forces. To take advantage of the opportunity to destroy the fleet, the U.S. launched 216 planes for an attack, despite knowing that the enemy was at the maximum range of their bombers and that their carriers would be recovering the aircraft after dark. The fliers sighted the enemy near dusk. With good surface visibility but limited time, they managed to sink one light carrier, badly damage a cruiser and three other carriers, and shoot down 65 of the 75 Japanese aircraft launched to intercept them. Twenty of the attacking American planes were lost in action; however, the night recovery was disastrous. Due partly to the pilots' receiving limited training in night carrier landings, there were 18 deck crashes. Of those aircraft that landed safely, half landed on the wrong carrier, and about 60 planes were forced to ditch at sea when they ran out of fuel. Still, most of the downed fliers and crewmen were saved. And even though losses were heavier than the day before, they were a small fraction of those suffered by the Japanese.

The next day, June 21, the battle ended when the U.S. called off a pursuit of the fleeing Japanese fleet. The highly one-sided Battle of the Philippine Sea—at least the action on June 19—became known as "The Great Marianas Turkey Shoot," after one of the fighter pilots exclaimed, "Hell, it was just like an old-time turkey shoot down home." Several factors account for the U.S. dominance in the air. The Hellcat fighter, developed after the war began, was far superior to the Japanese Zero; the U.S. had twice as many planes and a greater proportion of experienced and well-trained pilots; ship radar was very effective in picking up enemy planes and fighter-director officers were equally effective in pinpointing their range and bearing.

To both sides, the object of the Battle of the Philippines was the destruction of the enemy fleet. Although the U.S. failed to destroy the Japanese fleet, Morison concluded that the battle "contributed as much to victory as if [Japan's fleet] had been destroyed," for its air power was decimated and the six surviving carriers were useless for the rest of the war. The battle also gave the U.S. Navy complete control of the water and air surrounding the Marianas, thereby dooming Japanese land forces on Saipan, Tinian, and Guam.[136]

Air Group 60

During the Marianas operations, the squadron underwent a few organizational changes. Ralph Kalal replaced John Smith as Royce's wingman, and Smith became a section leader in another division. A new roster of officers designated Royce as the "flight officer." Other assignments included materiel, gunnery, safety, navigation, radio, and photographic officers. The flight officer is roughly equivalent today to the squadron operations officer. In this role, it is likely that Royce prepared daily flight schedules and supervised the maintenance of flight logs. As he told Becky, "This is a pretty big job, but I've been doing most of the work in that department for some time now. The skipper seems to think I'm doing all right."

Only aircraft from the fleet carriers took part in the pre-assault strikes in the Marianas and in the Battle of the Philippine Sea. During this time, however, the escort carriers were not idling their time away. After departing Kwajalein, Air Group 60 conducted combat air and antisubmarine patrols from June 13 to June 20. The first couple days were uneventful, but then they began to encounter more Japanese search planes than at any previous time. On the third day, June 15, Turret gunner Leon Bingham, in a torpedo plane piloted by Harold Jedlund, shot down a Japanese Mitsubishi twin-engine bomber known as a "Betty." A day later, fighter pilots shot down two more Betties, one credited to Kenneth Montgomery and the other to Royce Singleton.

The description of Royce's "kill" in the action report reveals aspects of the tactical art of air combat maneuvering. Royce led a division with Ralph Kalal as his wingman and Paul Barber and Dean Timm in the other section. The division was orbiting over base at 8,000 feet when they were "vectored out after a bogey" by the ship's Fighter Director Officer (FDO). A bogey refers to a blip on a radar display or visual sighting whose identity is unknown. The FDO indicated that the bogey was flying low, so first Barber's section and then Royce's dropped to 5,000 feet. When Royce reached this level, he heard Timm call "Tally Ho," which signified that he sighted the bogey.

Timm identified it as a Betty, 2 o'clock below, distance two miles and at an altitude of between 800 and 1000 feet, reported to base and gave chase. Timm and Barber immediately attacked when in position, both pilots making flat side runs and both hitting the Betty in the fuselage well forward. In the meantime, Singleton and Kalal came down through the clouds a short distance away and came into position for an attack. On his first run, Singleton made a flat side attack from about 60 deg. to 20 deg. and hit the starboard engine setting it on fire, pieces flying into the air. Kalal followed Singleton in on a flat beam run from 45 deg. to 30 deg., his shots going into the fuselage. The Jap then ducked into a cloud. Singleton called Barber and Timm to circle the cloud about halfway up while he and his wingman stayed below. About a minute and a half later the Jap stuck his nose out of the cloud, but on seeing our planes near him he ducked back in. The Jap then began ducking in and out of the clouds, the fire apparently having gone out, trying to get away, but each time someone saw him he would fire a short burst. After about two minutes of these tactics, Singleton got in one good long burst. A few seconds later the Betty came out of the clouds burning and in a steep dive continuing on into the water where it exploded on impact. There were no survivors and no identifiable debris.

The action report noted that the Japanese pilot "used good evasive maneuvers including tight turns and steep climbs, skidding and good use of cloud cover." It also stated that "Japanese aircraft still seem to burn fairly easily."[137]

After the landings at Guam were postponed, Air Group 60 remained in the Marianas, at first flying patrols and searching for enemy aircraft. On June 19, torpedo pilot Guy Sabin, on antisubmarine patrol, spotted a surfaced Japanese submarine about a mile away as he came out from behind a cloud. Sabin quickly began a dive and called his radioman to arm the bombs. Apparently, the sub sighted the Avenger at the same time, because it immediately crash dived going straight ahead. Flying right up the sub's wake, Sabin was able to drop his bombs a split second after the periscope disappeared. The bombs exploded in line with the sub's course and, soon after, an oil slick about 100 feet in diameter coated the water.[138]

The streak of wins and no losses came to an end on June 20, when an Avenger from VT-60 was shot down. The incident occurred during a pre-dawn launching for routine CAP and ASP. Six torpedo bombers went first, followed by eight fighters. John Smith, who was among the fighters that day, reported that "the torpedo bombers proceeded into their search sectors" on ASP, "while the fighters rendezvoused to make their [CAP] as a unit." As the fighters passed 10,000 feet, "several pilots noticed a fire on the water" to the west; so, they started down to investigate. When they got close, at 1,500 feet, the "whole sky seemed to erupt with shell bursts," and the fighters quickly departed from the area.[139] As they learned, the antiaircraft fire was from their own forces, and the fire on the water was one of their air group, the Avenger of Lieutenant (jg) Paul Higginbotham and his crew, Radioman William Barlow and Ordnanceman Robert Wolfe, who were shot down by the same nervous gunner.

Unintentional combat deaths from so-called "friendly fire" have occurred in every war in which America has fought. One source characterized friendly fire as so prevalent as to be "normal rather than exceptional."[140] Reliable estimates of its incidence are not available, although it appears to account for somewhere between 2 and 25 percent of all casualties.[141] The numerous causes include faulty information, poor visibility, inadequate training, misidentification, and stress; however, the fear, uncertainty, and excitement of combat may be the most important factors.[142] In the Higginbotham incident, it was the first time in this operation that the planes had taken off before dawn. As Green Peyton noted, "the vulnerable troopships in the convoy were anxious about the Jap bombers flitting around in the dusk after sundown and before dawn." It was not the first time that "trigger-happy gunners" had taken shots at friendly planes, albeit "without doing any damage."[143] Smith further noted that all the planes were equipped with a system that identified them as friendly, which led him to conclude that the incident was the result of a "nervous mistake."[144]

Late on June 20, the *Sangamon* and *Suwannee* were detached from CarDiv 22 and sailed north to replace two other escort carriers off Saipan. Heavy antiaircraft fire, combined with aerial combat, had depleted the Wildcat fighters supporting the Saipan invasion. The Hellcat fighters, which only the *Sangamon*-class escort carriers embarked, also offered greater speed and firepower than the Wildcats. So, beginning June 21, Air Group 60 engaged in close air support of ground troops on Saipan and provided air strikes against Tinian.

As Air Group 60 flew missions over Saipan and Tinian, many planes were hit by vicious antiaircraft fire. On June 23, Royce's roommate John "Rabbi" Shea received significant damage to the tail section of his plane that prevented him from making a carrier landing. Fortunately, he was able to land at Aslito airfield in southern Saipan, which the Marines had

secured on June 18. In the next few days, three other VF-60 pilots were
forced to land at Aslito, which became an emergency haven for pilots
unable to reach their carriers.

Much of the damage received over the islands was relatively minor and
easily repaired; however, some of it was lethal as three *Sangamon* planes
and one from the *Suwannee* went down. The *Suwannee* pilot lost was
Lieutenant (jg) John Campbell Simpson, one of Royce's closest friends in
VF-60. Simpson was hit on June 25 during an operation in which eight
Hellcats, one flown by Royce, made strikes on Tinian airfields. According to
Dr. Phillips, Simpson "had spotted a group of guns firing up at our planes,
requested and obtained permission to strafe this area, then led his section
down, guns blazing. Batteries off to one side, which had not fired before,
opened up on him with a hail of antiaircraft fire. They scored." When last
heard from, Simpson said, "I have a hole in my wing big enough to crawl
through and most of my elevator has been shot away. Will climb and bail
out." But he could not control his plane, as it went into a spin and hit the
water. A friendly destroyer picked up Simpson's body a day or two later,
and he was buried on Saipan.[145]

Simpson was a native of McKeesport, Pennsylvania. He played football
at Davis and Elkins College in West Virginia, graduating in 1942. Green
Peyton described him as "one of the closest friends I had in Air Group 60."

> Built like a truck driver or a coal miner, with a ruff of close-cropped,
> silken black hair growing down over his forehead, he had an imag-
> inative mind and a modest passion for doing small kindnesses to
> people of whom he was fond. At Los Alamitos, when the squadron
> was stationed there, my wife and I and The Lip and Becky were
> neighbors of Simp and his affectionate, small, tempestuous wife,
> Mary Edith [M.E.], in a tourist court. Simp would rise early in
> the morning, go to breakfast by himself, and return with coffee,
> sandwiches, and newspapers.[146]

As June was coming to a close, Japanese forces were steadily forced toward the northern tip of Saipan, and a significant number of Army air force P-47 fighters had arrived. As both developments reduced the need for Air Group 60 to fly close support missions, they shifted to their usual CAP and ASP. Finally, on July 4, the escort carriers remaining off Saipan departed for Eniwetok to replenish their supplies and prepare for the invasion of Guam.

Japanese troops remaining on the island were trapped and running short on supplies. On July 7, they mounted a banzai charge—a suicidal attack made when a battle is about to be lost—even though some were "armed only with bayonets lashed to bamboo sticks" and others entirely unarmed. The attack continued for 15 hours, with approximately 4,000 Japanese and over 400 American lives lost.[147] Two days later, on July 9, U.S. forces officially declared victory.

Because of the fierce Japanese resistance, the Battle of Saipan proved very costly. U.S. losses at Tarawa pale in comparison. Of the 67,451 U.S. troops employed at Saipan, 3,426 were killed or missing in action and another 13,009 were wounded.[148] The Japanese lost at least 23,000 soldiers, and an untold number of civilians died by suicide or in the crossfire of battle. Tinian and Guam would soon fall at a lower cost, completing the annexation of the Marianas and placing Japan within range of the new B-29 Superfortress bombers.

And so, the war heated up for Air Group 60 just as Royce was led to believe that they would be coming home after one more "push" (namely, the Marianas operation). In this context, Royce's letters express feelings about his personal commitment to the war that were widely held among those in combat. For example,

I still think we'll be home by the time I said before. If our wants had anything to do with it, we'd leave for the States tomorrow. We've all had about all we want of this stuff for a while. (May 30)

We had "Dr. Kildare's Wedding Day" at the movies last night and I saw Mary Lamont (Laraine Day) get hit by a truck again. How fraught with danger must be the life of a civilian! We have all decided that we've had our share of this gravy train and are quite willing to relieve some poor aviators who have been forced to stay in the States for too long a time. It is only just that we should endure our share of rationing, standing in line, dodging automobiles, etc. Don't you think so? (June 5)

It seems almost too good to be true that we may get to come home sometime soon – and yet it is logical to think so. We are practically the senior squadron out here right now. (June 6)

Two and a half years earlier, the consensus among Americans after the Japanese attack on Pearl Harbor was that U.S. entry in the war was a defensive necessity; the main goal was to prevent the conquest of the nation. But by June 1944, with the sense of national danger long passed and the outcome of the war all but a foregone conclusion, a sociological study of the American soldier showed that the main goal of servicemen became getting the war over with so that they could go home.[149] Furthermore, combat soldiers who were asked "how they felt about going into combat again" frequently responded, as Royce implies, "I've done my share; it's someone else's turn." "It was not that the men were not patriotic," according to the authors of the study. Rather, most servicemen did not have a feeling of personal commitment to the war and felt "that limits should be set to what was demanded from the individual in the way of sacrifice." While personal responsibility may have driven Royce to enlist in the Navy a month after Pearl Harbor, his desire to be home, reunited with Becky and his son, was stronger now "than any motivation to make a further personal contribution to winning the war."[150]

-12-

ANTICIPATING ROYCE'S RETURN: June 1944

I N EARLY JUNE, Royce and Becky wrote to one another in response to letters received in late May. But when the *Suwannee* was inaccessible to mail delivery while in the Marianas, neither heard from the other for more than a month. Royce didn't hear from Becky again until July 7; Becky finally got a letter on July 14. When the mail stopped arriving, both of them also curtailed their letter writing, although this may have been simply because they both were very busy during the same period of time. Becky often wrote in the evenings, which became more difficult as the baby demanded more time. And on the war front, VF-60 began an intensive period of flying. As John Smith described, from June 14 until July 4, when the ship made a quick run to Eniwetok to replenish supplies, they "were in the air almost every day. . . . An average flight took about four hours, but flights longer than five hours were not uncommon, nor was a schedule of two flights in one day." Pilot fatigue from this regimen "was further compounded by regular standing alert duty (ready to launch in ten minutes) and by lack of rest due to night intrusions by Japanese aircraft."[151]

It is also possible that Becky and Royce thought it was less important to write because they believed they would soon see one another. Becky said as much in mid-June:

> *You'll probably wonder when you get the letters I've written recently and look at the dates, what has happened. But everything is fine except I'm about to go crazy now that I have an idea when you are coming home. Up until lately your coming home always seemed so far away and I just wouldn't let myself think about it because it just made your being gone harder. But now when all of a sudden you say you are coming home soon, I can't do anything, not even write letters.* (June 15)

> *You are still wondering, no doubt, why my letters are few and far between. I can't rightly explain 'cause if ever I had anything on my mind constantly it's you. I think about you all the time and plan toward your coming home, but I can't sit down and write a letter. It won't matter, of course, if you do get to come home when you think, but I will be sorry if you are delayed and then don't have many letters from me.* (June 19)

Throughout the month of June, the letters show that Becky and Royce are mutually absorbed with the thought of Royce's homecoming. Every letter Becky wrote ends with a reference to his imminent return:

> *I love you, my darling, and am anxiously awaiting your return.*

> *I love you dearly and can hardly wait until August.*

> *Royce II and I are so anxious for you to come home. I don't know what heaven is like, but I'll bet it's not any better than it will be when we're together again.*

It just seems too good to be true that you may be coming home soon. I guess I'll be the happiest person alive when that great day comes.

Royce also often made such references:

We've been hearing some pretty good rumors lately. I think we may all be surprised how soon we get back to our loved ones. It will be wonderful to be with you again. Besides, we will have added happiness in our little son.

I am just counting the days until we can be together.

I will be so glad when we are together again, and I can tell you all the things that are in my heart. You know I'm not adept at putting in writing what I should like to say. I love you and miss you more than you can imagine, but I'll have to tell you all about it when I get home.

It seems too good to be true that we may be seeing each other soon. I'll let you know ahead of time if I possibly can. I am practically wild to see you and Royce.

Each of them wrote about what they might or should do upon Royce's return. One thread concerned Royce's subsequent duty assignments.

I am pretty sure I'll have to come back out [i.e., to the Pacific War]. . . . After another time out, I should be able to get shore duty. (I hope, I hope, I hope!)

What would you like for me to do when I get back to the States? I was thinking of trying to change to twin engine fighters. I'll probably have to get into Night Fighters to do so, but I've been flying the same type of plane a good while now. Of course, I'd rather instruct than anything but that looks pretty hopeless. I'll tell you right now – If I don't ever get back out here, it will be all right with me.

Becky's response to this comment is ironic.

Darling, I don't know what to say about your job the next time you go out. That's up to you. I want you to do something that is as safe as possible. Nothing is safe in the war really, but don't go getting into anything more dangerous than flying a fighter off a carrier. I prefer an instructor's job, but I guess that's out. You do as you think best, honey. I just hope this dang war is over before you have to go out the second time. Are you going to ask for duty in Seattle when you get back? I don't care where we go just so Royce and I can be with you wherever you are sent.

The irony is that few feats are more difficult and riskier than landing on an aircraft carrier. Night landings were so difficult that they were avoided as much as possible.

At another point, each of them looked a little further into the future after Royce returned. Royce mentioned that Seattle "is one of best places I've ever been. I've thought seriously of going either there or Alaska after the war. That is the best place for advancement, I think." Becky responded,

You said you liked the idea of being stationed at Seattle. I really do, too. 'Course I hate to be so far from home, but I'd rather be some place that I liked really well. You really surprised me when you said you had thought about Seattle or Alaska after the war. I thought you were set on staying here in Oklahoma and going to school and becoming a lawyer.

"I still intend to go through law school," Royce replied. "I just don't know whether I'll stay in Oklahoma or not. It has its advantages, and it has its disadvantages."

Becky started another exchange about Royce's homecoming by speculating about how they should greet one another when he arrives.

When you come home, honey, if you aren't able to get a plane and have to come by train, how about the baby and me meeting you in Amarillo and riding back with you. The streamliner makes the run from Memphis to Amarillo and turns around and comes back. The train from L.A. meets the streamliner and goes on to Topeka. Would you like that? I think it would be nice. You would have a chance to get acquainted with Royce too. What do you think about me bringing Royce to the plane anyway? I'd rather leave him at home, and you and I come out and see him after you get here. I don't know how you feel about it, but the first time you see your baby I think is kinda important and it's also a pretty personal and private thing between you and me. I'd like to show you our baby alone, without a crowd of people wanting to see your expression the first time you see him and all talking at once wanting to know what you think and "isn't he the cutest thing that ever lived" and "don't you think he looks like so and so." This is just my personal opinion, of course, and if you want me to bring him to the plane (if you fly) I will. It's up to you, darling. It's your leave and we're going to do whatever you wish.

"If I had my way," Royce replied,

I'd have no one but you meet me when I come home. I want to see you most of all and I don't want a public brawl either. Of course, the folks must come. Why don't you have Mina [Royce's sister] keep the baby and have everyone else meet me – if they're bound to. I know they'll want to. Even though I'm not the best of sons, I've been gone a long time. I think Mina would be thrilled that I want her to do this for us. We can see the folks for a short while and then go "home." Whatever you want to do is o.k. by me. I just want to get home mainly.

Of course, Becky continued to tell Royce about his son. Indeed, she often started her letters with something about the baby.

I'm beginning to think the Navy has forgotten you all, too. Darn I wish you could come home. I'm more anxious too now that Royce II is here 'cause I don't want you to miss out on his growing up. I've never seen a baby change so much in such a short time. He's getting fatter and cuter every day. Really, honey, he's got the cutest grin you ever saw. He squints his eyes up like you do and smiles so big. He has a dimple, too, by the way. He'll wink at you and wrinkle his nose when he grins, and you just want to eat him up he's so sweet. Did I tell you he smiled at your picture, honey? He loves pictures and just sits and stares at them when you hold him. (June 1)

Little Royce has been a problem the last couple of nights. Had to be rocked to sleep. Just when I think I'm going to get to sit down and write a letter he starts in wanting attention. And you would never guess – he gets it! (June 2)

We really have a spoiled young son, but I guess it can't be helped. He has to have attention all the time that he's awake. He knows he's cute, too, 'cause when he smiles, he looks all around to see if everyone's watching him. He tries his best to talk, too. He'll be "cooing" soon and almost laughs out loud now. I'm taking him to the doctor tomorrow for a checkup ... I'll find out his exact weight. He's really getting fat. His little ole cheeks look like balloons. (June 4)

Our young son is yelling his head off. He will not go to sleep after his 10:00 P.M. bottle. It's usually midnight before he's asleep every night. More fun. The doctor told me not to rock him, as I had been doing after his 10:00 o'clock feeding or I would be doing it until he was 4 or 5 years old. It's all right to rock him, she said, but not to sleep at night. But it sure is hard to let them cry it out. I don't think he's really cried himself to sleep yet. I usually end up giving him more milk or water to go to sleep or I have to practically hit the family in the head to keep them from talking to him or picking him up. Honey, how are you going to like having a human alarm clock? Royce is really one. He has to be fed at 6:00 A.M. and changed during the night, too. I'm going to make you get up with him when you get home – won't you have fun? He really is fun, though you won't mind getting up with him or changing him and all his clothes and the bed clothes when he's made a mess right when we're in the middle of dinner. That happened tonight, by the way. You don't mind anything he does really. As a matter of fact, you most always think he's cute – whatever he does. (June 9)

Your son is definitely spoiled. I call him "yours" whenever he's bad. You'll probably be saying when he throws one of his tantrums (and he's doing just that already), "just like your mother." Honestly, though, this hot weather we've had lately is hard on him, but he doesn't sleep much during the day and cries all the time that you're not holding him or at least talking to him. The minute you give him all your attention he shuts up. Happy Day. I let him cry it out today. I had too much to do and couldn't be bothered with him. He just screamed at the top of his voice, then he would look around to see if anyone was watching him. Then he'd fuss awhile then he'd get mad again and finally he dropped off to sleep. There was nothing wrong with him – just spoiled, so there's only one thing for me to do and that's to let him cry it out, because he's learned he can get his way by crying. As soon as he's a little older and can play with toys, he'll be able to amuse himself. He won't pay any attention to playthings right now, but he loves pictures. He'll just stare at them. (June 15)

Little Royce is really getting big and cuter all the time. He weighs around 13 lbs now. He's been awfully good lately. It's been terribly hot but he's getting along just fine. I've been keeping him on a comforter on the floor. It's a lot cooler. The room upstairs is so hot during the day and his bassinet is too small for him. I bought a bed for him, but I don't get it until tomorrow. It's second-hand, but what I wanted. It looks in a couple of places like the little girl who had it had tried to bite a hunk out of it or had taken a toy and banged it against the side of the bed. The sides let down though and you can raise the mattress to three different levels. The mattress on one side is for winter and the other is covered with cool material for summer. I paid $25.00 for the bed and the mattress. The one I wanted at Brown's was $45.00 all together and today I priced one at Harbour Longmire's that was $29.95 for the bed and $10.00 or $12.00 for the mattress. I really would like to have had a new one for him because he will use it for several years and the other children can use it too. But they are so expensive. I'm going to have the mattress sterilized – renovated I believe is the word. And I'm going to wash the bed in Lysol water. I'm not going to take any chances on it with the baby. He's been sleeping with me lately. The last couple of days he has learned to turn over on his side and can almost turn over on his stomach. If it just weren't for getting his arm out from under him, he could do it. He scoots, too, when he turns on his side and kicks and can push right off the palate I put down on the floor. So we can't leave him on the big bed anymore and go off and leave him. He's going to be crawling soon, I'll betcha. (June 19)

Toward the end of the month, Becky reported that the baby's picture appeared in the *Oklahoma City Times*. The paper ran a regular feature during the war called "Pix for Pop," in which they displayed a picture of a baby whom the father has never seen. "I guess we rate or rather Royce II does," Becky said. "He made the front page. His picture was on the front of the Saturday Times two columns wide. It's the cutest picture, honey, but I don't think it's as pretty as he really is. I'm sending you the front page in a separate envelope so you can see what it looked like."

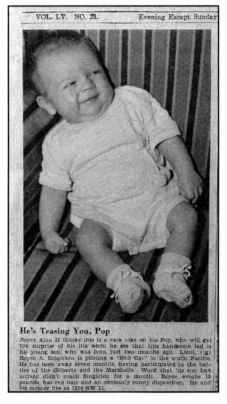

VOL. LV. NO. 29.   Evening Except Sunday

He's Teasing You, Pop

Royce Alan II thinks this is a rare joke on his Pop, who will get the surprise of his life when he see that this handsome lad is his young son, who was born just two months ago. Lieut. (jg) Royce A. Singleton is piloting a "Hell Cat" in the south Pacific. He has been away seven months, having participated in the battles of the Gilberts and the Marshalls. Word that his son had arrived didn't reach Singleton for a month. Royce weighs 13 pounds, has red hair and an obviously sunny disposition. He and his mother live at 1816 NW 31.

Photo of Royce II that appeared in the *Oklahoma City Times*, June 24, 1944

At Royce's urging, Becky began looking for an apartment in June. As she and Royce had encountered on the West Coast, however, apartments were hard to find. Several forces created a national housing shortage during the war. Between 1939 and 1944, war mobilization added 11 million people to the armed services and another 7.7 million to the civilian labor force;[152] large numbers of these people were on the move to military bases and war plants; and, as if this were not enough to increase the need for housing, federal policies established by the War Production Board put stringent limitations on lumber and building materials for nondefense construction. The greatest shortages occurred in war boom communities in the Sunbelt region, but most areas of the country experienced a sellers' housing market, especially metropolitan areas like Oklahoma City, which witnessed growth at military installations and war plants.

Before the end of the month, Becky wrote several times about her search for an apartment, mentioning two obstacles. The first was cost. "There are some apartments here if you want to pay the price, but no more 'Seaside' rents for me. I'm going to put my name on some waiting lists." Later, she "found a duplex that they wanted $100.⁰⁰ for with only water and garbage paid." She didn't take it, she said, although "we may have to pay that . . . before it's over with." The second obstacle was that some landlords wouldn't accept renters with children. As she wrote on June 25, "I'm having a Dickens of a time finding a place to live. I'm really beginning to lose my faith in people. They don't want children. Imagine not wanting a tiny baby – as if he could hurt anything."

Two days later, however, Becky revealed in her last letter in the month of June that she had successfully secured a place for them to live.

June 27, 1944

My Dearest Husband,

I've found a place for us to live. Darling, it's too much to pay for rent as per usual, but it's a nice comfortable place and that was what I've been looking for for us. I want to do everything I can to make this leave the happiest thirty days of your life. It's too bad we have to spend so much of your hard earned money to do so, but I've honestly *tried to get us something nice and yet reasonable. Before I go any further and keep you in suspense any longer, I've rented a five-room house for $85.⁰⁰ per month. No bills paid. Sounds terrible, but not any worse than we've had to do in the past. Just too bad, of course, we have to keep on doing it. I've looked, been disappointed, insulted and everything in trying to find a place to live. People are so independent they don't want children – even tiny babies. One woman didn't want to rent to me and the baby, because she was afraid I wouldn't keep the yard up since I didn't have a man around the house all of the time. So today I almost hugged this young woman when I found out she wanted someone in the service and didn't mind a baby at all. Her husband is overseas, and she sympathizes with these service people. She preferred me to others who wanted it.*

There are five rooms with lovely furniture. There is a beautiful table-top range and a large refrigerator and that's really what I've been looking for. A nice place to cook for you. There are two bedrooms – one for you and one for me – Oh, you don't want it that way! Ok. then we'll use one for the guest room. One of the bedrooms and the kitchen are on the south side of the house. It's just a darling place and I know you'll like it. I'll get it July 1, and then I can really start getting ready for you. The house really doesn't look like much from the outside, just a small white frame house, but Mrs. Hicks certainly has it fixed up nice on the inside. I'm really thrilled over it, honey, but I hate to pay so much. However, I'll really try to get by as cheaply as possible until you come home.

I had a letter from Beedie today. She hadn't had her baby when it was written – June 20, but if it wasn't here by yesterday (June 26), she was going back to the hospital, and they were going to operate. I hope they don't have to take it, because you can't have over two children that way. That's all they may want, however. She said Paul wanted her to be in California August 1. I hope she doesn't try to *make the trip and with a tiny baby too. She shouldn't travel that soon, but she probably will. Also, Neva Paul and Madge Walters wrote her that their husbands say the same thing. So, I'm really looking for you home in August some time. I can hardly wait. Our bank balance in the statement today was $1,738.32. I'll get two more checks before you get home so it should be close to $2000.^{00}. Ok, sweetheart? You said you expected $2000.^{00} by August. We should have it. How are we doing?*

Little Royce is fine. Growing like a weed. The paper sent me his picture to send to you. I'll enclose it in my next letter after your folks have a chance to see it. It's so much clearer than the one in the paper. I love you and miss you, too.

Your loving wife always,
Becky and Royce II

In early June, Royce wrote,

I just finished reading "Mutiny on the Bounty," which was pretty good. I had seen the show and had read a sequel to it, "Pitcairn's Island," long ago. I've decided to do no gambling. I've only gambled two or three times since we left the last time (and I'm about even). I probably will have only a couple hundred dollars when I hit the States – but that will get me home by plane. Anyway, since I'm not gambling, I have a lot of time for reading.

In addition to doing more reading, Royce mentioned a few films he had seen, including *All This and Heaven Too,* "a wonderful movie" which he had seen before but "enjoyed just as much this time as I did the last," and *Lifeboat.* Royce also told Becky that he had been writing more letters, answering letters from friends and family who had written to him.

As the anticipated date of Royce's return drew closer, his tone changed. He had less to say about life on board—a life he had little to say about in the first place—and more about getting back home. His longing in this regard is palpable. Before leaving for the Marianas, on the morning of June 10, Royce wrote the following letter, about which he said in another letter written later the same day, "I probably should neither have written nor mailed." He hadn't heard from Becky since May 30 and knew it would be several weeks until he received any more mail.

June 10, 1944

My Darling Becky,

Believe it or not I've just been awakened from a dream of you and home. I've been on a standby watch in the ready room, and I fell asleep. I don't need to tell you how wonderful it was to see you. Bob and Kathleen were there, too. You looked a little worn – I suppose you had not fully recovered from the baby's being born. Maybe I've been worrying about you subconsciously. I can hardly wait to see you, darling. The dream was sort of crazy in spots, but I was certainly on the ball in most of it. I was eating breakfast when I saw you first – and was so glad to see you I forgot to swallow what I was chewing. (Isn't that crazy, but it's what I dreamed.) Our meeting was a very tender one. I assure you our real meeting will be, too. I may embarrass you some by my joy at seeing you. Incidentally, if you bring the baby to the plane to meet me, have someone else hold him until I've met you in the proper manner. I'm going to embrace you in front of the populace of Oklahoma City if they happen to be there. I hope you won't mind, but I've been away from you such a long time! I know it isn't necessary to tell you how much I miss you – both as a wonderful companion and as a mate. Your niche in my life has grown to be quite a large one in the past year. I know this is just as you would want it to be and it is as I wish, too. More and more each day I realize just how very much you mean to me. Life for me would be pretty barren without you. I made the observation the other day when John D. and I were talking about furloughs that my plans were to be with you, which was all I wanted. I wondered what I'd have done if I had not been married. I just couldn't imagine such a thing. Isn't it nice that that is all I need to plan for – being with you. I hope that they have some good entertainment while I am at home. I should like to hear some good music – and also dance to some good music while I am there. I know I'll be awfully rusty on my dancing, and I never was so good – please don't mind too much. Incidentally, be careful if you do act as hostess at any of these USO affairs. I trust you completely, it isn't that which makes me say this. But you will be the object of many passes, some of the boys may even try to paw you around a little. I know what I am talking about. Although I never did anything like that, I've seen it done numerous times. I know you want to get out very much – I do too. I certainly can't blame you for going out. But you must not blame me for worrying about you, for I shall certainly do so now. I am sorry I mentioned anything about that, darling, but I can't help it. Maybe I am too possessive or something, I don't know. I just can't bear the thought of anyone even trying to touch you.

Well, I guess you were beginning to grow tired of that last paragraph. It kinda got out of hand. I hope you don't mind. I guess I said too much. Maybe I'm blue. I don't know just what's wrong, I know I miss you like the dickens. I love you so much. My heart is so full that I just can't tell you how much you mean to me. I wish that you see fit to turn down those invitations to USO dances – but not those of your friends like the couple next door, etc. It will only be a little while and I'll be home. I really shouldn't mind your helping the USO out, I know. But I'm only telling you my feelings, I can't help them.

Please write me soon about our young son. I know he must be getting to be quite a husky young man, now. Tell me all about both you and him.

I must close. This letter has not been a good one I know. I'm very sorry about that because it may be the last for a good while. I guess I'm just too homesick to write a good letter. If it offends you in any way, please forgive me. I love you more than life itself.

Yours Always,

Royce

The next day, before the ship departed for Operation Forager, Royce wrote one more, brief note, which he hurried to get "in on the last mail boat." "I'm feeling fine again and am in much better spirits," he said. He did not write again until June 28, when he told Becky, "I have a lot of news for you when I get home – some good, some bad. I am as well as can be, but I am ready for home any time they say the word. I know it isn't necessary to tell you, but I'm really eager to see you and that young son of ours." The "bad news" refers to the loss of John Simpson on June 25. Becky would not learn about Simpson's death until August.

-13-

BATTLES OF TINIAN AND GUAM: July 1944

O N JULY 4, not having received any mail in a month, Becky and Royce wrote to one another. It was a quiet day for both of them. The *Suwannee* was on its way to Eniwetok for a few days. "I suppose it won't be many years," Royce said, "before this day [the Fourth of July] will be worrying us as it worried our parents – wondering if that son of ours has burned himself with firecrackers, etc." He reiterated that he has had very little time for writing. Although he again said he had a great deal to tell Becky, he added, "as usual, there is no news the censor would pass." Royce reported that he recently read *Rupert of Hentzau*, a sequel to *The Prisoner of Zenda*, which was made into a film he had seen several years earlier, and that tonight would be the first film showing aboard ship in some time—*Something to Shout About* (with Don Ameche and Janet Blair). He continued,

I don't have any idea when we'll get to come home. I'm just hoping it won't be too much longer. I miss you so! I certainly hope I don't have to come back out for a long time when I do get back. You and I surely have a lot of happiness in store for us. I hate to be away from you, but I truly believe this separation has done us good. It has certainly made me realize just how much I care for you. I can hardly wait to get back to you and Royce II. I love you more than anything on Earth.

Finally, he appended this postscript: "I've read this letter and I can see it isn't very good. I guess I'm a little 'torn up' inside. I'll try to do better next time. I love you."

Becky's letter on the Fourth updates Royce on the house and other news.

July 4, 1944

My Dearest Sweetheart,

Here I am in our cute little house. I've moved in, the baby is asleep, but before I go to bed, I wanted to write to you and send you our son's picture. This is the one the paper sent me to send on to you. I thought it would be larger, but I guess they made it to fit into the "father's" billfold. It's better than the one in the paper. When they enlarged it for the paper, he looked six months old. How do you like that dimple, darling? Pretty smart looking boy, isn't he? Looks just like his dad. If you think he looks fat in this picture, you should see him now. I may take him to the doctor tomorrow, and I'll find out how much he weighs. It will probably be around 15 lbs. He has doubled his birth weight in three months when the average babies only double their weight in five months.

I moved some of our stuff Sunday [July 2] but didn't move in really until yesterday. Mina came over and helped Virginia and me. Mina and I scrubbed all the kitchen cabinets and got everything put away. Virginia straightened the rest of the house around. We didn't do much today. I still have my clothes to put away and cleaning to do. Just to glance at the house, it looks ok, but there is a lot of cleaning to be done. I'll have it looking real good by the time you get home. I don't know what I would have done without yours and my folks and my friends. You should see all the things everybody has lent me for the house. I haven't bought anything for it yet except groceries. Linens, dishes, and cooking utensils aren't furnished. Your mother let me have her Community Plate Silver, glasses, sherbets, wear-ever aluminum skillet, cups and saucers to finish out my pastel pottery set that I had broken and can't buy, and preserves and jam. Margaret let me have her aluminum cooking utensils, mixing bowls, everyday silver, kitchen silverware, waffle iron, etc. And Mother has given me a bunch of stuff. So, with my linens and the stuff I have, I'm really fixed up.

(The baby was crying out in his sleep, bad dream I guess, so I had to go in and pat him till he quieted down.)

I'm by myself tonight, but there will probably be someone staying with me from time to time until you get home. It will be fun having a place of my own, but I'll bet July passes slowly since I have a place and will just be waiting for you to get here.

I keep listening to the news hoping things will kinda die down out there, but you all have really been busy for almost three weeks now. This must be the "push" you were talking about. Margaret thinks Erman [her husband] is in the invasion of Saipan, and I wouldn't be a bit surprised but what you were. We also heard about the Bonin Islands today.

I have your picture here on the desk as I write. It looks so good, but how much better you would look in person. I can hardly wait, darling, until we can be together again. I miss you so. And I love you more than ever. I never want you out of my sight again after you get home. Would it do any good for you to apply for instructor's duty? Or would you want to? I want you to do just what you want to and what you think best.

I love you with all my heart. Take care, darling. Tell John D hello and tell him also that I intend to write him.

I guess Paul is walking on air – being the father of a baby boy is something to be pretty proud of, isn't it, precious? You tell him all about it, that is, if you can get a word in edgewise. I received Beedie's announcement Saturday. I haven't heard how she got along. We're waiting, darling. Hurry home.

Your loving wife always,
Becky and Royce II

When the ship arrived at Eniwetok on the morning of July 7, Royce reported, "lo! and behold! our mail was waiting for us. Naturally, we were all very, very glad. I received letters up to June 28." For the next three days, he responded to Becky's letters. For example,

I'm now showing everyone the picture from the paper, and they all think it's swell. He's the cutest kid I've ever seen. You've made me the happiest guy on earth and no kiddin'!

I'm afraid I jumped the gun a little on when I'll be home but keep the apartment [i.e., the house] anyway. It will be worth any cost to have a home of our own – even for a little while. It just can't be too long. We all feel that we deserve to go home soon.

I hope Bob and I can be at home at the same time. We'll be more than glad to let him and Kat have the "guest room." We surely won't need it!!!!

I won't mind getting up in the middle of the night with the baby – that is certainly better than having the Japs get me up!

It just can't be too much longer until I get to come home darling. You don't need to worry about my leave being the happiest month of my

life. It will be wonderful, but I expect many, many more just like it. Oh, if we could only be together hereafter – with no more separations. Do you realize that we will have lost nearly a year of marriage? If we live to be seventy, that's still over 2%. We've given quite a lot to this old country, don't you think?

Say, you're doing ok on that bank account. I think we can save a good deal while I'm home in the States, too. I'll be making about $370 a month, I think. Do you think we could save 50 to 75 of that each month, besides a war bond? If we can get an apartment reasonably, it shouldn't be too hard. It'll be nice to start out with a surplus this time instead of being practically flat broke. Incidentally, when I make lieutenant, we'll really do o.k. I think I'll make about $430 a month. We won't be doing so bad for a couple youngsters, will we? Say! I thought I told you to spend that $100 for clothes. Of course, you may want to get something this fall, so I guess it's o.k. to wait. Anyway, I'm proud of you!!

Royce wrote on July 8, "I was blessed with quite a number of letters when" the ship hit port, including

one from your dad and one from your Aunt Anne – and I have answered both. Your Aunt sent me one the loveliest poems I've read in ages – "Paternity" by William Rose Benet.[153] She must be a very nice old lady. Evidently you have been spreading some pleasing propaganda about me. She seems to think I must be o.k. I hope all these people you've told about me aren't too disappointed when they see me in the flesh.

Another letter from Royce's mother Gussie elicits this note to Becky:

I may as well tell you – Mother is crazy about you – and she idolizes that baby. If you continue to be as nice to her as you are now, you'll be doing wonderfully. Mother and Buddy have always thought very well of you, but now, oh! I don't know how to say it, but you've just turned out to be everything they ever expected a daughter-in-law to be. And I could ask nothing more of you as a wife. Incidentally, I'm ready to get home and see if you can do all these things about the kitchen. I believe you, of course. I just want to try you out. If you're as good as you say, I'll give you a steady job. All you have to do is pick up things after me, cook for me, and make me happy. Do you think you'd like that job?

Royce told Becky on July 9, "The last mail closes this evening, so you probably won't be hearing from me for some time. Don't worry about it." He mentioned that for the first and only time while at sea he attended the ship's church service, and he enclosed a copy of the program. "You might read Mark 10:2–12," he said, "I think you'd enjoy it. It makes a person realize a little more just how truly wonderful marriage can be." Finally, Royce repeated, "it looks like we should be home in not too long." From then until early August, he wrote two more brief letters, leaving Becky to believe that it won't be too much longer before they'll be together again.

On the War Front

After a couple days at Eniwetok in early July 1944, CarDiv 22 headed back to the Marianas. Having captured Saipan, U.S. forces needed to invade Tinian and Guam to secure the Marianas. Rota, the smallest geographically and least populated of the four inhabited islands, had lesser military value, with one small airstrip. Therefore, although subjected to air and sea attacks, it was not invaded and was left in Japanese hands, who surrendered after the end of the Pacific War. Tinian was too close to Saipan to ignore. Not only was the island a danger to the new bases in Saipan, it also had a major airstrip and plenty of level ground for expansion. Runways constructed by Navy Seabees after its capture made the North Field on Tinian the largest airport in the world in 1945, when it was destined to go down in history as the launching point for the atomic bombings of Hiroshima and Nagasaki.

Air Group 60 had contributed preliminary air strikes and bombing in June that softened up the Tinian Island defenses; however, they were not involved in the invasion of Tinian, which began on July 24. The major issue was where to land. With limited options, U.S. commanders feinted a landing at a site on the southwestern side of the island, which they knew the Japanese would be well prepared to defend. Instead, Marines landed at two small beaches on the northwestern coast. An assault on these beaches was highly risky: The landing area concentrated troops on a narrow front, and lava walls and banks that enclosed the beaches had to be blasted to provide exits to the interior. But the tactical surprise worked. Japanese forces were not posted nearby but at more obvious landing sites. And relentless bombing by land (from artillery on Saipan), sea, and air kept the Japanese at bay until the U.S. had landed and moved enough troops, tanks, and weapons across the lava barrier to turn back a counterattack.[154]

Once U.S. forces were ashore, the ultimate seizure of Tinian was not in doubt. By the end of the first day, over 15,000 Marines and soldiers were gathered on Tinian. From there they moved steadily south, finally declaring victory nine days after the assault began, on August 2. Still, the Japanese defended Tinian as elsewhere at all costs. Only 252 Japanese were taken prisoner; 5,000 were buried and another 4,000 were unaccounted for. Among U.S. forces, 389 were killed and 1,816 wounded.[155]

The Guam land assault began on July 21. On the one hand, the taking of Guam was far more difficult than Tinian. It is the largest island in the Marianas, with much more rugged terrain; it had formidable coastal defense guns and underwater defense emplacements; and the Japanese garrison numbered 19,000. On the other hand, the delay in the original date of attack, as Morison notes, "gave United States forces a chance to deliver the most intensive and prolonged pre-landing air bombing and naval bombardment that any Japanese held position ever received."[156] Aircraft from the fleet carriers had bombed Guam on June 11–12 and a week later during the "Turkey Shoot" (i.e., Battle of the Philippine Sea). The island was bombed again on July 4. Then, starting on July 8, it was subjected to 13 days of continuous naval and air bombardment prior to the landings. In addition, the Underwater Demolition Team blew up obstacles planted by the Japanese that blocked the entrances to the two beaches where U.S. forces landed.

U.S. forces landed at two beachheads on the west coast of Guam. Aided by naval bombardment and the rapid placement ashore of Marine artillery, the northern force of 20,000 Marines made it ashore on the first day, withstood a Japanese counterattack on the second day, and then moved steadily inland over hills and cliffs. Once they thwarted a second counterattack on the fifth day of fighting, the northern force gained full control, and this assault phase effectively ended. The southern attack force of over 30,000 troops encountered stronger initial resistance in which several amphtracs were disabled by enemy fire. But a Marine brigade followed by Army units established themselves ashore, held their line against a night counterattack, and after a week, had linked up with the northern sector. Thereafter, organized resistance from weakened Japanese forces gradually dissipated until, after three weeks, on August 10, the island was declared secure. A large number of Japanese soldiers—at least 9,000—escaped into the dense jungle. Most of them were killed or captured by the time Japan surrendered in September 1945, although it took decades to apprehend the remaining holdouts, with the last known survivor discovered in January 1972.

CarDiv 22 was one of two escort carrier divisions that supported the assault on Guam. From July 12 until August 1, Air Group 60 was active every day except two—July 19 and 28, when the ship loaded ammunition in the harbor off Saipan. At first, they flew ASP and CAP. These missions were soon followed by fighter-bomber strikes on Guam and Rota. Then, the pilots made strikes in support of troop landings and movements. Designated targets included enemy troop concentrations, barracks, pill boxes, caves, buildings and installations. Flight schedules were heavy; two flights a day were common. In fact, VF-60 flew more hours in July (over 2,000) and made more carrier landings (590) than in any other month at sea.[157] Royce wrote on July 18, "I've flown 22 hours in the last three days. That's quite a lot for a fighter pilot."

As a consequence of this heavy airtime, pilot fatigue was a problem, which, John Smith believed,

> contributed to the . . . operational accidents that occurred during this period. In one instance, a TBM did not stay airborne after a free-run (non-catapult) takeoff because the pilot pulled up too sharply. There were no injuries [when it crashed into the sea], and by the grace of the fates, all three of the crew were picked up. On the VF side, both Frog La Fargue and Rabbi Shea went into the water during aborted landings.[158]

Both pilots were rescued. About Shea's accident, on July 20, Royce told Becky that Rabbi "is living on what is commonly called 'borrowed time.' All he has to show for it is a little cut on his head, however. I'll tell you all about it when I get home." Smith described Rabbi's story.

> When he hit the water, his left wing impacted first, causing the plane to knife downward. As Shea later gave a firsthand account, he was rigged for a carrier landing with canopy open and harness unstrapped. Thus with the release of his safety belt and the unplugging of his radio earphones, his egress from the plane took only a few seconds. Even so, the plane must have dived deeply during that short time, because as Shea swam to reach the surface he

found himself reaching the point where he could no longer hold his breath. He therefore triggered both carbon dioxide cartridges to inflate his life jacket and quickly popped to the surface. Indeed, one of the pilots who was observing landings from the bridge said that he rose so fast that he cleared the water by 10 to 15 feet before falling back. This may be a slight exaggeration, but Red Rynearson, Rabbi's wingman who was in the landing pattern behind him, verifies that he rose clear of the water.[159]

The other part of the story was Rynearson's actions when Rabbi crashed into the water.

[He] immediately aborted his landing approach and circled over the pilot in the water. The *Suwannee* continued steaming into the wind, which carried it away from its normal station. The ship became impatient and issued repeated calls for Red to return to the pattern and land. These calls were politely ignored, and Red returned to the ship only after his section leader was safely aboard a destroyer.[160]

In other words, Red disobeyed commands to return to the ship, an act of insubordination that is a punishable offense. His sense of obligation to secure Shea's safety reveals the strong bonds that form among members of Navy squadrons. Similarly, social cohesion among small units in battle, such as Army and Marine squads and platoons, is believed to be a primary factor in sustaining and motivating soldiers to fight.[161] Fortunately, Red was able to rationalize his decision to those in command, as Smith described.

When Red was queried afterward as to why he ignored the ship's calls, he explained that a man in an inflated Mae West life preserver is a very tiny object in a very large ocean and is easily lost in a running sea. To Red's way of thinking keeping Rabbi in sight seemed a prudent thing to do. Essentially all aircrew would agree; certainly the skipper bought it and protected Red from any reprimand from higher authority. But he did point out to Red that destroyer escorts had reported many submarine contacts in the vicinity of the carriers during their operations off Guam as well as off Saipan and Tinian and that it was dangerous for the carriers to unnecessarily hold a steady course for any prolonged time.[162]

After the air group launched its last strike on Guam, on August 1, CarDiv 22 departed for Eniwetok in company with the rest of its task group for a welcome break.

U.S. casualties on Guam—over 1,700 killed and 6,000 wounded—were half as many as those on Saipan. Japanese deaths totaled over 18,000. Within a few months, Guam became the command post for Western Pacific operations, with the island population swelling by nearly 200,000 military personnel in preparation for the liberation of the Philippines.[163] Gaining control of the Marianas was decisive in the Pacific War. By putting the U.S. within striking distance of Japan, it gave the U.S. an overwhelming strategic advantage. The loss of Saipan alone, according to Morison, "caused a greater dismay in Japan than all her previous defeats put together."[164] Prime Minister Tojo and his cabinet resigned. And even though Japan would not consider surrender, knowledgeable Japanese understood that their ultimate defeat was inevitable.

On the Home Front
Throughout the month of July, Becky's letters show that she used news about the war to try to determine when Royce would return. On July 9, she reported, "We heard today over the radio that the Battle of Saipan was over. What wonderful news. Maybe you are on your way home. We all have

our fingers crossed." Later in the month, she had a chance meeting with a Navy fighter pilot who has just returned from the Pacific.

> *His squadron was land-based and was replaced by Marine fliers. I told him that you said you would be home in August and then wrote it would probably be a little later. He said that might be due to the fact that it took a lot longer at Saipan than they figured. He was really encouraging and thought you would be home right away.*

A few days later, she also wrote, "I'm looking for you as soon as the campaign in the Marianas is over. Our papers tell us that they are still using carrier planes over Guam. My guess is that you are there or near there."

Becky finally received mail from Royce on July 14. Her letter written to Royce on the 15th expressed some concerns, followed by a surprise about an available apartment.

> *I was really glad to hear from you, honey, and even though you think it will be longer until you come home, it's good to know you are glad we have a house and that everything is all right with you. In the last letter you wrote, you sounded pretty blue. Nothing you said in particular – just the sound of the letter. Have you lost any fighter pilots? Several things you've said made me think that, such as your having good and bad news to tell me, etc. Who are they? I haven't heard from M.E. [Mary Edith, whose husband, John Simpson, was –unbeknownst to Becky—shot down over Saipan in June] in ages – that worries me. Beedie writes to several of the girls, and I know if anything had happened, she would let me know, because I had a letter from her yesterday. But I can't understand why I haven't heard from M.E.*
>
> *Well, guess what? I think I've found an apartment, smaller and cheaper. Bill and Vivian Freeman were over by us playing bridge. Bill was taking some of the neighborhood kids out for an airing and saw*

*my car, so stopped by. He happened to mention his mother having a
garage apartment she was renting when we got to talking about this
place and all. So he called her, and she said she would like to have
me! I know her and she's the sweetest thing. She rents an apartment
in her house and then she has these three apartments in the rear. The
one that is vacant is the most desirable she says. I haven't seen it yet.
It has a living room, bedroom, kitchen, breakfast nook, and bath.
$50.^{00} per month, water and garbage paid and no yard to keep up.
It has a southeast exposure, is on the ground floor, and is supposed
to be cool. If I like it (I'm to go and see it in the morning), I'm going
to rent it and sublet this one to get my money back. Rather, I'm
going to tell the landlady's sister (Mrs. Hicks is out of town) that I'll
run the ad and show the house and she can pass on the tenant. The
apartment will be available Tuesday. She has redecorated, she said,
and if it's cool and comfortable, the difference in rent will be swell.
Don't you think? I'll write you tomorrow if I decide. The address will
be 604 NW 20th Street. We won't have an extra bedroom for Bob
and Kathleen, but we could manage. There are several advantages
to this house, but if the other place is as nice as I think it will be, the
advantages of this house will not be worth $35.^{00} more, plus <u>all</u> the
bills and the upkeep of the yard. I sure hate to leave this little house.
I'm getting rather attached to it. It's real cute, but not worth $85.^{00}.*

In the following days and weeks, Becky filled Royce in on the apartment.

*Remember the apartment we had in Seaside at the Golf View Motel?
Well, Mrs. Freeman's apartment reminds me of it. Her apartment
is extremely nice. I'm really crazy about it, so I guess I'll move again.
That difference in rent is quite a bit. I haven't talked to my landlady's
sister yet. I don't think I'll have much trouble about it. I hope not
'cause I think we should take the cheaper place. She caters to Service*

people, so she can't expect much notice. She won't lose any rent on it if I rent it before I move and let her choose the tenants. Sounds easy anyway, doesn't it?

The new place is one of three gar-apartments – two upstairs and we'll be down. It has a southeast exposure and with the apartments overhead we won't have the direct sun off the roof of the afternoon sun. There are two south and two east windows in the bedroom.

. . .

I finally got ahold of the woman who is taking care of this place. She was real nice, said she didn't blame me and I'll get back some of my rent. (July 16–17)

It looks like I'm not going to get much rent back. My landlady is going to rent the house when she gets back in town next week, which will be practically the end of the month, so here I am keeping up two places. I don't know when Mrs. Freeman will start charging me rent. I haven't been over to pay her, but, of course, it's standing vacant and she's losing rent on it. It will be cheaper for us in the long run, though, to have the smaller place even if I have to keep up both places until the first of the month. I'm afraid I'll never want to live in someone else's home again since I've had a place of my own. I really like it. (July 21)

I still haven't moved but hope to this week. I only had to pay a third of a month's rent at the apartment and even if I don't get some of the rent back from this house, our rent for two months with me keeping up two places part of this month will not be as much as it would be to stay here for that long. This month it cost me $85.⁰⁰ here and 16.95 on 20ᵗʰ Street and next month our rent will be $50.⁰⁰, so you can see all that is not as much as paying $85.⁰⁰ for two months. If the landlady gets back in town within the next day or two and rents *this house, I still can get some rent back. I'm paid up until the 2nd of August.* (July 24)

As in June, Becky reduced her letter writing to Royce in July, although she picked it up mid-month after receiving mail from Royce and deciding to move to the cheaper apartment. After telling Royce about the apartment, Becky continued,

I started giving Royce cereal Saturday and he's taking it just swell now. He didn't spit up any of it today. He takes it twice a day along with his bottle, morning and evening. I'm supposed to increase it gradually, but I believe tonight he could have eaten twice as much as I gave him. In another three weeks he'll start eating his fruit (canned). Then when he's four and a half or five months old, he'll start taking canned vegetables, I think. Did I tell you he weighed 14 lbs., 10 oz. Friday and is two feet long? Say, he's doing ok, isn't he? Don't know whether I should tell you this or not, but I imagine your mother has or will. But I let Royce fall off the bed. You can't leave him alone on the big bed anymore at all. He didn't hurt himself, but it scared him and he cried just for a little bit. It scared the fool out of me. I was in the kitchen when I heard him hit the floor and I almost fainted. Mother liked to have had a fit, but your mother said he wouldn't be right if he didn't fall off the bed a couple of times. I had him in his playpen today and if I went in and put him back in the middle of it once, I did it two dozen times. He scoots all over the place and bangs his head against the side and then yells bloody murder, then when you pick him up and put him back in the middle again, it makes him mad, 'cause you didn't pick him up and hold him, and he had another breakdown. But he's not spoiled – much!! He'll be worse, too, when I move 'cause everybody in the apartments around us work and so go to bed early. So, I won't be able to let him cry himself to sleep after his 10 o'clock feeding. I don't hardly anyway. If he doesn't go to sleep on his bottle, I usually put him to sleep by rocking him. He sleeps thru the night when you do get him to sleep. He slept until 9:30 Sunday morning.

Some of my letters I just go "hog-wild" on the baby and others I hardly mention him, but I figure you kinda like to hear occasionally how much I love you and that you are all I would ever desire in a husband. Also, you are the sweetest, most thoughtful, and most handsome man I've ever known. Seriously, darling, I mean it. I do love you with all my heart. I don't know how I could live now if it wasn't for you. It doesn't seem possible now that you haven't always been right with me – in my thoughts at least. Mina and your mother tell me all they write about anymore is the baby, so I know you get all that news. Do you like to read about how your wife adores you as much as I love reading your sweet letters? My vocabulary is limited, even on sweet nothings, but I could say "I love you" over and over again and never run down or get tired. You'll hear it an awful lot when you get home. Do you mind?

A few days later, Becky had more to say about the baby.

Guess where I am? Over at your [parents'] house. I left the baby here today when I went to town. The girls wanted me to meet them for dinner and a show, so I just left him here and came out to spend the night so I wouldn't have to move him. Your mother and Buddy went to the show this evening and Mina got to take care of him by herself. They said he was good. He's been awfully fussy lately. I think he's trying to cut teeth. He's pretty young for that, but I cut teeth early and your mother said Robert had 4 teeth at 4 months. From 5 to 7 months is normal. He chews on his fist and sucks his lower lip like his gums hurt him. He learned to spit. We've probably mentioned him spitting up, but that isn't what I mean. He's not tossing his cookies; he just spits now and dies laughing. He thinks it's so funny. He's really getting cute, but also more difficult. He's at a bad age where he can move around by turning over kicking, but he hasn't learned to play with his toys real good and can't sit up and so he's not very well satisfied with anything. He's developing so fast that he may be sitting alone in six weeks or so. They don't usually though until six months. He's almost 3½ months old now. It doesn't seem possible, does it?

Becky continued by reporting the film that Sandy and Gussie had seen that evening: *Pied Piper* with Bob Wills. "I remember seeing the *Pied Piper* in Seaside," she says, although "it seems to me that you had the duty, and I went with M.E. and John." This leads her to again ask about John Simpson: "How is John, by the way? I haven't heard from M.E. in ages. Neither has Beedie. I've noticed that John hasn't censored any of your letters since the first of June. Has anything happened?"

Earlier in the summer, Becky mentioned that her parents' next-door neighbors, Claude and Lucy Beeler, were teaching her how to play bridge. "I'm crazy about it and only learning now," she says. "I'll probably go nuts when I get really started playing. It's so fascinating." On July 24, she wrote, "I played bridge tonight at the Gas Co. Everybody down there has the bug and is learning to play." A couple days later, she played again when she hosted a "slumber party" for the "war women." A derivative of Whist, the modern version of contract bridge came into being in the 1920s. As David Owen pointed out, it "was an ideal populist pastime for the Depression and the war years. It was sociable and challenging, yet the only cost was the price of a deck of cards." By the time Becky was introduced to the game, it was being played in an estimated "44 percent of American homes."[165] By the fall, Becky had taken it up in earnest.

As the month came to a close, on July 30 Becky reported, "I moved today. I know you'll like this little apartment. It's not arranged like the one at the Golfview Motel in Seaside, but it reminds me of it. It won't be

as much work, and I'll be able to spend more time with you." The letter
ends, however, on a down note.

> *I really had a blow today. You remember Mary, don't you? Well,
> her husband has been in everything in the army practically and
> finally made the air corps and received his wings June 27. Mary has
> been with him in California ever since and today he was killed in a
> plane crash. Mary is out there all by herself with a car to drive home.
> Dick's mother has Mike, their little boy. It seems like Mary has had
> the tough breaks. She lost both her mother and father when she was
> young and now her husband.*

In Royce's last letter of the month, written on July 23, he told Becky
that he has received letters written as late as July 10. He continued,

> *I'm glad you got moved into the house ok. I wish you'd have Virginia or
> someone stay with you until I get home, however. I don't like to think of
> you being by yourself. I don't believe I could take it if anything should
> happen to you, and I've learned to take a good deal. You mean every-
> thing to me, and that's all there is to it. I love you with all my heart.*
>
> *Eggbert is writing Beedie right now. He is certainly happy to
> be the father of a son. I'm not exactly downhearted about it myself.
> They are calling his boy "Mickey" and he said that was going to stop
> when he got home.*
>
> *We have been very busy lately. For the first time in my life my
> rear end has actually ached. I'll surely be glad to get home and get
> off it for a while.*
>
> . . .
>
> *There is so much to tell and so little to write! I can hardly wait
> to see you! Until then, take the best care of yourself and our young
> son. I love you.*

-14-

Sojourn in the Admiralties:
August 1944

AFTER DEPARTING THE Marianas in early August, the *Suwannee* stopped first at Eniwetok for three days, where "war-weary" planes were traded for replacements. According to John Smith, whether due to shoddy workmanship or the abrasive coral dust on Eniwetok, nearly all the replacement aircraft had problems. In a few days, the *Suwannee's* maintenance crews did a magnificent job of rectifying the problems, but without their hard work, Smith said, "a great many of the aircrews would not have come back."[166]

Royce wrote to Becky three times between the departure from the Marianas and the brief stopover at Eniwetok. He did not know when or where the next operation would be, but he knew it would be a while longer before they rotated back to the States. The first letter, dated August 2, begins,

> *I know this is going to be a very disappointing letter. You can imagine how much I hate to write it. It looks like I was too optimistic on the time of our getting back. It looks now as if I may make it home in time for your birthday [November 19]. I don't know what to tell you to do*

about the house. It doesn't seem very practical to keep it for five or six
months at 85 dollars a month when we'll only get to use it twenty
days or so. I know this news is heartbreaking – it certainly was to us.
We've been working harder than we ever did before and we all were
just sure we'd be on our way home soon. Maybe they <u>have</u> forgotten
us. Our morale is so low nothing could cheer us up. There is just one
consolation that appears to us now. Doc Phillips says that if we do stay
out here much longer, he thinks all of the original air group will get
shore duty. That would surely be hard to take!

Three days later, on August 5, Royce wrote,

It is practically certain that I won't be home until your birthday. I
don't know what to tell you to do about the apartment. Since I wrote
the last letter, I have received some more mail and found that you
have moved to a cheaper place. If it isn't too expensive, you may as well
stay if you want to. We're all pretty disgusted. Maybe I'll get home in
time to see a football game. If not, I should be at home for Christmas.

. . .

You're right about mother telling me a lot about her grandson,
but I like to hear all about him, so you add a little in each of your
letters too. It looks like he'll be dating the girls (nearly) before I get
to see him, so I have to know how he's doing.

It is wonderful to hear from you that which I want to hear so
much. I love you so very dearly! I've often been a little sorry for the
irritability on my part while we were at Long Beach [during training
at Los Alamitos]. I suppose my nerves were a little frayed. I was sort
of "on edge" to get out here and get it over with. I don't think you'll
ever have to worry about me being like that again. If I have to come
back out, I'm just going to make the most of every precious moment

I am with you. You are going to hear so many times over "I love you" when I get home.

I have more bad news for you – the worst yet. The reason Simp hasn't censored my letters is that he has been killed – June 25th. We had to wait until we were sure the Navy had broken the news before saying anything. I am going to write M.E. as consoling a letter as I can. I know she must be heartbroken. He was shot down by anti-aircraft fire. I was with him, but my luck has been good so far. I have only been "shot at" – not hit. You'll probably want to write M.E. We were all pretty close. Maybe it isn't good to be too close to anyone in war time. That isn't my opinion, however.

This "disappointing" and "bad" news is followed by a short letter from Eniwetok. "We have received no mail," he said, "so there isn't much to write about."

We are in port at the moment and are doing as little as possible. We had a good movie – "Claudia." You and I saw it in Long Beach, but it was good to see it again. I've been in several very sentimental moods lately. Sometimes I feel like I'd give an arm just for a glimpse of you. I'll probably hang around you so much when I get home, I'll become a pest. Do you think you'll mind?

Incidentally, it looks like we'll have quite a lot of money in the bank by the time I get home. It doesn't look like I'll be home for some time. Save what you can. A nice, juicy bank account may come in handy. I'll probably have two or three hundred dollars when I get back, but I'm thinking we may need an automobile. If you'll manage another hundred for each month after August 1, we'll get a nice car when I get home. I know you can do it. You've certainly been doing ok so far!

There is no news. I love you more than ever – and miss you more
than ever. Take care of yourself and our young son.

In the early days of the month, Becky was caught up in preparations
for her sister Virginia's wedding and in attending the funeral for Dick
Brown, the husband of her friend Mary. In an August 2 letter, she wrote

I'm really going in a mad whirl. Virginia set her wedding date for
August 19, then changed it today to September 2. So, I guess the big
event will come off and it's going to be pretty big too. She already has
her white satin dress and it's beautiful. We're going crazy getting
dresses for the attendants. I'm to be Matron of Honor and my dress
will be different from the rest and I think I've found what I want. It's
perfectly beautiful. She's also going to have a candle lighter and two
bridesmaids. She's going to have her reception in the backyard. I'm
hoping you are here, so you can be in it. Bob would probably have you
as an usher and you could watch me come down the aisle. Wouldn't
that be fun? I told your mother I wanted her to sit right on the aisle
and hold Royce, so I could see him as I came down.

We're still waiting for Mary to get here. It seems they had car
trouble in Arizona, and they expect them in tomorrow. Dick's body
arrives tonight or tomorrow night. I've forgotten. We (Margaret,
Verla, and I) are going to take some food over there tomorrow. I'm
going to make a meat loaf, Margaret is baking a cake, and Verla is
fixing a congealed salad. Dick's mother is already here with Mike.
Margaret took him this afternoon and I may bring him home with
me tomorrow afternoon and give them a rest. I don't know when the
services will be held yet.

Becky ended the letter with this postscript: "Do you realize you have
never seen me in a long evening dress? I hope you'll be here for the wedding.

My dress will be pink – like it?" A few days later, she received a letter from Royce written in mid-July. She responded to Royce's letter, but she also again referred to the wedding and funeral.

> *Rabbi must have had a narrow escape. You tell him to be careful 'cause you have an awfully cute kid to show him one day soon. Can't you tell me who it is you have lost, Royce? It seems like you are trying to tell me something has happened in your letters recently. I can't help but think you've had some pretty disheartening experiences from the way you talk.*
>
> *. . .*
>
> *Well, it looks like Virginia and Bob will be getting hitched the 16th of this month. Bob got a leave beginning the 13th, so we are having to rush everything up. You should see my dress. It's beautiful. Sure wish you could be here. Mother bought my dress for me, 'cause she said she wasn't able to give me a formal wedding. The wedding is going to be held at Wesley Methodist Church, and the reception in our backyard.*
>
> *I went to Dick Brown's funeral today. It was strictly military with guns and everything – I brought Mary over here the first night she was home. She was so nervous from the drive home and people running in and out at her house. She seems to be getting along fine now. Dick's best friend drove Mary back here. He sure was a swell fellow.*
>
> *Honey, don't you worry about me staying alone. I like to. As a matter of fact, I don't know if I'll ever be able to live at home again. There's nothing to be afraid of here in the apartment anyway because there are four apartments in the garage here, and then the big house in front with neighbors on either side and back of us. I haven't been closing the door at night – just locking the screen 'cause it's so hot.*
>
> *I can hardly wait for you to come home, darling. I love you so much and miss you, too. Royce is getting cuter every day. He's the*

best little thing. Just laughs and talks (coos) at everyone. Hurry home sweetheart and write as often as you can.

Eight days later, on August 13, Becky wrote again, first apologizing for being remiss about writing: "You could sue me for a divorce, and I wouldn't blame you. The way I've been writing you is a disgrace. But, darling, after Wednesday night [the date of Virginia's wedding] there will be no excuse for neglecting you, and as far as that goes I don't have a real good one now." Getting ready for Virginia's wedding and the backyard reception, she said,

All I've done is pack the baby and all his equipment over to Mother's or your mother's and then race off to town or work out at our house getting ready. Mother has done a lot to the house, and it really looks good. There has been a lot of shopping to do, and a shower Friday night with another one coming up tomorrow night, the rehearsal and rehearsal dinner Tuesday P.M. and the wedding Wednesday. Then rest. Oh joy!! Wish you could be here, honey. I think you would like my pink dress.

Then, on August 16, Becky reported that the wedding plans went off track and responded to sad news.

August 16, 1944

My Dearest Darling Husband,

I missed you so much tonight, darling. Virginia was married, but not as we planned. Monday she got a good case of the jitters, I guess you would say, and backed out. We called everything off with Bob and his folks both here. Then late yesterday, she changed her mind again and was married tonight in a beautiful little home wedding that reminded me a lot of ours. We really went to town today making all the arrangements on such short notice and it turned out perfectly lovely. There were just close friends and the family present. They were married in front of the fireplace which was decorated beautifully. Dorothy Dersch lighted the candles, I was the matron of honor, and Paul Reed . . . was the best man. We also had a reception with cake and punch afterwards. I wore the pink dress (long) I was to wear in the big church wedding and carried a beautiful bunch of flowers. There was a photographer here making pictures so you can see how

Wedding photo of Virginia Caldwell and Robert Parnell, August 16, 1944

pretty it all was. In one of the pictures taken in front of the piano, I believe you were caught. Your picture was sitting on the piano, and I lowered my bouquet so you would show. I wanted you in it too, because you were really here with me all the time in your spirit. I thought about you constantly and like someone said, I felt like I was being married all over again. Bob is terribly sweet, and he'll make Virginia an awfully good husband. I hope everything turns out ok.

My darling today I got the news and even though I've known it for some time, I wouldn't admit it to myself. Simp is dead and yet I can't believe it. M.E. loved him so and I grieve too for her. I don't believe I've had anything strike me quite so forcibly as it did. You know, Royce, I've had Simp and M.E.'s picture out on the dresser ever since I came home. Even though M.E. and I haven't corresponded as much as Beedie and I have, I've felt so close to her and John because we were such good friends. When you live with someone as we did with them, it really strikes home. It's too late to tell John how very much their friendship meant to us, but I hope to be able to tell M.E. I really worry about M.E. You know how very devout she was. You don't suppose she'd consider going into a convent, do you? I don't want her to. She told me many a time that if anything ever happened to John, she would never marry again, and I believe her.

Darling, I'll pray every night that you can come home soon. The props were kinda knocked out from under me hearing that you wouldn't be coming home as you thought together with the news about Simp. It can't be true. I thought of nothing else lately and dreamed you were home several times, and I haven't decided what to do. I think I'll let things ride awhile. I would like to keep the apartment and maybe, if I really tried, I could keep expenses down and live reasonably. I certainly haven't done so hot lately. There seemed to be everything coming up at once. I'll let you know about the bank balance as soon as I can. I'm behind on my bookkeeping.

By the way, nobody knows why Virginia and Bob didn't get married as previously planned. Everyone thinks his orders were changed – alerted for overseas duty – and they put it off. Even your folks think it, so don't say anything.

Little Royce was there – at the wedding. He was all dressed up in his white suit that I got him to wear when you come home. I decided he would have outgrown it by November or Christmas and would have to have a new one to greet his Daddy in anyway. He's all boy, though. He got bored with everything and went to sleep while his Aunt Virginia was getting married. Everybody thought he was darling, of course. Lucy next door kept him for me and brought him over all dressed up.

Did I tell you that I'm just about back to the size of the girl you married? Yes, sir, I weigh the same, 110 lbs. The only difference I'm about an inch larger in the waist. I'm going to see what I can do about that.

I love you, Royce, with all my heart. I'm praying for your safe return and hope that it's not too far off. Darling, you are the one person in my life, the only one and there could never be another. I love little Royce, but the love for your husband and your child is so different. We're waiting anxiously for you.

Love and kisses,
Becky and Royce II

By this time, Becky had received letters from Royce written in early August. The day after the wedding, she told Royce that she was "home" again.

This apartment seems like home now because I got it for you and me, darling. And if it's all right with you, dear, I'll keep it for now. I'm going to make out a budget and really try to live by it and save $100.$\underline{^{00}}$ every month. I'll write you all about it when I get it planned.

You are so terribly sweet to tell me that I've done well so far when it (bank acct.) really isn't what you were expecting. I know I've fallen short of your expectations as far as money is concerned, because I'm still your extravagant wife. Do you love me anyway? I love you more dearly every day, because you are so patient, understanding, and by the far the most wonderful person in all this world. There may be many more like me who are proud of their husbands and as in love with them, but there is no one any more so than I am.

I am so glad you want to buy a car when you come home. There may be some who think we are foolish but if it were just you and me traveling around together, it would be different. We could manage. However, with little Royce, we must be careful, and it will be so much easier and better for him if we can have a car. Some may say I should stay here with him, but I think that he should be with his Daddy as much as possible and vice versa. Little Royce is around women too much anyway and he needs his Daddy. Virginia and Bob took care of Royce the other afternoon and Bob said he didn't know when he had so much fun. . . . With the experience Virginia has had with Royce and Bob crazy about kids, they shouldn't do bad at all as parents. I can hardly wait until you and I can really start being parents. This long-distance, remote-control stuff isn't so good, is it, my darling?

I haven't written M.E. yet. I probably will do that tomorrow. I'm thinking of asking her to come here for a visit. I'm almost sure she wouldn't, but I'd really love to have her, and it might do her good. You know, darling, I'm really worried about her.

. . .

Margaret is having a birthday party for Tammy – 1 year old – tomorrow afternoon and Royce and I are invited. We'll tell you all about it. This will be Royce's first party. Margaret had a letter from Erman today and he said he was on Guam. He told her all about it. Said it was about three times as bad as the Marshalls. He said it was *the first time he had ever gotten close enough to fire on the Japs (he drives a loading barge), and he said he hoped he'd never have to do that again. They had to clean out a Jap pillbox or something. If you are anywhere near Guam look Erman Winner up. He's a Marine PFC with the 2nd or 4th division — I've forgotten.*

On "Vacation"

Four days out of Eniwetok, on August 13, the *Suwannee* arrived at Seeadler Harbor. MacArthur's forces had taken it from the Japanese in March, and it now served as the major staging area for further operations in the western Pacific. Before the ship anchored at Seeadler, the air group flew their planes ashore to an airfield on the nearby islet of Pityilu, where they were quartered for the rest of the month. Located along the equator, Pityilu was hot and wet. It had been a coconut plantation prior to the war. The Seabees carved out an air strip between rows of coconut palms and installed Quonset huts for living quarters, mess halls, offices, warehouses, and an officer's club.

Despite the equatorial climate, Green Peyton described Pityilu as the nearest thing to a "South Sea Island paradise that the air group had seen . . . after ten months of wandering in the Pacific."[167] The crews could rest here and recover from the intense action at Saipan and Guam. Pilots waded in the reef, collected shells, and fished from self-made outriggers. And some of them visited the well-stocked officer's club, where they could nurse "their ration of three bourbon highballs apiece."[168]

A day after arriving in the Admiralties, Royce told Becky that he received several letters from her. His letter to Becky is longer and more upbeat than any he had written in some time.

August 15, 1944

My Darling Becky,

. . . We are on a nice little vacation and the people on the island are treating us very well – although the facilities aren't too good. I went out

this morning in shorts and hunted shells on the reef and I look (and feel)
like a broiled lobster. However, it was worth it, and I have some lovely
shells which I shall bring home to you. I intend to go out again before we
leave and get enough small ones to make into a necklace. They are really
beautiful. Even the fish are brilliantly colored. You would be amazed at
the sea life around these islands. We've caught a couple of small squids.
They can really cover the ground on their tentacles incidentally. I could
have caught enough crabs to make you a very nice Crab Louie. I saw
a puffer fish, which we have been taught to recognize as poisonous (for
eating, that is). Gordon Peel, whom you have met – he's from Oklahoma
City and you met him at Corpus. He went to Central State at the same
time as Bob and I. Well, anyway, he is stationed here in a PV (Ventura,
Dump will know what it is) squadron. He went with me and gave me
the word on getting the shells.

Oh, yes! I found out that Bob is at Biak (maybe). He must be
doing that night bombing on the Philippines we've read of in the
paper lately.

We had a good movie tonight, which I had seen, naturally –
"Gentleman Jim." Of course, it's always good to see Errol Flynn and
Alexis Smith. We also found out via the newsreel that the 8th Army
was pushing Rommel back in North Africa [Royce is being sarcastic
here about the datedness of the films and newsreels shown aboard
ship, as he surely knew that this occurred in 1943].

I don't know why, but I'm in a very good mood tonight. My
morale has been low for some time. There is no telling when I'll get
to come home to you, so I can't understand why my spirits are high.
(I haven't been drinking either—not a drop.) I did laugh a lot at the
movie, and that's good for a person, I hear.

. . .

I tried my hand at poker again. I had a hundred dollars on the
books, so I drew it with the intention of making a small fortune. P.S.

I only lost 98 dollars. I bought a box of candy and a box of gum. My luck wasn't too good, incidentally. You know that old saying – lucky in love and unlucky at cards. I must say I've been very lucky in my love life – except, of course, that the **** Navy has deemed it advisable to keep me separated from the sweetest wife in the world for a helluva long time now. If you won't be bored by my repeating – I adore you. I miss you very much but mostly I just dream and daydream about you. I guess it's really building "castles in the air," but I really have bright hopes for the future. It looks very rosy to me. I can hardly wait to see you, and I won't mind too much your having to spend a lot of time with the baby. I will say this though – with me and the baby both around you're likely to have all your time occupied.

Be sweet, write often. Take care of yourself and our young son. It can't be too much longer until you'll have two Royces at home – I hope, I hope, I hope.

Your Loving Husband Always,
Royce

The flying schedule was light at Pityilu. There were no flights at all during the first full week. After that, the flight log shows several days of aerial gunnery practice, which was interrupted by a novel flight in which the entire air group observed a departing U.S. submarine. As John Smith described, the "sub was proceeding from the Admiralties to its assigned patrol area and had been requested to dive and surface a couple of times after reaching deep water to demonstrate to the air group personnel how this maneuver appeared from the air." Most "of the pilots had never seen a submarine in actual operation at sea."[169]

Being in port expedites the delivery of correspondence. By mid-month, both Becky and Royce had received letters from one another postmarked in early August, and by the end of the month, Royce learned from Becky about Virginia's wedding. As usual, his receipt of letters prompted his writing. He told Becky, "I'm sorry I led you to believe I'd be at home so soon," and he inferred from her letters that she seemed "to be sorta blue. I thought I'd be home when I said but sometimes things don't happen as people wish. Keep a stiff upper lip – it just can't be too much longer." He also said,

> I know this "mad whirl" you are all in must be a happy one. I know that I won't be there for the wedding, so wish Virginia and Bob best of luck – much happiness – for me. I should like very much to be there – if only to catch a glimpse of you in that dress. You'll doubtless be the most beautiful thing at a beautiful affair. You would be that to me if I were there. Think of me and all the happiness we can share when I come home. (August 19)

> I'll tell Rabbi you said to be careful, but I don't think you need to worry. Besides the time he nearly got his neck broken, he got about half of his tail feathers shot away before that. . . .
> How true was your statement that we've been out here long enough!!! Everyone agrees with you, but apparently we are too good at our assigned work. That's the story they hand us. Maybe they think a little flattery will make us feel a little better. . . .
> I won't worry about your being alone. Keep that apartment of Mrs. Freeman's if you can. But I'll miss you like _____. You won't mind, will you? I'm practically going nuts (and of course I don't have far to go) to see you and the baby. Eggbert and I have decided we'll be at home in time to send the kids off to school, anyway. (August 24)

> I just received a couple of letters from you mailed August 18. I'm glad to hear that the wedding came off ok. I'll bet you that Bob was just as glad it wasn't a big affair. I'm glad you and I did it the way we did. Those big shindigs scare the Dickens out of me.

Seriously, it did sound nice, and I wish I could have been there.

I don't know whether I would have M.E. come out or not. It might just make things a little harder for her. I intend to write her a long letter when I get home.

I'm glad to hear that you're back down to your "fighting weight." When I got those snapshots of you and the baby you appeared to have gained a good deal around the waist. I had already planned on running you around the block every morning, but I guess it won't be necessary.

. . .

Hey, I saw a guy who's been with Bob for the last year and he said Bob sank a 5000-ton cargo ship several nights ago. How's that? (August 27)

At the end of the month, Royce reported that Bob Hope put on his USO show at Pityilu. "It was very good, but I was sure ready to start home when it was over. He made one good crack about the scarcity of women: 'Boy, are the odds terrific – 700 to 1 – 800 to 1 – 1000 to nothing. Never in all history have so many chased so few for so long for so little.' We had to sit in the rain about half the time, but it was worth it." According to John Smith, "Some of the air group bumped into Hope at the O-Club . . . later in the day and found him to be as witty off the stage as on."[170]

Royce told Becky not to tell his mother, but his brother Bob "is supposed to come thru here in a day or so and I sorta expect to see him. If I do, I'll write all about it and she'll be thrilled for a week. It's been about 19 months now since I've seen him."

On the Home Front

After Virginia's wedding and learning of John Simpson's death, in addition to the prediction that Royce would not be coming home soon, Becky wrote to him every day for the rest of August, except for two days when she was composing a letter to M.E. On August 25, she said, "I spent all evening trying to write M.E. and was feeling pretty low after I finished. I haven't mailed the letter and don't think I shall. It doesn't sound right." She wrote to M.E. again on August 30: "This time I mailed it. I asked her to come down here, but I doubt that she will. Sure wish she would."

Post-wedding, Becky also said she's "getting restless again" and wanted "to be on the go." This restlessness expressed itself in many ways. For example, she told Royce,

> *I went with Mother to her dentist today and could have had a job as receptionist . . . if I had had anyone to leave Royce with. I think your mother would be more than glad to keep him, but you get rather attached to the little devils and I don't believe I could leave him every day as much as I would like to work. I'm restless now that I think you won't be coming home right away. I want to go to work, take a trip or something, but I know that I should stay here and keep the apartment and care for Royce. Margaret is going to California around the 20th of September, and I'd love to take Royce and go along. I have so many relatives I could visit out there. I guess it would be silly. If it's not too hot next week, Royce, your mother and I may go to Duncan with Sandy – that is, if he makes the trip.*

As occurred before the baby was born, Becky was constantly active. Following the wedding on Wednesday, August 16, she and Royce II went to Tammy's birthday party on Friday. Afterward, Virginia, Bob, Margaret, Verla, and Becky went swimming at Spring Lake. On Sunday, Becky had dinner at the Singletons'. After her mother gave her a bunch of tomatoes and she made a trip with Gussie to the market on Monday and Tuesday, she spent the better part of three days canning chili sauce, peaches, apricots, and peach and apricot preserves. Becky attended a "hen party" Tuesday evening, had lunch with Verla and Margaret on Wednesday, and saw a film with them—*The Canterville Ghost* with Charles Laughton, Robert Young, and Margaret O'Brien—the next night. She was invited to a luncheon and bridge on Friday, August 25. And, the following week on consecutive nights, she hosted her parents and then Margaret, Verla, and Mary for dinner. Becky may have decided to host her dinner parties because she needed to cook a ham she had purchased. As she told Royce, "I bought a ham before they were put back on the ration list to bake when you came home, but when I found out it would be a while before you got here, I decided I had better go ahead and cook it."

Becky's letters in the last half of August mainly provide details of these events. In other news, she reported

Verla's husband was wounded in France and is in a hospital in England. She had a letter from him Saturday saying he had lost all his personal belongings but didn't mention what happened. Then today she received a telegram from the war department saying he was slightly wounded. I guess I'd just pass out completely if I ever got a telegram of any kind.

There also was some news about Royce II.

Honestly, Royce, little Royce is a case. He wants everything he sees now and can hold out his arms to you or to something he sees. He scoots all over the floor and loves paper. You can't leave a newspaper, magazine, or anything near him without him trying to tear it to shreds and put it in his mouth. This evening I was holding him on my lap and he wouldn't be still. He wanted to get ahold of the arm of the chair. He'd wiggle and squirm and try to bite down on it. If he doesn't have a tooth pretty soon, I'm going to be surprised. He has a habit now of sticking his lips out and spitting. Of course, we think he's about the smartest kid in "these here parts." He knows or rather recognizes us and can tell strangers. You can hardly get him to smile at someone strange. He'll just stare a hole thru them or look around as unconcerned, like he was saying, "Will you please go away and not bother me." He's going to be sitting up soon, I think. His little back is strong. We'll pull him up to a sitting position and if we hold on to his hands and help him, he'll push right on up to a standing position and does he love it – of course, we tell him how smart he is and he just laughs. Mother is afraid I'll make him bow-legged, but his legs are so straight. (August 19)

Today is a red-letter day, darling. Royce did something new. He ate cereal sitting up in his highchair. He's been taking his cereal just like he does his bottle, lying down. But I decided he was old enough to try it in his highchair since he's sitting up real good with support now. He did very well, too. He seemed to enjoy it. He was in his highchair when I was having breakfast, and when someone else is eating, he has to eat, too. So I gave him some of my prune juice. He drank it out of a glass, and it was the cutest thing you ever saw. He'd start working his little old mouth before I'd ever get the glass up to it and he'd try to hold the glass. He'd put his head back so he could drink good, and he'd keep it back when I would take the glass away so he could swallow. He was really darling. I got so tickled at him. I've given him prune juice before, you know, as a laxative, but this had a little lemon juice in it and he made the awfullest face, but he was holding his arms out for more right away. (August 21)

Toward the end of the month, Becky gave Royce a financial report and a proposed budget to manage her expenses. She acknowledged that "we have been standing still for two months," with a current bank balance of $1,813.72. Royce had asked her in early August if she could save $100 per month. Incorporating that amount into her budget, she said, left her $125 to live on, which she broke down as follows:

Rent	$50.00
Utilities	6.00
Groceries	40.00
Recreation	7.50
Incidentals	11.50
Car	10.00
	$125.00

In explaining the amount of these items, Becky emphasized the bare-boned nature of her estimates. The cost of groceries, she said, is "ridiculous. You wouldn't believe that it's possible to go in a store and spend as much money as you have to and come out with so little. You'll probably think I eat an awfully lot, but with what little I eat and the little entertaining I do, it takes every bit of that." For recreation, she eats "downtown two or three times a month and [goes] to the show about once a week – 55 cents each time." "Incidentals include insurance, gifts, magazines, necessities." "There's no room for clothes." And during the month of December, with the need to purchase Christmas gifts, she "won't be able to save anything."

For two months, Becky eagerly anticipated Royce's return in August. Learning that he would not be returning so soon seems to have made her restless, which was manifested in a full, if not hectic, schedule of daily activities. In addition, she wrote to Royce more frequently—almost every day—and, as indicated by the following letter, may have reminisced more about their last times together.

August 27, 1944

My Darling,

Does it seem to you almost a year since you left? In some ways it doesn't seem possible that it could be that long since we were together and then, when I get to thinking about it again, it's been an awfully long time. Coming home and working, then waiting and planning for the baby, and now taking care of him and running around all the time, has made time fly. Looking for you home this month since May has helped, too, but now the disappointment of your not coming home and not knowing when to expect you has sorta made time stand still. When I think how long it's been since you held me in your arms, it seems forever and, then again, I can be thinking about you and feel like you are very near and that I can almost reach out and touch you. I'm so glad for that – it makes it so much easier. Even though you have been away a long time, you are still with me as plain as if it was yesterday when you left. That's real love, isn't it, darling? Do you remember what we did the last night we were together? I can tell you. Crash, Barclay, John, M.E., and you and I had dinner together, then we went back to the motel and played poker, only John and M.E. didn't play. John did for a while, though, didn't he? I won some money, remember? Unusual for me! We played until 12 or 1 o'clock. To some people that probably sounds funny – playing poker on our last night. But we didn't care – just so we were together. The next morning, I'll never forget, you said you had been awake for some time before I woke up, hoping I would awaken, but I didn't – not until it was time for us to get up. I'm still sorry for that, 'cause I've often wondered what you thought about during that time, holding me in your arms. Will you tell me some time, darling? You were wonderful when you told me goodbye, and I tried to be brave. M.E. told me she hoped she could do as well when she told John goodbye. Later, she told me she did. I'll never forget when M.E. stopped through here on her way home, she kept Mother and me laughing all thru dinner recalling incidents that happened while we four lived together. I only hope now that she can still do that and be happy for her memories. They were sweet, and for that she should thank God.

This is a rambling letter, isn't it, darling. I just wrote my thoughts for a change and, though this sounds rather disconnected, you can probably fill in and make these memories as real to you as they are to me.

Perhaps I shouldn't live so much in the past. They always say, look to the future. But even though I know our future is going to be bright and happy, mainly because we'll be together, I can't help living over again the happy days we've had. Our future is so uncertain as to when it will begin that I love to look back on the seven months that were so sweet, but I know when this war is over and we are together again, the years ahead will be even sweeter.

I love you, my darling. And I'll wait for you as long as it's necessary. I only hope that you'll be coming home to me and Royce soon. We want to see you so much. Write often, my dearest.

Your loving wife and son,
Becky and Royce II

-15-

ADVANCING TO THE PHILIPPINES: September 1944

AFTER NEARLY A month's rest at Pityilu in the Admiralities, the air group flew back aboard the *Suwannee* in early September. It was then that the men learned they soon would be on their way to the Dutch East Indies. Royce wrote to Becky twice before the departure. The first letter replied to letters from Becky mailed in late August.

September 7, 1944

My Darling,

I'm sorry to have neglected writing you lately, but I've just been with Bob for a few days. Wreckage is strewn everywhere.

I just received three more letters from you when I got back – up to August 28. One of them is the very best letter I have ever received. However, instead of immediately writing an answer to that one, I'll answer them in order.

We haven't had "Lost Angel" aboard ship. I'd love to see it though. I remember very well seeing "Journey for Margaret" with you.

I'm ready to go to work on all that good food you are preparing for me. Any time the Navy's ready, I am. . . .

I haven't written M.E. yet. I intend to when I get home, however. I think she'll be o.k. even though it might take some time. There are many things more terrible than death.

I shall be delighted to play bridge with you. I'll charge you a kiss for each point you lose – and jump you to a grand slam on every bid. Them's my only terms.

And now I'm back to this wonderful letter. (They're all wonderful – this one is perfect, however.)

It is so hard to put one's thoughts on paper. I think you'd probably like to know what I thought that last morning before you woke up. I had just been mentally kicking myself when you awakened. Not until then had I realized just how very much I loved you. (I also realized how big a heel I'd been on several occasions.) Of course, I don't remember my thoughts perfectly – they were sorta jumbled up and sentimental. I had no worries for the future. I was a little disappointed to realize I'd not be with you during the last months you were pregnant. Somehow, I feel that that must be a very wonderful period in a man's life. I hope I don't have to be gone any more at a time like that incidentally. My darling, my heart was so full that morning that it just can't be expressed in words. I can say that I loved you very much that morning – and I love you more and more as time passes. Everything will certainly be perfect when we are together again.

I remember that last night too. It may have seemed a little odd (or silly) to some people. But feelings were a little too deep that night for what most people might call normal reactions.

Now here I am all mixed up. I love you – please write more of your "rambling" letters. They are wonderful.

Your Always,
Royce

Two days later, Royce wrote again before the ship weighed anchor. "Mail closes today," he said, "so I have a chance to write you again before there is a lapse in the mail you receive from me." He had received two pictures of Royce at 3½ months, wished he could have been there when Becky had his folks over for dinner, and was glad to hear that Beedie was coming for a visit. "Incidentally," he added, "Eggbert went with me and Bob while Bob was here, and Bob really liked him. Bob looks good – although a little thin. He said he'd get his weight back at rest camp."

On the Home Front

By September, Becky's letters dwell somewhat less on the timing of Royce's return. Still, her desire to see him is so strong that she continually looked for signs that his tour will end. "According to the papers," she wrote on September 5, "the outer defenses of the Philippines are being bombed quite systematically now," which prompted her to ask, "Can you answer this question? Will you be in the Philippines? Or will you get to come home before it begins or at least before it ends?" In one letter, she expressed feelings of exasperation and resentment when others discouraged her from believing Royce would soon be home.

> *I've had more people tell me that I may as well quit looking for you for a long time – that they could have told me you wouldn't be here by this month and that you couldn't possibly be home by Christmas. It makes me fightin' mad to hear anyone say such a thing – Absolutely. I could start pulling hair when they begin talking that way, because they don't know a damn thing about it. Most people who have husbands or sons in the Navy or Marines [say] they stay months and years, but as I tell them, I've yet to hear of a fighter pilot and especially one based on a carrier who stays much over a year. . . . Gad, all I live on anyway is hope and if I couldn't look forward to your coming home and hope it will be soon, I'd just curl up and*

die. Pardon me if I rave awhile. But what I can't stand nowadays is discouragement from anybody. Hells bells there is enough of that every day without some pessimistic idiot shooting off his mouth. Pardon me, honey, I have to throw a good one every once in a while. I just got back from a hen party where Margaret said some of those things. I guess I shouldn't let them bother me. I'm just going to quit going to those things. They are beginning to get me down. What I wouldn't give for you right now, darling. I need you so. Ordinarily, I enjoy girls' company. But they are beginning to give me a pain in the neck. The only thing that worries me is that when you do get home, if I'm not careful, these man-crazy females will mob you. Mind if I'm possessive, darling?

In the first half of the month, Becky mentioned Royce II only once, when Royce's sister Mina spent the day with her.

Mina and I are both writing you. We have been all evening getting the refrigerator defrosted, the groceries put away, dinner over with and the dishes done. Little Royce has played a big part, too. We couldn't get him to sleep after his six o'clock feeding, as he had to be entertained off and on. We put him in the highchair while we ate and gave him some toys. Mina didn't get much eating done, however, for picking up toys. He'd throw the toys on the floor as fast as she gave them to him.

I took the baby to the doctor today. He's getting along just fine and he's eating everything now. He can have egg yolk, canned baby fruits and vegetables, besides his cereal, fruit juice, and bottle. I fed him some fruit tonight for the first time along with his cereal. I gave him a few spoonfuls of cereal, then stuck a spoonful of apple sauce in his mouth, and he didn't know the difference until the second bite. All of a sudden he stopped in the middle of it and made the worst face and then went on eating. After we visited the doctor, I went by the store, then to the Gas Co. and then up to Buddy's office. Mina and Buddy took him home. He slept some but after I picked Mina up and we came over here (also took him to the grocery), he was wide awake and didn't go to sleep until a while ago. He was so tired that he was restless, and I thought he never would go to sleep.

Mina and I went together and bought him a car seat. You hook it over the back of the front seat, and he can sit up and see everything. That was his 5th (mos.) birthday present from Mina. She gives him something every month.

As usual, Becky's letters described her busy schedule. At least weekly, she played bridge, took in a movie, and had dinner with the war wives. For example,

I'm getting to be a regular bridge fiend. Gosh, do I love it? It's more fun and I'm getting a little better all along or at least I think I am. According to your latest report on poker playing (-$98.00), you had better take up bridge and drop poker.

. . .

Margaret is having the girls over for dinner tomorrow night. Then we'll probably go to the show. "Going My Way" with Bing Crosby is on, but you haven't been able to get within blocks of the theatre for a week, because it's been so crowded. Jean and I saw "Bathing Beauties" Monday and I thought I'd die laughing at Red Skelton giving an imitation of a woman getting up in the morning. It was really good. (September 6)

Saw the cutest show tonight, "Two Girls and a Sailor" with Van Johnson, Gloria DeHaven, June Allyson, Jimmie Durante, Harry James and his orchestra and several others. It was really good. . . . It

must be kinda' old 'cause of the songs. They sing "Sweet and Lovely," and "Paper Doll" and "Take It Easy." Have you ever seen it? It had a lot of the stars of "Fleet's In" and had the same cast as "Bathing Beauties" with a few more added. Van Johnson is kinda scrumptious – he reminds me of you, darling, and Harry James and that trumpet – Oh man!! Remember the singer (female) who can really sing with that deadpan expression – She's not bad looking. Then Ben Blue danced, June Sturbis played the piano, Lena Horne sang, Carlos Ramirez sang, and the Wilde twins were in it. Do you remember them at the squadron party in Hollywood? They were blond and really good looking. It (the picture) was a scream. (September 7)

At their dinners, the war wives invariably shared the latest news about their husbands, which Becky reported in her letters. After getting together on September 7, Becky wrote,

Margaret had 3 letters from Erman today. I don't know how he knew, but he said you were headed for someplace and it wasn't home. So help me, I wish I knew what was going on. Something big must be going to break now. He told Margaret he had a narrow escape this last time (Guam). His tractor was evidently knocked out, 'cause he got a new one, she said, and when his tractor is wrecked, he becomes a machine gunner and in one of his letters to Margaret, he told her how he had machine-gunned a Jap pill box for the first time.

Verla had a letter from the War Department today saying that on August 9, the reports on Dee were good and he was improving (wounded, you know). She had a letter from him written the tenth of August, before she ever received the wire, that was the last she heard.

Becky also told Royce that Virginia was home now. Her husband "Bob is on his way overseas. They certainly weren't together long. I don't know what Virginia will do – work, I guess." Virginia may have had thoughts about returning to school. For within a week after Becky told Royce that Bob had left, Virginia and Becky visited Oklahoma A&M. Both were members of the same sorority, Alpha Delta Pi. The occasion for the visit was the culmination of the annual sorority rush, a selection process in which potential members attend sorority events, sororities extend bids, or offers to join, to those they would like to become new members, and potential members decide whether to accept or deny the bid. Virginia and Becky arrived in Stillwater on Saturday (September 9). That night, Becky wrote,

Guess where I am? Virginia and I decided all of a sudden to come up here to Stillwater for Bid House. Rush was over last night, but we came up to see the new pledges and you ought to see them. We really got the cream of the crop. We got 25 pledges. It was really exciting. Makes me wish I could go back to school while you are gone, but couldn't leave our little "Joe."

Royce is with his grandmothers. Your mother came after him early this morning and Mother was going to get him this afternoon. We expect to go back to the city tomorrow.

. . .

We played with a "weegie board" this evening and it said you would be home in four weeks. How about that?

We also played bridge tonight. I'm getting a lot more confidence in myself now and am playing a lot better, I think. Maybe tonight it was just because the kids I played with didn't know much more about it than I did.

. . .

I've showed everyone here your and the baby's pictures and, of course, they think I'm awfully lucky to have you both. They think you are so handsome and little Royce is cute.

On Tuesday following her weekend in Stillwater, Becky wrote again about her activities, at once expressing uneasiness about and rationalizing the value of her "galivanting around."

This evening I went to an alumnae meeting, and Virginia and I told them about "Rush" and the new pledges. I was one of the assistant hostesses at the meeting tonight. I guess I'll pay my dues and be active until you come home. We meet once a month.

. . .

I stayed at home last night and plan to again tomorrow night. I don't like to be running around all the time. Thursday I'm going to Margaret's brother's wedding. Your mother will keep Royce, I guess. Mother kept him tonight. Friday, Mary is going to have us for dinner. We are having our little weekly dinners again. Vivian (Freeman) called me to play bridge tonight but had these other plans already. Also, Jean Ash called. She lives with Ruth Prickett from the Gas Co. and they wanted me to come over and bring Royce. Dorothy Williams and her fiancé were going to be there. But I couldn't do that either.

Guess you see where my time goes. I could be going all the time if I wanted to. Everybody wants me to come and see them and bring Royce, but he's too much trouble to do that very much. I don't feel particularly like I'm doing anything worthwhile unless it is caring for Royce. I wish I could be out working for a rainy day instead of galivanting around. Royce keeps me busy, and I could make a full-time job of him and the house etc., but I guess I'd go crazy if it weren't for being able to get out and "go." That is what made time pass so fast when I was pregnant and while I'm waiting for you. I know that when you come home, I won't care a thing about going unless you want to go someplace. Perhaps there is one exception to that – I do want to "show you off."

Becky ended this letter by referring again to the Philippines. Enclosing a newspaper clipping from the paper, she asked, "Were you in on this? We've also had the report on the big raid on the Philippines where a convoy and many other ships were sunk. I suppose you were there, too. I'll sure be glad when the Philippines are all over." Becky erroneously inferred that the escort carriers in CarDiv 22 were involved in the actions of aircraft from the fleet carriers. Although the *Suwannee* was not "there," it soon would be. In the meantime, the ship was on the way to an operation some 350 miles southeast of the Philippines.

Preparing for MacArthur's Return

By September, Allied forces had positioned themselves for an invasion of the Philippines. Lying about 500 miles east of Indochina (now Vietnam) between Formosa (now known as Taiwan) and Borneo, the Philippines is an archipelago of over 7,100 islands stretching more than 1,000 miles from north to south. The islands are clustered into three major groups: Luzon, Visayas, and Mindanao. The population center is Luzon, the northernmost and largest island; the southernmost and second largest island is Mindanao.

The Japanese gained control of the Philippines in May 1942 following a surprise attack and invasion in December 1941. In March 1944, the United States Joint Chiefs of Staff decided to invade Mindanao before the end of the year. Further advances were, however, the subject of continuing debate as the J.C.S. discussed Pacific and Far Eastern strategy. Chief of Naval Operations Admiral Ernest King proposed to capture Formosa and bypass the rest of the Philippines, in particular Luzon, whereas General MacArthur was determined to liberate all the Philippines as soon as possible.

Although MacArthur contended that there were sound strategic reasons for invading Luzon rather than Formosa, his position also was a matter of personal sentiment and honor. He had a long history with the Philippines. His father had been a military governor there. It was his first assignment after graduating from West Point in 1903; he had two tours there in the

1920s; and he returned in 1935 when he was appointed as military advisor to the Commonwealth Government.[171] From then until 1942, MacArthur remained in the Philippines. Retiring from the U.S. Army in 1937, he became the Philippine field marshal while building a citizen army. When Japanese aggression in China and French Indochina heated up in the summer of 1941, President Roosevelt recalled MacArthur to active duty and incorporated the Philippine army into the newly established United States Armed Forces, Far East, under his command.[172]

After the Japanese invaded Luzon in December 1941, MacArthur and his forces retreated to the Bataan Peninsula and island of Corregidor. But as supplies dwindled and the Japanese advanced, Roosevelt ordered MacArthur to evacuate the Philippines. In March 1942, he and his family and members of his staff fled in a daring escape aboard PT boats, evading a Japanese blockade and mines on a 580-mile journey over rough seas to Mindanao, and then proceeding to Australia by air. Upon arriving in Australia, MacArthur's first words to reporters were that he had been ordered to "proceed from Corregidor to Australia for the purpose of . . . organizing the American offensive against Japan, a primary objective of which is the relief of the Philippines . . . and I shall return."[173] He would often repeat that promise in public appearances over the next two and a half years.

By August 1944, the Joint Chiefs still had not decided which route to take for the final offensive against Japan. American progress westward across the Pacific had been steady. East of the Philippines, central Pacific forces, under Admiral Nimitz's overall command, had gained possession of the Marianas. And to the southeast, General MacArthur's forces had advanced beyond Hollandia to the Vogelkop peninsula in northwest New Guinea. In early September, the Formosa–Luzon debate was still unresolved; however, it was decided to invade Mindanao on November 15 and Leyte on December 20. Preparatory operations were planned to establish land-based air support for the Mindanao invasion and to neutralize Japanese forces east and southeast of the Philippines. Admiral Nimitz's Pacific Fleet would support a Marine invasion of Peleliu in the Palaus, 470 miles east of Mindanao. And to the southeast, 350 miles from Mindanao, General MacArthur's Army would invade Morotai in the Molucca Islands. D-day for both operations was September 15.

Peleliu was targeted because it had an airfield that the enemy could use to launch attacks against the U.S. fleet invading the Philippines. It was captured with far greater difficulty than anticipated as the Japanese invoked new tactics of defense, which they would use for the rest of the war. To prolong resistance to amphibious assaults, Japanese forces offered minimal resistance at the beach and fell back to organized defensive positions beyond the range of naval bombardment. Well-fortified and operating from a system of interlocking caves, a garrison of 10,000 Japanese troops fought to the death. U.S. forces secured the Peleliu airfield area within a few days of landing, but casualties were high and would remain so as fighting continued in the central highlands for the next two months. One Marine regiment suffered 70 percent casualties, and the total number of U.S. casualties exceeded 8,000, including 1,500 killed in action.[174]

In selecting Morotai, MacArthur bypassed the larger, nearby island of Halmahera based on the leapfrogging principle, or "hitting 'em where they ain't," which U.S. forces had applied at several other points in the Pacific War. Halmahera had excellent natural defenses and a large Japanese garrison of 37,000, whereas Morotai was believed to have only 1,000 troops. Taken at much lower cost, Morotai could cut off the larger force on Halmahera by sea and air.[175]

The *Suwannee* did not take part in the invasion of Peleliu. Instead, it supported the landings at Morotai as part of Task Group 77.1, which comprised six escort carriers, including the four *Sangamons* in CarDiv 22. The task group weighed anchor in Seeadler Harbor on September 10 and rendezvoused with the attack force on September 13, thereafter providing antisubmarine and combat air patrol over the convoy. The landings at Morotai were unopposed, and with negligible subsequent opposition, combat operations for ground troops amounted to a series of patrols to hunt down Japanese parties.[176]

With so little opposition on Morotai, VF-60 missions were limited mostly to sweeps to neutralize airfields in Halmahera. The pilots' sorties were routine, except for a remarkable air–sea rescue. On September 16, fighter pilot Ensign Harold Thompson from sister ship *Santee* was shot down by antiaircraft fire while making a strafing run on Japanese barges in Wasile Bay, Halmahera. Parachuting into the bay, Thompson found himself 300 yards from shore with a badly torn left hand, a life preserver that could be only partially inflated, and Japanese guns shelling him intermittently. A PBY Catalina rescue plane that soon arrived was driven off by heavy fire in an attempted rescue, but was able to drop Thompson a life raft, which he managed to inflate and clamber aboard.

To support Thompson's rescue, dozens of aircraft, including 12 Hellcats from VF-60, were called upon. Royce was among the first pilots to arrive. For several hours, under intense antiaircraft fire, the fighters continually strafed the beaches and gun positions. As planes circling above the bay ran low on gas, replacements came from the *Suwannee* and other carriers, seventy-five miles away. Thompson at first drifted toward shore, but as the pilots attacked the shoreline, he paddled farther out into the bay and tied his raft to the anchor chain of a barge, which afforded some protection.

When radio reports of these events reached Admiral Daniel Barbey, Commander Amphibious Force, Seventh Fleet, he arranged for a coordinated attempt to rescue Thompson with PT boats, which had arrived that morning at Morotai. As the boats approached the narrow entrance to the bay, they encountered a hail of coastal gunfire and were forced to withdraw. Fighters then began working over the batteries covering the entrance, and Avengers from the *Sangamon* dropped smokescreens. Under this cover and using evasive maneuvers to dodge Japanese fire, the PTs dashed into the bay, retrieved the downed flier, and then retired full speed. Enemy shells chased the boats as they zigzagged out, at one point crossing an enemy minefield. Finally out of range, the PTs had been under almost constant shellfire for two and a half hours, and Thompson had been in the water, under fire, for eleven hours.[177]

"One of the more amazing things about this rescue," historian William Y'Blood noted, "was that no one was hurt on either boat, and the PTs themselves suffered only superficial damage."[178] Long before the PTs arrived, however, VF-60 lost two planes and a pilot. The lost pilot was Ensign William Bannister, who had joined the air group in March when additional Hellcats replaced the group's bombers. Bannister was hit by flak on a strafing run. Too low to bail out, he was killed when he impacted the water at high speed not far from Thompson. The other Hellcat pilot shot down was Ensign Paul "Big Red" Lindskog, who had reported in June at Guadalcanal. After antiaircraft fire ruptured his oil line, Lindskog had enough power and control to land his plane on the water far away from the shore, where a seaplane rescue could be safely carried out. Big Red was taken to Morotai after his rescue. And, according to John Smith, with so little action on Morotai to report, "the press who were covering the invasion needed some spice. Apparently, VF 60's young birdman spun some good yarns for them when he was interviewed."[179]

Every crew member of the two PT boats volunteered for the rescue mission. In recognition of their valor under extremely hazardous conditions, Lieutenant A. Murray Preston, who led the mission, received the Medal of Honor, four crew members received the Navy Cross, and the rest of the crew were awarded Silver Stars.[180] Royce—and presumably other pilots who supported the rescue—was awarded an Air Medal.

Over the next five days, Royce and other pilots from VF-60 flew more strikes on the Halmahera airfields, as aircraft from the escort carriers kept away Japanese planes while construction began on an air drome at Morotai. Poor weather slowed the construction, but permanent fighter aircraft began using the fields on October 4, when the operation was declared over. CarDiv 22 was released on September 26, leaving the other two escort carriers to finish the job.

The development of the air base at Morotai proved to be more important and timelier than anticipated. In support of the Morotai and Peleliu operations, pilots from the fleet carriers struck targets in the Philippines in early September. (This is the news that Becky alluded to.) When they encountered no opposition at Mindanao and hardly any in the Visayas, Admiral Bill Halsey, who commanded these strikes, recommended that the Mindanao landing be canceled and forces go directly to Leyte, an island in the Visayas. The Joint Chiefs quickly approved an October 20 landing at Leyte.[181]

Beginning D-day at Morotai, Royce flew every day for a week, mostly sweeps over airfields in Halmahera. He finally got a break on September 22 when, on standby in the ready room, "while listening to beautiful music," he wrote, "I could not resist the urge to write you a letter and tell you once again how dear to me you are. If you were only here." His letter refers briefly to his recent combat experiences, including the air–sea rescue, although it lacks any of the details necessary for Becky to decipher exactly what he has been doing.

> Although I did not care to stay out here any longer, it has not been in vain that I did stay. I have been privileged to take part in what appears to me to be one of the most miraculous events of the war out here. I don't think I could tell you in a letter (the censor, you know), but you'll get the complete word when I get home.
>
> We have been flying a good deal lately, but it has been interesting – nearly _too_ interesting. We've seen so much of the Jap "AA" [antiaircraft fire] that it doesn't bother us much anymore, however. We are continually amazed at the Japs' manner of doing things. They must indeed be a strange people.

He went on to boast about the squadron and commanding officer Lieutenant Commander Harvey Feilbach.

I'd give anything if you could know our squadron now. It is larger, you know, and I think it is one of the best out here. Incidentally, the skipper has turned out to be one of the best, too. Perhaps being through so much together has made us all a little more cooperative.

After the *Suwannee* departed Morotai, Royce wrote another brief note.

September 28, 1944

My Darling Becky,

> *We're headed for some more rest and cold beer, and you may be sure that we'll enjoy both. None of us will be very happy out here until we head for home, however.*

> *I've been doing a little poker playing lately (and I got back that $98). Shea and I are sweating out this automobile. When I have a good winning streak, we decide it'll be a Buick, and when I lose, it works back down to a Ford. Right now, we think it'll have to be nothing bigger than an Oldsmobile. Seriously, if you do as well as I asked, we'll be able to get a good one, I think. I'm all for getting a new one. What do you think?*

> *There is no news, as usual. I seem to miss you more all the time, but I guess that's not news anymore.*

> *I love you very much and can hardly wait 'til I'm in a position to make it very apparent to you. Maybe it won't be too long. Take care of yourself and our young son.*

> *Always,*

> *Royce*

In the second half of the month, Becky wrote twice more. Her first letter mentions letters from Royce's brother Bob.

September 21, 1944

My Dearest One,

I don't know how you feel about it after you shot down that Jap bomber, but it scared the something or other out of me. We are so proud of you, darling. But let the other guy get the next one, honey. That's just too close for comfort. I realize that you are out there fighting, but, gad, not until you read something like that do you realize just how much you are out there and in it, too. Bob wrote us about it yesterday and it also came out in the paper. I'm enclosing a clipping. You darn guys anyway. You write about what Bob has done, and he writes about what you have done, but never a word about yourselves. We think you are both tops, but it's darn near time for you to come home. The Navy had better get on the ball. Bob writes that he thinks you will be home after the mission you have been on the past couple of weeks. I'm almost afraid to hope. I don't want to be disappointed again. I'm praying it's true, darling. It must be.

Guess what! Royce sat up yesterday. Just as big as you please. He was crawling along and all of a sudden sat right up. I almost fainted. He did it right by the stove and I was afraid he'd fall back on it, and I jumped up and he jumped, too. He stayed all night with your mother last night and was so good she said. I had dinner over at Verla's and we went to the show afterwards. We saw a putrid picture, "Hail the Conquering Hero," and so Margaret and I got up and went and saw "Gaslight." It was so good, but "creepy." Today one of the girls who lives next door, her friend, and Virginia and I went to the U.S.O. to the Service Wives luncheon. It was nice, but you will never guess who was there to entertain – Mary Lou Brown. Honey, if you thought her voice was good once, you should hear it now. She was wonderful. Why she can sing as good as Deanna Durbin ever did. Talk about swooning. I almost did. She sang Always, Stardust, Sweet and Lovely, A Pretty Girl is Like a Melody, Donkey Serenade, I'll

Walk Alone, and The Kiss Waltz. She recognized me, and I talked to her later. She's leaving next week for Chicago to study, and she has a job there. I'd give anything if you could have heard her. I told her all about you and showed her the baby's picture. She really puts expression into her singing and is cute as a bug. This evening I went to a surprise birthday party for Jean Ash. She was surprised too. We played bridge and, oh, you should have seen what I did once. We got the bid and took only one trick. Oh, it was terrible. Hey, what's that you said about jumping all my bids to little slams. If you do, you'll go down sure as anything. You'll learn that I'm conservative in my bidding, especially after tonight.

Darling, here's something I think you'll like. It expresses what I'd like to and what I've tried to put into words for you.

Why do I love you?
I love you not only for what you are
But for what I am when I am with you.
I love you not only for what you have made of yourself
But for what you are making of me.
I love you for ignoring the possibilities of the fool in me
And for laying firm hold of the possibilities of the good in me.
Why do I love you?
I love you for closing your eyes to the discord in me
And for adding to the music in me by worshipful listening.
I love you because you are helping me to make of the lumber of
*   my life*
Not a tavern but a temple, and the words of my every day not a
*   reproach, but a song.*
I love you because you have done more than any creed to make
*   me happy.*
You have done it without a word, without a touch, without a sign.

You have done it by just being yourself.
Perhaps after all that is what love means.[182]

I am enclosing a picture of Tommy's birthday party – August 20.
Margaret is the one in the very middle. Mary and Mike are second
on the left. The first baby on the left is a little girl exactly a year older
than Royce. She and Royce weigh the same now, and she wears size 2
shoe. Royce has just about outgrown that size and soon will be wearing
a three. Can you imagine?

I love you, darling. I'm proud of you too. Bob says you are one of
the best liked fellows in your outfit, but he needn't tell me that 'cause
I already know it. He told us all about your reunion. Your mother
and I just cried. It sounded so wonderful. Write again.

Love and X's,
Becky and Royce II

As the month closed, Becky sent Royce professional photographs of
his son. "This is Merry Christmas or 'sumpthin'," she said. Aside from
describing the photographs, Becky wrote,

Well, honey, I'm just waiting – Bob said you would be home soon –
after a twelve-day mission. It's been way over twelve days. The raid
on the Philippines (Manilla) was over a week ago tomorrow, so I
should be hearing from you soon now. I wish it would be a telephone
call instead of a letter. I can hardly wait, darling. Royce is going to
have a tooth before you get here if you don't hurry.

. . .

I love you darling. By the way, if you should walk in on me in the
next few days, you would be sorry. It's my time – skipped a couple of
months. Same old story.

-16-

Operation King Two Begins: October 1944

URING THE EARLY summer months, Royce and the rest of the air group thought they would be relieved after the Marianas operation. By the end of July, they would have been at sea for more than eight months, and the normal tour of duty for a Navy air group was six to eight months, after which they ordinarily were rotated back to the States for reorganization and training. When Air Group 60 left Morotai, they once again anticipated that they would be heading home. Upon their return to the Admiralties at the end of September, however, they were disappointed to learn that they would participate in the invasion of the Philippines.

Members of Air Group 60 were led to believe that their tour was extended because, as John Smith put it, "of the efficiency of the *Sangamons* in their role of close-air support."[183] This resonates with what Royce wrote to Becky in August: "Apparently we are too good at our assigned work." In fact, three of the four *Sangamons* in CarDiv 22 were the only escort carriers in the U.S. fleet to carry F6F Hellcats, which made them superior to other CVEs. As Admiral Richard Conolly, Commander of the Southern Attack Force for Operation Forager, stated,

The importance of CarDiv 22 to this Force cannot be overemphasized. . . . This class of carrier is very well suited for work with an amphibious group because, in contrast with the other type of CVEs, the *Sangamon, Suwannee, Santee* and *Chenango* (1) are able to carry a well balanced complement of Avengers and Hellcats (the latter aircraft being far superior to the FM-2 in its combined ability as a fighter, strafer and bomber), (2) are equipped with a thoroughly reliable engineering plant, (3) have a larger oil and gasoline capacity, and (4) are most useful as refueling sources for smaller vessels of the attack force.[184]

And that is not all. The location of the Philippines increased the likelihood of Japanese night air attacks, which had occurred often in the Marianas. Therefore, as preparation for the invasion at Leyte, Rear Admiral Ralph Ofstie, Commander of the Task Force of Escort Carriers that supported the Palaus invasion, recommended that the *Sangamons* be adapted for night operations.[185] The commanding officer of CarDiv 22, Rear Admiral Thomas Sprague, chose Air Group 60 for this task, because he perceived them "to be the most proficient."[186] And so, on October 4, VF-60 was deployed to Pityilu to practice night field carrier landings.

Unfortunately, the idea of night patrols or interceptions was misguided on several levels. To begin, two planes and one pilot were lost during the night field carrier practice. The first accident occurred when the pilot landed without extending his landing gear, which in the darkness was not detected by the landing signal officer until after he had signaled the pilot to cut (i.e., reduce power) and proceed with the landing. As the plane skidded along the runway, no one was hurt. The second, fatal, accident seems to have occurred because of a crucial difference between the runway elevation of the airstrip at Pityilu and the deck of the carrier. As Smith explained:

The airstrip at Pityilu . . . extended from water's edge at one end to water's edge at the other; thus, there were no obstacles at either end. However, the runway elevation was only two to three feet above the water level. This contrasts with the flight deck of the *Suwannee*, which was about 70 feet above water level. So while a plane could safely descend several feet below optimum flight path in a carrier approach, it could not do so in a field approach to the island.[187]

Late in the practice runs, Ensign Charles Lamb, another of the Hellcat pilots who had reported at Pearl Harbor in March, got too low in his approach. When his wheels hit the water, the plane flipped upside down on the reef, and Lamb was trapped in the cockpit, close to the coral and "in water that wasn't more than hip deep." When pilots observing from the shore rushed to the plane, "he was still alive but couldn't get out." Their desperate attempts to break the skin of the cockpit failed, and by the time a mobile crane arrived to raise the plane and extricate Lamb, he had drowned.[188]

A few days after the night practice, four VF-60 pilots, Royce, Earl Helwig, John Shea, and John Smith, were selected for the first flight of the new night program. They launched before dark, patrolled through the night, and landed safely at dawn. Shortly thereafter, Admiral Sprague changed his mind and made the *Santee* the night duty carrier. Smith speculated that Sprague might have been motivated to make the change by the loss of two planes during night practice. But the *Santee* also seemed "like a step in the right direction." It was the only carrier in the division that carried FM-2s (an improved version of the F4F Wildcat), which could "be brought aboard with less hazard than the faster and heavier F6Fs aboard the other *Sangamons*."[189] Several nights later, however, it was shown "that the entire concept of a night fighter without radar on board was fruitless." As Smith recounted:

Harold Funk, the skipper of the *Santee*'s fighter squadron, was launched at night with his wingman to intercept an intruder. Ship's radar vectored them onto interception several times. On some of these vectors they passed close enough to the intruder to visually observe the enemy's hot exhaust stacks, but they were completely unable to maintain contact long enough to fire a shot. The results caused the concept to be scrubbed until radar-equipped fighters became available.[190]

Following the night-flying trial run, the air group finally went ashore for several days of "rest and cold beer." Royce had received a batch of mail upon his return to the Admiralties, and he proceeded to write in response to Becky's letters.

> *I always arrange your letters in order according to date and the first was the financial report. I am a little disappointed, but don't let it worry you. I could never be angry with you because of that. You are so very nearly perfect to me in all other things that I'd be quite a heel if I quibbled with you over a few dollars. Just do your best – you're improving all the time.*
>
> *It is perfectly ok with me to wait some time before our next off-spring. I leave all that up to you. I think it would be better to wait until we're settled after the war too. I'll be satisfied if I can get back to see you and Royce before he starts to school.*
>
> . . .
>
> *It's awful that Bob [Parnell] has to go back overseas. I thought he didn't have to go. The sad thing is that Virginia had better be prepared for an eighteen or more months waiting period. The Army darn near forgets about them compared to the Navy (which doesn't rate too high in my book right now!)*
>
> . . .

If that "Weejie Board" is correct, I'm going to have to really get going to make it in time. I'm afraid it's a little off.

. . .

Hey, don't spend too much on that old car. Keep it running, but no paint jobs, etc. Hear?

. . .

I got a good laugh out of your being scared about that little tangle with the Jap bomber. For your information, that is the easiest piece of work I've had to do. The Jap gunners in the plane weren't any good – and old Eggbert was in there too – plus two more. Our whole division worked it over. I just happened to set it on fire on one of my runs. None of us even got hit. If I had nothing more dangerous than that to do, it would really be a safe war.

I'd certainly have enjoyed hearing Mary Lou. She will go far with a wonderful voice like that. I'll bet it was good to hear her.

That was a very welcome piece of literature you sent to me [Davies' poem]. You may be sure that I feel that way myself.

Well, I've answered all your letters – and only 5 pages. I'm a helluva writer, am I not? And I sit around and think volumes and volumes.

I'm enclosing a picture the ship's photographer made. He doesn't have portrait lights and what he had made my face look greasy, but it's not too bad. At least you'll know I haven't changed too much. I still love you more than anything. I'll write again very soon.

I don't know when Bob will be home, but his squadron (most of them) think they'll get home in December.

We did have a party. I even forgot to tell you that Crash Wertenbaker was with us. We ran into him at the Officer's Club and, naturally, we all got together. He hasn't changed a bit.

There is so little to do in these parts that Bob and I didn't get to do much. We just had a good "bull session."

A week later, Royce wrote:

October 8, 1944

My Darling Becky,

I just received a couple more letters from you. Pictures #3, 4, 5, and 6 were in them. I'll let you know when I get the others.

Say, we've really got something, haven't we? That baby looks like the healthiest thing I've ever seen. He's really something. I'd give anything to get to see him – and his mother. Things are looking better, too. I wouldn't be at all surprised if we spend our first Christmas together this year.

I've been visiting with Bob again. I guess I won't see him again until we get back to the States, though. He left this morning for another tour. He's afraid he may have to do some more night bombing, but I don't think he will. Incidentally, he sank two ships (1300 tons) in his last tour up there. He sank another about the day I wrote you he'd sunk the first one. I sure hope he gets something out of it. I think his squadron and VFB-33 are going to get the Presidential Unit Citation, but they deserve something individually.

. . .

I still haven't written to M.E. yet. If you write her, tell her that I shall write her as soon as I get home and can write an uncensored letter. I think she'd like to know just what happened, where John is buried, etc.

I don't know how you're going to be able to take care of me and the baby when I get home. After a few days of seeing everyone, I'd sorta like to go on a little trip – just you and I – a kind of honeymoon. What do you think about it? You might start thinking where you'd like to go if the idea agrees with you. Or, if I should get orders to Jacksonville, Miami, or somewhere, I'd like to go a little early and see a few places – New Orleans, Baton Rouge, some of Mississippi and Georgia. We can do this if I get orders to Florida. I feel sure I'll get shore duty. If I don't, it won't be too bad because I'll probably get it after another six months at sea. Think these things over because I want us to have a little time all by ourselves. After all, you're the most important thing in the world to me – and I'm too selfish to share you all the time.

Take care of yourself and our young son. You're everything to me.

Yours Always,

Royce

Royce speculated about the time of his homecoming in two short missives. First, he told Becky, "I don't know when I'll get home but it's ok to guess and I say you can expect a call within nine weeks. Remember that it takes a helluva long time just to get home from where we are – and I know you can make a good guess on that." Then, on October 11, in his last letter written in the month of October, he said, "Mail closes in an hour or so. For this reason, you'll not receive any mail from me for some time after this letter. Don't worry about it. We're all really ready to go because we hope to get home after this, incidentally."

The censor on the first letter, Doctor Phil Phillips, wrote this note in the margin: "Becky, We've had lots of fun out of Lip! He goes around holding the pictures up before him just staring at them with a gleam of pride in his eye and grin on his face! Honestly, though, they're grand pictures – and that boy!!! What a boy! He has a twinkle in his eye almost as bright as his Daddy now has!"

On the Home Front

Becky's letters in October express hopeful and cautiously optimistic thoughts about Royce's imminent homecoming. At the beginning of the month, her state of mind about Royce's return is reflected in her ambivalence about whether to send him a Christmas present. When she sent photographs of their son, she wrote, "You will be home by then, no doubt, so I am sending you the pictures early to wish you season's greetings three months early this year." A week later, however, Becky decided to go ahead and send a Christmas box. "Thought, maybe," she said, "you would make it [home] sure enough, if I didn't count on it and sent you something."

On the one hand, Becky tells Royce, "Well, honey, I've planned on your coming home so many times and have been disappointed that I'll believe you are here when I see you. Of course, I'm thrilled to death that you might make it by Christmas, but I'm not going to plan for it." On the other hand, her letters show how she is preparing for his return. Late one night after the baby is asleep, she says,

> *I had a brainstorm and moved all the furniture in the living room to make room for Royce's playpen. Then I cleaned out dresser drawers etc. in the bedroom to make room for your things. There still are two big drawers in the chifferobe, two in the dresser and a shelf in the bathroom cabinet reserved for you.*

In another letter, after describing a couple that lives in one of the apartments near hers, she tells Royce how to get to their apartment and how to contact her when he returns.

> *For your information, dear, I live in the rear of 604 NW 20. As you come up the driveway, there are two garages and to the left an apartment (#1). That's me. There are two apartments over the garages and me. And then there's a tiny apartment back of the garages where Margaret and Henry Peterson live. As I've told you, I have no phone and I use Mrs. Freeman's and Margaret's. They are real nice to call me to the phone anytime. When you do hit the States, call me at Mrs. John Freeman's or Henry Peterson's, both of 614 NW 20th. If no one*

answers, I know Betty would call me and her phone is listed under her folks' name: Major Robert McCormick.

On October 11, Becky reported that the baby had a cold.

Royce has the sniffles today. It really turned cold all of a sudden, so I started giving him a prescription Dr. Levy gave me and rubbed his chest and throat good before I put him to bed. I hope he's better tomorrow. He's trying to cut his other lower front tooth, so he's been pretty cranky today. Your mother had to put up with him all day. Virginia had her tonsils out, and I spent a lot of time at the hospital and downtown. I'm going to stay in now, though, and try to get Royce over this. I just swore up and down Royce wasn't going to have a cold this winter, but with the weather like it's been you don't know how to dress children from one hour to the next.

The baby's cold was lingering five days later, when Becky described the difficulty of playing cards while caring for young children.

Our young son still has a cold. It doesn't seem to bother him too much though. He is kinda funny, but as active as ever. You almost have to hit him in the head to get him to go to sleep. Betty Brown, next door, Lucy, Virginia and I played bridge tonight. Royce was so sleepy, so I put him in his bed. It was an hour and a half until time for his bottle and he just yelled his head off. Finally, I had all of that I could stand, so I stuck him in his highchair with a cookie which he got all over himself and the floor. Anyway, I ended up giving him his bottle early. So I gave him his medicine, greased his throat, and got him ready for bed and gave him his bottle. He went to sleep on it and then we got a little bridge playing done. You just wait until you come home, and we try to entertain. One night Lucy had her little girl here (2 years), Betty brought her baby (3½ months), and together with Royce and trying to play bridge, it was a mad house. What will you and I do with four? Probably go stark-raving mad, but it will be fun.

Royce said "Da" today. Of course, he knew what he was talking about, too, you know. When he fusses, it sounds like he's saying "mum-mum-mum" all the time. Makes you feel good to think he says that anyway.

A few days later she reported,

Your young son is certainly getting his share of the bumps these days. He pulls up on everything now and nine times out of ten falls before it's over and bumps his head if I don't catch him. He has learned to pull up in his bed so now when I put him to bed, I can usually go in and find him standing up gazing around. And does he think he's smart! He'll laugh, squeal, and spit when he pulls up – just tells you all about it.

Don't think he doesn't have a temper either. The other day he embarrassed me to death in the grocery store. He's usually so good natured and everything, but he certainly has a mind of his own. I had put my groceries in his buggy, and he was having a big time playing with them. But when I went to take the things out to be checked, he liked to have had a fit – started crying and when I gave him my purse to play with, he slapped at it and knocked it out of my hand. Of course, everybody was watching him. It made me so proud of him. I could have spanked him really. You know, he looks and acts so much older than a six-month baby that you feel sometimes he's old enough to know how to behave. I'll sure be glad when you get home to help me with him. He's a handful now, but that's only half of what he's going to be later on.

I know he'll be walking by the time he's eight or nine months old. He's also going to need a haircut before long, but I'm not going to have it done until you get home. Even if it gets down to his shoulders.

Despite Royce's misgivings about Becky volunteering for USO events, Becky began working at the USO club on Sundays. After working there on October 8, she told Royce,

I work at what is called the snack bar, where you make sandwiches, malts, serve cold drinks and coffee to the fellows. I couldn't have picked a busier time, I don't imagine. They are three deep around that counter all the time and I really work. All I get to say to anyone is "May I help you?" or "Would you care for something to drink?" Today I worked the 3 hours straight without stopping for a minute's rest. It's nice to have something to do every week outside of my everyday work, but I only wish it were something where I could use my brain instead of my hands. The whole time I'm working I'm thinking, "If I could only look up and see a certain somebody in a Navy uniform, complete with Lt(jg) bars and, no doubt, ribbons across his chest. Darling, I think of you every minute I'm there, because I'm reminded of you constantly by those fellows there who are probably no happier than I am away from their loved one. That's why I wanted to do something to help. I hope you don't mind and please don't worry.

Two weeks later, Becky wrote,

Today was another day at the U.S.O. Virginia went today and she liked it. Betty, next door, went with me last Sunday and today her sister Jean went. They are going to take turns. One of them has to stay home with Betty's baby, Carol Jean. They really keep you busy

down there. You don't have time to think even. Everything becomes
mechanical. Guess that's why I like it. Except seeing all those guys
makes me think of you even more, if that's possible. Your mother is
going to work Wednesday. She works whenever they call her. But I
have a certain time – between 1 and 4 on Sunday.

By the middle of the month, Becky had received the picture that Royce
sent as well as his letter of October 8 informing her that he had received
the photographs of his son. "You know, honey," she said,

that was the first picture I had had of you since last Christmas when
you sent the one of you and that Duncan boy from San Diego? You
really look wonderful, darling. My same sweet Royce – you haven't
changed a bit except you look better. It looks like you have gained
weight sure enough. Your face is fatter. You do look like you have cold
cream on your face, though. But there couldn't be anyone to tell me or
show me a better-looking man than "my husband." I'm kinda sold
on you. The baby's eyes are exactly like yours. I've never seen such a
resemblance. I just can't keep from looking at your picture. I'm so glad
you sent it. I've been wanting a recent one but had no idea where you
would have it made, so didn't mention it. (October 11)

I was so happy to hear that you received some of the pictures. The
two you didn't get, #1 and 2, are of Royce and me together. They
were larger and I had to use a large envelope, so the odd shape may
be the reason it didn't go thru as quickly as the others. One picture is
me feeding Royce and he's sitting in his highchair; the other is of me
holding him and he's standing on his feet. He really is something,
isn't he, darling? Yes, he is really healthy, but has a cold right now.
It doesn't seem to bother him much, however. And, by the way, Royce
has two teeth now. I hope he waits a month before he cuts his two

upper front teeth to give himself and me a rest. He's always cranky
when he's cutting teeth.

. . .

Darling, I must have been sending you thought waves or some-
thing, because taking a little trip by ourselves is exactly what I've
had in mind and had written you about. Mother says after you get
here and see Royce, you won't want to leave. I don't think we should
go far, but it would be so wonderful even if we could go just for a few
days by ourselves. What do you think of Dallas or Kansas City? St.
Louis wouldn't be bad. If it were summer, we could go somewhere
in the mountains in Arkansas or Missouri. How about flying? We
could make hotel and train or plane reservations as soon as you get
home, or I could make them when I know you are in the States. I
think you have to make reservations for those things at least two weeks
ahead. Gosh, I'm getting all excited just thinking about it. Won't it
be wonderful? (October 15)

With the presidential election approaching, Becky also passed along
this advice:

Honey, cast your vote for Dewey. He can't be any worse than Roosevelt.
And I don't see how he can help but be a darn sight better. You'll
be getting a ballot. You may as well vote. I'm telling you I'll have a
fit if Roosevelt makes it. Sandy thinks Dewey will beat him. I don't
know if I ever told you, but I'm registered as a Republican. I didn't
have you here to discuss it with, so I did what I thought was right. I
definitely was not influenced by any one person.

In 1944, President Roosevelt was running for an unprecedented fourth
term, and Becky's father ran in the Republican primary for a nomination
for the U.S. Congress. Yet, this was Becky's first mention of politics in her

letters. Earlier in the summer, Royce attached a couple of anti-Roosevelt jokes to a letter, about which he said sarcastically, "I think your dad will like these literary gems." It appears that he was not following the election closely when, on October 8, he told Becky, in reference to a letter he wrote to her father, "I hope your dad didn't think too much about my saying I didn't like Dewey's mustache. I really don't know anything about him." Indeed, Becky's endorsement of Dewey may well be a reaction to this comment.

It is hard to imagine, contrary to her claim, that Becky was not strongly influenced by her father and perhaps Sandy, an anti-New Deal Democrat. Their views as well as Becky's are partly a matter of economic class. Gallup opinion poll data from 1937 to 1943 showed that support for Roosevelt was strongly related to economic class, with less favorable ratings from the middle and upper classes, although class differences weakened during the war.[191] While Roosevelt won a fourth term handily, Dewey got a greater percentage of votes than the Republican candidates in the three previous presidential elections.

On to Leyte

As the *Suwannee* left Seeadler Harbor on October 12, it is unlikely that Royce and his shipmates were giving much thought to the presidential election. The ship was one of 18 escort carriers that would support troop landings on Leyte Island in the central Philippines. Briefed on their mission, the air group knew that the scope of the operation far exceeded any other invasion in which they had been involved, and they may have anticipated more air strikes than usual. However, no one knew the clash at Leyte would evolve into the largest naval battle ever fought and the *Suwannee* would fall victim to the first Japanese organized kamikazes, "a tactic that would eventually kill more American sailors and sink more American ships than any other used in the war."[192]

The *Suwannee* sailed on tranquil seas for the first couple days, but then encountered a violent storm—the outer edge of a typhoon—that lasted for over three days. There were no flights during the storm, and "it was even dangerous to go on deck." As big as the ship was, it "pitched and rolled over large angles," the danger of which was explained to John Smith "one morning at breakfast by one of the ship's officers":

> A carrier is relatively top heavy and is susceptible to capsizing if the roll is too severe. In the case of the *Suwannee*, the critical angle of roll before capsizing was computed to be 27 degrees. This officer informed his listeners that he had been on watch the previous night during a period of particularly violent rolling when the inclinometer, which measures the degree of roll, actually reached this maximum angle. He said she hung at this precarious balance point for heart-stopping seconds, apparently trying to decide whether to right herself or go over. Then a big wave hit her down side and upset the delicate situation to move her toward the upright position.[193]

The storm caused minor damage to several ships, the most serious being the loss of a mast by a destroyer in the *Suwannee*'s unit. The troops were to go ashore on October 20, with initial bombardment and air strikes to begin on the 17th. Because of the weather, however, the first strikes were not launched until a day later.

The invasion of the Philippines brought together naval power that had been operating under separate commands: the Seventh Fleet of MacArthur's Southwest Pacific forces and the Third Fleet of Nimitz's Central Pacific forces. MacArthur's campaign had been fought in areas and on islands accessible to land-based aircraft. With few exceptions (Hollandia being one), it did not require the naval warships essential to the Central Pacific island-hopping campaign. Commonly known as "MacArthur's Navy," the Seventh Fleet therefore consisted mainly of troop transports, destroyer escorts, PT boats, and submarines. For the Leyte operation, it was greatly expanded, with dozens of warships transferred from the Pacific Fleet, including six battleships, eight cruisers, numerous destroyers, and 18 CVEs that included the four *Sangamons* of CarDiv 22. The Third Fleet consisted of the massive fast carrier strike force, with 17 carriers escorted by an armada of battleships, cruisers, and destroyers. The combined forces totaled slightly fewer ships than had assembled off Normandy, but its battleships and carriers gave it more firepower.[194]

The island of Leyte is located on the eastern side of the Visayas group, in the heart of the Philippines archipelago. It is separated from Mindanao to the south by the Surigao Strait and from the island of Samar to the northeast by the San Juanico Strait. The island is long, narrow, and irregularly shaped, about 110 miles long by about 40 miles at the widest point. Rugged mountains cover the southern end of the island and form a backbone in the center that divides plains on the east and west coasts. To the east of the island is Leyte Gulf, an irregularly shaped bay bounded by various islands. Deep water approaches from the Gulf and beaches and lowlands along the coast provided excellent points of entry for amphibious landings. Seizing Leyte would put the rest of the islands within striking distance of MacArthur's forces, and, applying the leapfrogging strategy, would bypass and isolate Japanese forces on Mindanao.

According to the Leyte plan (codenamed Operation King Two), the Seventh Fleet, commanded by Admiral Thomas Kincaid, would carry out the actual assault while the Third Fleet, commanded by Admiral William Halsey, would conduct pre-invasion air strikes in Formosa, Okinawa, and northern Leyte and be prepared to destroy the enemy fleet should the opportunity arise. The fleet of 18 CVEs was to operate approximately 100 miles east of Leyte, beyond the Gulf in the Philippine Sea. Each of the three escort carrier groups was known by the radio call sign of their commander: Taffy 1, Taffy 2, and Taffy 3. The Taffys' general operating areas were 30 to 50 miles apart. Taffy 1, consisting of the four *Sangamons*, the *Petrof Bay*, the *Saginaw Bay*, and their destroyers and destroyer escorts, was stationed in an area southeast of Leyte Gulf, off northern Mindanao.

Taffy 2 operated from east of the entrance to Leyte Gulf and Taffy 3 northward off Samar's southern tip.[195]

On October 18 and 19 the escort carriers' primary responsibility was neutralizing enemy airfields in the Visayas and northern Mindanao. Taffy 1 focused on airfields on the islands of Negros and Cebu in the western Visayas, where they destroyed many enemy planes on the ground. They also targeted installations and shipping in the vicinity of Leyte Island. Royce sank a small transport; other VF-60 pilots sank freighters and PT boats, destroyed trucks, and strafed buildings and gun positions. On the first day, Royce's plane was hit in the tail region by AA fire but made it back safely to the ship. The air group saw no enemy planes in the air over the first two days, with a notable exception on the second day. Starting back to base after making anti-shipping strikes, Ensign Billie McManemin and Lieutenant (jg) Wilbur Schmall spotted and downed a Japanese fighter known as a "Tony."

The huge amphibious force entered the Gulf on October 20. At dawn, as the transports moved into position, the battleships and cruisers delivered a pre-landing shore bombardment. The assault troops landed on beaches in two main areas, one in the northernmost part of the gulf and the other 15 miles to the south. A third, much smaller unit, landed on Panaon Island off the southernmost point of Leyte. Throughout the day, planes from the escort carriers kept watch over the Gulf and supported the landings, with each Taffy assigned to one landing force.[196] Taffy 1 supported the Panaon Attack Group. Some pilots in Air Group 60, including Royce's division, performed CAP while others provided direct support, destroying trucks and buildings in southern Leyte.

Panaon was occupied without opposition by 10:15 a.m. Meanwhile, to the north, both landings were easy compared to previous amphibious operations in the Pacific. By early afternoon, the Japanese had retreated inland, and MacArthur and his entourage waded ashore. Along the beach, the signal corps arrived in a weapons carrier with a portable transmitter, so that MacArthur could announce, "People of the Philippines, I have returned. By the grace of almighty God, our forces stand again on Philippine soil—soil consecrated in the blood of our two peoples."[197]

More than 100,000 U.S. troops were ashore by the end of the day. Over the next few days, the army secured the beachhead. As they began moving into the foothills and mountains, however, the fighting became more intense. Slowed by heavy rains that created a muddy morass in the lowlands, well organized enemy defenses in the foothills and mountains, and Japanese reinforcements that landed on the west coast, major fighting in Operation King Two would grind on for another two months.

From October 21–23, Air Group 60 continued to fly local CAP and ASP as well as seek out and destroy enemy aircraft and other targets of opportunity in the western Visayas and northern Mindanao. Strikes were made on several airfields, where VF pilots strafed and destroyed 24 operational planes on the ground. On the 23rd, VF-60 lost a man when Lieutenant (jg) Earl Helwig's Hellcat was shot down by antiaircraft fire. Unable to bail out until he was down to 300 feet, he hit the ground just as his parachute opened. Skin, as he was known by his radio call sign, had roomed with Royce early in the tour. He had been "serious about flying"; intending to make the navy a permanent career after the war, "he had applied for a commission in the Regular Navy."[198]

To this point in the Leyte operation, planes from the escort carriers had encountered few airborne enemy planes, and the Japanese Navy had not been spotted anywhere near the Philippines. But tensions began to build when Admiral Thomas Kincaid "sent the following dispatch to Tommy Sprague" at 1:22 a.m. on October 24: "Possibility large enemy air attack may be brewing. Until otherwise directed cancel western Visayas strike. Increase target CAP to 36 fighters with additional 16 fighters in Condition Eleven [ten-minute launch notice]."[199] Reports soon followed that Japanese warships had been spotted heading northeast toward the Philippines. What became known as the Battle of Leyte Gulf was about to begin.

-17-

BATTLE OF LEYTE GULF: October 1944

BEFORE OPERATION KING Two began, intelligence sources had predicted that the Japanese would not offer strong resistance and Japanese fleet action was unlikely.[200] They could not have been more wrong. Throughout the war, the Japanese had longed for a "decisive battle"—a victorious major fleet engagement that would drive the Americans to settle for a negotiated peace. They had prepared for such a battle at Midway and had committed the combined fleet again at the Battle of the Philippine Sea. These battles were devastating defeats for Japan, but both were largely carrier-plane attacks; neither involved an engagement of warships. The Imperial Japanese Navy, with its formidable fire power, was still largely afloat—in large part because Admiral Raymond Spruance chose to remain near Saipan in support of the U.S. troops and not pursue the retreating Japanese fleet at the Battle of the Philippine Sea.

By the end of summer 1944, the Japanese were certain that U.S. forces were preparing to invade the Philippines. Because the loss of the Philippines would cut off the Japanese lifeline to fuel supplies in the Dutch East Indies, they decided that they must make a do-or-die stand. Japanese commanders knew they were outmanned and could not count on air support, but their navy, with the two largest battleships in the world, was a potent force. When word came on October 17 that U.S. forces were preparing to land at Leyte, the Japanese activated a plan, named *Sho-Go* (Victory Operation) Number One, for a decisive battle.

Sho-Go brought together almost the entire Japanese fleet. After the Battle of the Philippine Sea, they had anchored their most powerful warships at Lingga Roads, bordering Sumatra, to be near that crucial source of fuel oil. The remainder of the fleet, including what was left of their aircraft carriers, retreated to the Inland Sea of Japan to train replacement pilots.

According to the *Sho-Go* plan, the combined fleet would attack American forces at Leyte Gulf from two different directions. The Center Force, commanded by Admiral Takeo Kurita, would pass through the Philippine Archipelago via the Sibuyan Sea and San Bernardino Strait north of Samar, then proceed south along the Samar coast to Leyte Gulf. The Southern Force, with the combined fleets of Admirals Shoji Nishimura and Kiyohide Shima, would take the Sulu and Mindanao seas to Surigao Strait and enter the Gulf from the south. While these two forces attacked, a Northern Force, commanded by Admiral Jisaburo Ozawa and consisting mainly of the Japanese Navy's few remaining carriers, would enter the Philippine Sea northeast of Luzon and lure America's Third Fleet north, away from the action converging at Leyte Gulf.

Dependent on surprise, timing, and deception, *Sho-Go* was a desperate attempt to destroy U.S. landing forces at Leyte and cripple the American fleet. But timing was off from the beginning. Japanese planners had predicted that U.S. forces would strike in the Philippines in mid-November, which was correct—until the landing was suddenly moved to October. When the Japanese finally learned when and where the Americans were about to land, it was too late to bring together their warships to attack the U.S. fleet when it was most vulnerable—as troops were being boated ashore.

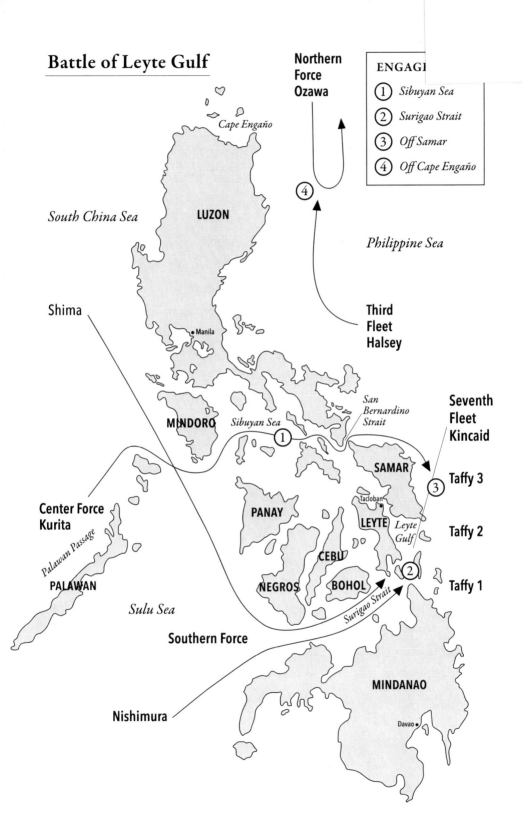

Battle of Leyte Gulf

Northern Force Ozawa

Cape Engaño

South China Sea

LUZON

Philippine Sea

• Manila

Shima

Third Fleet Halsey

MINDORO

Sibuyan Sea

San Bernardino Strait

Seventh Fleet Kincaid

SAMAR

Taffy 3

Center Force Kurita

PANAY

Tacloban •

LEYTE

Leyte Gulf

Taffy 2

Palawan Passage

CEBU

PALAWAN

Sulu Sea

NEGROS

BOHOL

Taffy 1

Surigao Strait

Southern Force

MINDANAO

Nishimura

Davao •

Four Battles in One

Japanese movements resulted in four separate naval battles and related skirmishes, all of which occurred outside Leyte Gulf. Air Group 60's direct involvement in these actions was limited. In roughly chronological order, the battles ensued as follows.

Battle of the Sibuyan Sea. Hostilities began on October 23, as Japanese ships approached the Philippines from the southwest. Two U.S. submarines patrolling the Palawan Passage made radar contact with Admiral Kurita's Center Force shortly after midnight. Remaining on the surface during the dark night, the submarines reported their sighting and then stalked Kurita's ships to maneuver into a favorable firing position. Just before daybreak, the subs slipped under the water and fired a barrage of torpedoes that sank two heavy cruisers and crippled a third. Although diminished by these losses, Kurita still had a formidable force, with five battleships, nine cruisers, and thirteen destroyers. By late afternoon, his force was well clear of Palawan Passage and expecting to cross the Sibuyan Sea the next day.

At dawn on the 24th, Admiral Halsey ordered a comprehensive reconnaissance of all eastward approaches to Leyte Gulf. Around 8:00 a.m. he got word that a large Japanese fleet was headed east, about to enter the Sibuyan Sea and apparently bound for San Bernardino Strait. Halsey's Third Fleet was widely deployed, east of Leyte Gulf, east of San Bernardino Strait, and east of the island of Luzon. The only conceivable route to a surface engagement was through the narrow San Bernardino Strait; however, because its waters were presumably mined and its channels known only to the Japanese, Admiral Nimitz had ordered that no ships were to enter the strait without his permission.[201] Halsey therefore immediately ordered a massive air strike from his carriers.

The air–surface Battle of the Sibuyan Sea thus began at 10:30 a.m. when the first wave of aircraft reached the Center Force. For the next five hours, Hellcats, Helldivers, and Avengers from the Third Fleet made 259 sorties, relentlessly attacking through intense antiaircraft fire. AA fire hit several planes in the initial attacks, and 18 American planes eventually were shot down. Still, they kept coming. Early waves targeted the super-battleships *Musashi* and *Yamato*, although initial torpedo hits did not penetrate the ships' great steel plates, and bombs seemed to have little effect. As the second and third waves concentrated on *Musashi*, however, repeated blows weakened the exterior hull, and when two torpedoes hit the same spot, the inner hull gave way and flooded the number four engine room.[202] By the end of the attacks, American planes had hit the *Musashi* with "a minimum of 16 bombs and at least 11 (and possibly as many as 15) torpedoes."[203] The ship sank in the early evening, taking with her over 1,000 of those aboard.

At 3:30 p.m., Kurita ordered his ships to reverse course, possibly to take them out of range of the attacking aircraft. When two hours passed without further attacks, Kurita reversed course again and headed for San Bernardino Strait. Pilots had reported to Halsey that Japan's Center Force was "seriously impaired." However, though weakened, it was still very powerful. The loss of *Musashi* was costly; another cruiser was disabled and could not continue; but damages to other ships did not diminish their fighting ability.

Battle of Surigao Strait. During the early morning reconnaissance on the 24th, Halsey's planes also spotted Nishimura's Southern Force of seven ships in the Sulu Sea. Admiral Kincaid, whose Seventh Fleet, aside from the escort carriers, was anchored inside Leyte Gulf, correctly inferred that Nishimura intended to enter the Gulf via Surigao Strait. He ordered his staff to formulate plans for a night engagement. They had all day to prepare and more than enough fire power to take care of the Southern Force.

The U.S. battle plan literally worked to a "T." Surigao Strait is relatively narrow and runs north to south. Six battleships set up a battle line in Leyte Gulf at the northern end of Surigao Strait. From this position, at the top of the T, the ships could bring all their guns to bear on the enemy, while the enemy, with less room to maneuver, would be limited mainly to the use of their forward guns. South of the battle line, cruisers and then destroyers took up positions on either flank or side of the strait. Much farther south, a large group of PT boats patrolled the seas and reported contacts while attacking enemy ships. The PTs sighted the enemy before midnight; they did little damage, but their reports enabled the destroyers to position for attack. Beginning at 2:00 a.m. and for the next two hours, U.S. destroyers unleashed a torpedo attack that destroyed most of Nishimura's fleet. By the time his fleet was within range of the big guns of the cruisers and battleships, only three of Nishimura's ships were afloat. Of these, only the destroyer *Shigure* would survive.

Admiral Shima's Force, consisting of three cruisers and four destroyers, trailed Nishimura by forty miles. Nishimura had communicated to Shima that he was under attack, but Shima did not know the extent of the damage until he encountered burning ships and the retiring *Shigure* in the middle of the strait. Making a quick estimate of the dire situation, Shima retreated south. Thus, before daybreak, at 5:00 a.m. on October 25, the surface–ship Battle of Surigao Strait was effectively over. All that remained was the aerial pursuit, including Avengers from the *Suwannee*, of the fleeing ships. Shima's light cruiser, initially hit by a PT boat, was sunk in the air attacks.

The last two "battles" of Leyte Gulf were the result of a command decision by Admiral Halsey. After air attacks ceased in the Sibuyan Sea, a reconnaissance flight from the Third Fleet spotted Ozawa's Northern Force, 190 miles to the north. Halsey's original orders were to cover and support the invasion, but they also contained an overriding task: "In case opportunities for destruction of major portion of the enemy fleet is offered or can be created, such destruction becomes the primary task."[204] His options now were to (1) cover San Bernardino Strait with the entire Third Fleet; (2) divide the fleet, leaving part of it to block the strait while the remainder attacked Ozawa's Northern Force; or (3) strike the Northern Force at full strength and leave San Bernardino Strait unguarded.[205] History showed that Option 2 was the most prudent decision, as "Halsey had enough gun and air power to handle both Japanese forces."[206] But unaware of how weak Ozawa's force was, believing Kurita's force was no longer a "serious menace" after the damage inflicted by his pilots, and longing for a showdown battle, Halsey chose Option 3.

Battle off Samar. On the night of October 24–25, as Halsey's Third Fleet headed north to attack Ozawa's force, Kurita's Center Force sailed undetected through San Bernardino Strait and emerged unopposed on the eastern side. Halsey did not know that Kurita's force had reversed course, and, in any event, he believed it was "no serious menace." With the Seventh Fleet warships battling the enemy in Surigao Strait, the only obstacle between Kurita and Leyte Gulf were the escort carrier groups, which were "hardly a match for [Kurita's] still formidable array of battleships and cruisers."[207] The largest guns on the slow, thin-skinned CVE ships and their destroyer screens were five-inchers, virtual "popguns" compared to the 18-inch, 12-inch, and other caliber guns on Kurita's ships.[208]

Entering the Philippine Sea shortly after midnight on October 25, Kurita had clear sailing for the next six and a half hours as he headed east then southeast toward Leyte Gulf. At 6:30 a.m., American and Japanese forces sighted one another. The Center Force and Taffy 3 were only 20 miles apart. Moments after the sighting, Kurita made a fatal error when he ordered a "General Attack." Rather than form a battle line for the effective, coordinated deployment of his battleships and cruisers and use his lighter forces for immediate torpedo attack, his ships began firing helter-skelter at American ships.

Still, Taffy 3 was in serious trouble. The escort carriers were never expected to fight the main Japanese fleet. Based on a battle plan issued by Admiral Halsey on October 24, Admiral Clifton Sprague, commander of Taffy 3, believed that Halsey's ships were guarding the Strait. Surprised by the attack, he made urgent pleas for assistance. He also knew he must slow down the faster, superior enemy force, or he would be quickly wiped out. "I didn't think we'd last fifteen minutes," Sprague said, "but I thought we might as well give them all we've got before we go down."[209]

Almost immediately, Sprague launched every operational plane from his carriers. Then, as the enemy closed rapidly and increased the volume and accuracy of their fire, he decided that his only hope was to counterattack with torpedoes from his destroyers. For the next two hours, three destroyers and four destroyer escorts, plus planes from Taffy 3 and Taffy 2, fought valiantly against overwhelming odds. The destroyers inflicted minimal damage, and the planes hurriedly launched by Taffy 3 lacked the armament to destroy or sink enemy ships; however, the torpedo attacks and the strafing and bombing drew attention away from the CVEs and seriously slowed Kurita's advance. When planes from Taffy 2, armed with torpedoes and heavier bombs, began arriving in the second hour of the battle, two of Kurita's cruisers were hit and were dead in the water.

By 9:00 a.m. Kurita was on the verge of overrunning Taffy 3. He could not tell, however, that he "was winning the battle," and he didn't know that he "had the speed and power to overwhelm the Taffys."[210] His ships had sunk a carrier, two destroyers, and a destroyer escort, and had damaged the rest of the Taffy 3 escorts and carriers. But the Japanese had expected to encounter Halsey's Third Fleet. They misidentified the Taffy 3 force, believing that the CVEs and destroyers were larger ships, and the super aggressiveness of the American destroyers and planes rattled Kurita. He feared that heavier air attacks were on the way, and around 9:15, he ordered his fleet to break off the engagement and regroup as they sailed north. After three hours of maneuvering, Kurita changed course and sailed toward Leyte Gulf. But 20 minutes later, he suddenly changed course again and headed north for passage through San Bernardino Strait. Believing that his force would be annihilated if they entered Leyte Gulf, he abandoned his mission.[211]

Battle off Cape Engaño. In the meantime, at the crack of dawn, Halsey ordered an air strike on Ozawa's force, located off Cape Engaño on the northern tip of Luzon. The battle was aptly named after the cape, as the Spanish word *engaño* translates to "deceit" or "fraud" in English, perfectly capturing Ozawa's mission to lure Halsey away from the action at Leyte Gulf. The first strike, arriving at 8:00 a.m., quickly eliminated 18 Japanese fighters, all that was left of Ozawa's aircraft.[212] With only antiaircraft fire and the evasive maneuvering of the Japanese ships to contend with, American aircraft hammered away throughout the day. The first three of six strikes did most of the damage, as American pilots ultimately sank four aircraft carriers, a cruiser, and two destroyers.

Despite the toll in enemy ships, naval historian Thomas Cutler called the Battle off Cape Engaño anticlimactic. It was, he claimed, "almost mundane when compared to" the other battles at Leyte Gulf, and, though one-sided, it was "indecisive in its outcome."[213] By the second air strike on Ozawa's fleet, Halsey began receiving urgent pleas for help from Admiral Kincaid. At first, he was annoyed by these messages, as he assumed the Taffys had "enough airpower to hold off Kurita's damaged force until . . . battleships of the Seventh Fleet could sail up to relieve them."[214] He began to perceive the seriousness of the situation when he received a message from Kincaid that his battleships were low on ammunition. When a message arrived from his commanding officer Admiral Nimitz, asking him to clarify the location of his task force of battleships, Halsey divided his forces, detaching the battleship group to head south for Leyte Gulf and leaving behind two groups of fleet carriers to continue the air attacks off Cape Engaño. He was only 42 miles from Ozawa's force, he claimed, on the verge of a battleship engagement that he believed would annihilate the Japanese carrier force.

Air Attacks on U.S. Carriers

Sho-Go also brought into action Japan's aircraft. Ideally, these aircraft would have supported Kurita and Nishimura as their ships crossed the

Philippines. But because their inadequately trained pilots lacked the skills necessary for air-to-air combat, the Japanese decided to use most of their available aircraft to attack U.S. ships.[215]

On October 24, while the battle was being fought in the Sibuyan Sea, land-based aircraft scattered throughout the Philippines mounted numerous air attacks against U.S. carriers. Three raids, each of 50 to 60 planes based on Luzon airfields, were made against the northernmost task group of Halsey's Third Fleet. With one exception all these planes were successfully intercepted. As the Hellcats of the light carrier USS *Princeton* were returning on board, an undetected enemy plane emerged from the clouds and dropped a 550-pound, armor-piercing bomb that struck the center of the flight deck and passed through three decks before exploding. The blast entered the hangar deck, where flames enveloped six torpedo bombers and detonated their loaded torpedoes. Firefighters could not get the fires under control, and when the cruiser USS *Birmingham* came alongside the *Princeton* to assist, a tremendous explosion blew off most of the carrier's stern and rained steel debris down on the *Birmingham*, taking the lives of 229 men who had gathered topside to fight the fires and prepare for a tow. The *Princeton* could not be saved, although it suffered fewer casualties—108 killed—than the *Birmingham*.

Meanwhile, the Japanese also launched over 50 planes from airfields in the Visayas to attack ships in Leyte Gulf and the escort carriers east and southeast of the Gulf. Flying in small groups, virtually all these attempts resulted in heavy losses to the attackers. Every pilot in VF-60 was in the air that day, performing combat air patrol, and many of them shot down enemy planes. Royce's division, the first to take off on a predawn patrol, was the same group with whom he had flown most of his sorties at Leyte: Ralph (Kal) Kalal, Edgar (Eggbert) Barber, and Roy (Tex) Garner. As they were ready to return to the ship after four hours on station, they received a radio report of eight bombers "at ten o'clock heading towards Leyte." The action report credited the pilots with shooting down seven of the enemy planes, with the eighth shot down by AA fire from ship and shore batteries. However, Tex Garner recollected a slightly different—and more dramatic—account of the incident.

I swept the sky and spotted a formation of Lily bombers. I tally-hoed them. We dropped our empty belly tanks and climbed to intercept them. Lip Singleton and I set up one line of the formation while Edgar Barber and Ralph Kalal set upon the other wing of the Vee. We all rolled in at the same time. It was perfectly coordinated, and four Lilies were knocked down on the first pass. Each pilot had a bullseye.

After that run we whipped the Hellcats around for another target and for an instant all four fighters had the same bomber and fired at him—so long Lily. All four scrambled for another bomber. Lip burned one. Kal exploded one and the last bomber pushed over hell bent for our landing ships. I called on my Hellcat to give her all, closing very slowly. I was trying to get to him before he got to the fleet because there was no way he would miss 'em. I began to realize some of our AA was trying for him too. I either had to break off or go for him into our ships' AA.

I bore in firing all six .50 caliber guns. He began to smoke. I noticed the bomb bay doors open. There was no way he should have done that because that slowed him down enough for me to catch him. I closed to within four feet. I thought I'd ram him. I came across from his left engine, left wing spar, cockpit, right spar, right engine. On the sweep back, as I crossed the cockpit area, I saw like an accordion door open and the pilot appeared. The six guns cut him in half. The plane exploded with the bombs still on board.

I knew I was in a tight spot with all those ships still firing and if I pulled up I was a dead man. I pushed over, leveled off to about eighteen inches off the water and went zigging through the ships like a scared rabbit, hunkered down behind the armor plating and prayed. I was amazed when I reached the other side, wringing wet but still alive, with eighteen holes and nothing serious.[216]

By the time the engagement was over, Royce and Tex's fuel reserves were so low that they were diverted to land on the nearest available carrier, the USS *Franklin*, one of the fleet carriers in the Third Fleet. When they came back to the *Suwannee* later in the day, "they told of landing on a deck the size of the King ranch, where they taxied for what seemed like miles after landing just to get across the barriers."[217]

At the end of the day, CVE pilots claimed fifty-four planes destroyed and twenty probably destroyed. Yet, despite the evident success, "the appearance of so many planes worried Kincaid and Sprague."[218] Sprague had expressed concern about the vulnerability of his escort carriers before the Leyte operation began. Radar could not detect low-flying aircraft near land masses; therefore, "it would be relatively easy for aircraft to follow land until opposite the formation and then close it without being detected."[219] The next two days, this "threat would become a reality."

While the Battle off Samar was being fought, the Japanese introduced a new tactic to the Pacific War. Japanese air commanders had been thinking about forming a suicide squadron since the Battle of the Philippine Sea, which had cost over 300 planes and pilots. Attacks on airfields in the Philippines and Formosa in September and October further decimated Japanese air power to the point that fewer than 400 aircraft were available for *Sho-Go*. Given the shortage of planes and the critical situation in the Philippines, the time had come for desperate measures.

Deliberate self-sacrifice in the war was not new. According to the Japanese moral code, "voluntary death was better than living in shame. Suicide was regarded as an honorable act, free of the opprobrium often attached to it in Western countries."[220] U.S. forces had witnessed this moral code in action throughout the Pacific War. At almost every stop in the Central Pacific drive, they encountered fierce resistance, which often ended only after all or nearly all the enemy were killed or committed suicide. In some battles, Japanese resistance took the form of banzai charges such as the July 6–7 night attack by the doomed garrison on Saipan: Rather than surrender, soldiers mounted a last-ditch assault when the battle was about to be lost.

Thus, on October 20, the new commander of the First Air Fleet, Admiral Takijuro Onishi, organized "suicide attack units composed of Zero fighters armed with bombs, with each plane to crash-dive into an enemy carrier."[221] The act of deliberately crashing into American ships had occurred before; several instances were reported in the air–sea battles at Guadalcanal. But these acts resulted from the pilot's initiative in the heat of battle and accidental circumstances; Japanese pilots may have targeted enemy ships when seriously wounded or their planes had sustained catastrophic damage that prevented a return to base. Now, an air commander was officially sanctioning premeditated suicide missions. With aircraft inferior in quality to American planes and most pilots short on training and experience, conventional air attacks would rarely succeed. To assure that their "meager strength will be effective to the maximum degree," Onishi believed that inexperienced pilots could be trained to effectively dive their planes into enemy ships.[222] The name given to the new suicide unit, "kamikaze," meaning "divine wind," referred to a historic typhoon that had repelled a colossal Mongol fleet from invading Japan in the late 13th century.

The first organized attack by the kamikaze corps occurred early in the morning on October 25. Six planes took off from Davao in the southern Philippines and headed northeast toward Taffy 1. With heavy cloud cover, the planes were not sighted until they were very close. Around 7:40 a.m., before any shots were fired from antiaircraft guns, one of the Zeros crash-dived into the flight deck of the *Santee*. Crewmen were in utter disbelief as they witnessed their first kamikaze attack. On the *Suwannee*, radioman John DiGiovine remembered seeing the enemy plane descend toward the *Santee*: "I'm watching the plane come down . . . As he came down, I'm waiting for him to pull out and drop his bomb. Boom! He hits midship, and I thought, What the hell is he doing? Why didn't he pull out?"[223] Other kamikaze planes soon dove as the American gunners began firing. The *Suwannee's* gunners shot down two of them; however, a third plane regained control after being struck and, at 8:04, crashed into *Suwannee's* flight deck.

Both strikes had similar destructive effects. On the *Suwannee*, the "suicide plane," as it was labeled in the action report, crashed just forward of the after elevator, tearing a hole 10 feet in diameter; its bomb exploded between the flight and hangar decks, leaving another hole, 25 feet in diameter, in the hangar deck; and fuel from the plane's tanks spewed out, caught fire, and flowed to the interior of the ship through the openings the plane created. Fires were rapidly extinguished, and the hole in the flight deck was repaired by covering it with 1/8-inch steel plates. The after elevator was inoperable, and only two of the arresting cables were still in place, leaving a very restricted landing area—about 50 to 70 feet—to catch a plane's tailhook. But by 10:09, the ship commenced landing aircraft. It operated without incident for the remainder of the day and following morning, which John Smith credited to the LSO Bob Misbach and the skill of the pilots.[224] Overall, the physical damage to the ship was remarkably light.

The human toll, however, was considerable: 32 men were killed instantly and another 39 died of their wounds.[225] General Quarters had been called when the enemy planes were spotted, which meant that the crew immediately reported to their battle stations. Those stationed on the bridge "were jolted and tossed around a bit, but many in the hangar deck were instantly killed or seriously injured."[226] According to quartermaster Bob Mueller, "It was our custom during GQ to muster damage control and other personnel in that large, enclosed space beneath the flight deck. There were possibly a hundred sailors there that day. I don't believe any survived the explosion and fire."[227]

A few men did survive. The hangar deck had large open doors to one side, and the concussion of the explosion blew some of the survivors overboard. Flight director Erich Kitzmann was in the chow line when GQ was sounded and he rushed to the hangar deck. His experience gives an inkling of the horror witnessed on that day. He heard the crash of the kamikaze hitting the flight deck but did not hear the bomb go off. Moments later he surfaced in the ocean.

> I discovered that my dungarees were no longer on my body except my belt and shorts, no shoes or socks. . . . My face felt like someone had hit me with a baseball bat. [As] I regained my senses, it was apparent I was not alone. Mournful cries of help and despair were all around. A body came up near me without a head.[228]

The next thing Kitzmann remembered was seeing the bow of a destroyer, which called out, "Rendezvous in the rafts we are going to drop out, we'll pick you up later." In what "seemed like years," the destroyer returned to pick up survivors later in the afternoon. When seated in the wardroom, a pharmacist mate told Kitzmann that bleeding from his "shoulder, ankle, and groin . . . needed attention."

> I told him to take care of the man lying on the table. All that I recall was that his name was Manookan, and his ankle had been blown away.

> The Pharmacist Mate offered me a glass that contained some liquid medicine. After I drank it, I walked out on the after deck of the destroyer to identify the bodies of some of my shipmates. Sneed, from Reading, California, was lying there without a mark on this body. L. E. Anglin . . . was still alive with a hole through his stomach, begging me to put a 45 to his head to end his pain. It was at this point that the world seemed to spin and I dropped to the deck, out cold.[229]

An indelible memory of the hangar deck was impressed on Bob Mueller when he fetched coffee for those on the bridge as soon as the fire was out.

Since crossing the hangar deck lengthwise was the shortest route [to the wardroom], I took that path. I was probably one of the first to enter there except for those who fought the fire. I hesitate to fully describe the scene that met my eyes, of the broken and burned bodies of my shipmates. The picture shall always remain in my mind. I'm certain the end came quickly for them. Thankfully they did not suffer pain. As the ship rolled, water mixed with their blood washed over the tops of my shoes. I managed to complete the trip to the wardroom, but returned to the bridge by a different route.[230]

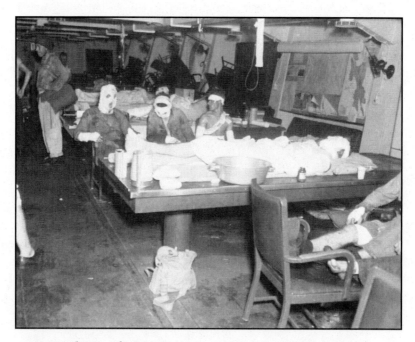

**Wardroom of USS *Suwannee* in use as an emergency sick bay
following the kamikaze hit on October 25, 1944 (Official
U.S. Navy photograph, in the National Archives)**

All serviceable aircraft were in the air when the kamikaze hit the ship, which was fortunate, because burning fuel from the ship's planes would have been even more devastating. Earlier in the morning, several VF-60 pilots took off pre-dawn for CAP over southern Leyte. Later, four Avengers armed with torpedoes, joined by Hellcats for protection, were launched to pursue the Japanese ships fleeing Surigao Strait. Royce was not in the air. According to John Smith, Royce and Quinn (Frog) La Fargue were on the flight deck when the antiaircraft fire began. Near the island when they saw the diving plane, Royce "sprinted for the bow while Frog leaped into the catwalk. Had the Judy not penetrated the flight deck before exploding, both would have been casualties."[231]

None of the pilots were among the casualties from the kamikaze attack on this day. As survivors, those on board were among the scores of volunteers who immediately began to help care for the wounded, placing them on stretchers and transporting them to the main sick bay and other areas that became emergency aid stations. Many volunteers directly assisted the doctors and hospital corpsmen in caring for the wounded. Royce may well have followed Quinn La Fargue, who recalled that, after moving casualties from an area on the flight deck, he made his way down to the sick bay, where he met Dr. Phillips. "He gave me some morphine and told me that if I met anyone in pain to give it to him. I proceeded to do that through most of the morning."[232]

Later that morning, a little more than an hour after Kurita's gunships had ceased their engagement off Samar, a second kamikaze unit struck Taffy 3. Flying at low altitude to avoid radar detection and catching Taffy 3 ships off guard, the Japanese fighters were not spotted until they began to make their runs on the carriers. All the Zeros but two were shot down by antiaircraft fire before they impacted the ships. The wing of one Zero just missed the island of the *Kitkun Bay* but crashed into the port catwalk and its bomb exploded, causing minor damage. A second Zero crashed through the flight deck of the *St. Lo*, spewed burning gasoline over the hangar deck and ignited several torpedoes and bombs. Seven tremendous explosions ripped the ship apart, and she sank in 15 minutes.[233]

The *Suwannee* pilots and crew were not involved in the main Battle off Samar, as the kamikaze attack prevented their planes from landing, refueling, and re-arming before the battle ended. However, they launched a group of planes in the afternoon that joined other CVE planes in tracking down Kurita's fleet before it reached San Bernardino Strait. A VT-60 Avenger made a hit on a cruiser with their last torpedo. Low on fuel after these sorties, several pilots from Air Group 60 landed at Tacloban, an airstrip in northern Leyte. Four of them returned to the *Suwannee* the next morning after obtaining gasoline and ammunition. Two pilots whose planes were disabled, VF-60 skipper Harvey Feilbach and Kenneth Montgomery, had to return via surface transportation and would not rejoin the squadron for several days.

Although the Japanese fleet was in full retreat, the battle continued the next day, October 26. Halsey's ships had finally arrived off the north coast of Samar. Shortly after midnight, his cruisers sank a straggling destroyer from Kurita's fleet headed for San Bernardino Strait. Later that morning, air attacks by Halsey's planes resulted in the loss of two more ships from the Center Force—a cruiser and a destroyer.

Halsey's actions on the 26th marked the "official" end of the Battle of Leyte Gulf. A significant aftermath was the rescue of over 1,000 seamen from Taffy 3 who had gone into the water when their ships were sunk in the Battle off Samar. In William Y'Blood's words, "What should have been a fairly routine, although extensive rescue operation turned into a poorly organized and badly botched effort."[234] Through misunderstanding about responsibility for the rescue, miscommunication, incorrect reports of the survivors' position, and other issues, most of the survivors spent two nights in the water before they were finally picked up.

Inexplicably, some notable accounts of the battle fail to mention arguably the most consequential action on the final day: a second kamikaze hit on the *Suwannee*.[235] The ship was struck shortly after noon, when landing operations were well underway to recover planes launched earlier in the day, including a division led by Royce, which had performed CAP over Leyte. Seven fighters and two Avengers were parked forward on the flight deck, and a third Avenger had landed and was taxiing forward. Another ten planes, fueled, armed, and ready for afternoon flights, were parked in the hangar deck. "Incoming kamikazes," according to John Smith, "had not been detected by radar because they had trailed closely behind the returning flight and were mistaken, therefore, as friendly."[236] One of the suicide planes crashed into the taxiing Avenger just as the pilot reached the forward elevator. Both planes exploded, instantly killing pilot Fred Beidelman and his crew, radioman Frank Barnard and gunner Arnold Delmenico.

The plane's bomb, apparently dropped at bridge height, exploded on contact with the deck. A few minutes later, a second explosion, possibly caused by another bomb, detonated. The explosions ignited fires that quickly spread to the planes spotted on the forward deck, which burned and exploded. The damage to the ship was much more severe than the first kamikaze hit, and the ensuing fires took several hours to get under control.

Indeed, if not for the heroic actions of many men, the *Suwannee* might well have sunk. In the Executive Officer's report to the Captain, Commander Schermerhorn Van Mater singled out numerous individuals for special praise.[237] One of those was Chief Shipfitter William Brooks, whose actions quickly quelled the fire in the hangar deck. Brooks had made his way to the hangar deck when he was knocked unconscious and injured by the second blast. As Van Mater described,

> Upon regaining consciousness, he crawled under the planes to the valves controlling the water curtain and the forward sprinkler system and opened them, thus preventing the fire on the forward elevator, which had been smashed down to the hangar deck level, from spreading and exploding the gassed planes on the hangar deck,

which in all probability would have made the fire uncontrollable, resulting in the loss of the ship.[238]

On the previous day, Brooks had donned rescue gear and made his way through smoke and fire on the hangar deck to open the valves on the same sprinkler system, which helped to subdue that fire.

On the flight deck, an inferno had erupted where the planes were parked, and burning gasoline flowed across the deck and over the catwalks on the ship's side. Several members of Air Group 60 were involved in fighting the fire. Both Quinn La Fargue and Roy Garner immediately manned hoses, one on each side of the deck and "went among the burning planes and amid the exploding ammunition, fighting the fire until it was subdued." In Van Mater's judgment, "The two pilots formed a team which ignored completely any consideration of their own personal safety."[239]

Other brave men risked their lives to aid the wounded and rescue their shipmates. Many of the plane handlers on the flight deck were killed outright. Those in the front portion of the deck who survived the blasts found it impossible to move aft as flames cut them off from the rest of the ship. Van Mater told the story of an unidentified sailor's attempt to reach a group of burned and wounded men trapped on the forecastle. After repeated failures to get medical supplies to them, the sailor

informed Chief Aviation Electrician Mate C. N. Barr that he would try to get through the flames to medical supplies because he could no longer stand the suffering of the wounded. Despite Barr's efforts to stop him, the man climbed to the 20-mm mounts just forward of the flight deck. A second later a torpedo-bomber directly in his path exploded and the man was seen holding on to the starboard side of the flight deck with one leg blown off. A moment later he fell into the water and was not seen again. Every effort to ascertain his name has proved unavailing.[240]

Scores of men on the front of the flight deck made it to the bow and, as the heat intensified, jumped overboard when an officer on the bow ordered, "abandon ship."[241] Many of those on the bridge were killed or badly injured by shrapnel from the explosions. These men, including the ship's captain, William D. Johnson, who was immobilized by shrapnel wounds, were among the first to be reached by those seeking to help the wounded. When pilots found Captain Johnson sitting on the deck against a bulkhead, he told them he was ok and to go fight the fire and save the ship.[242] After the fire was under control, rescue efforts centered on those trapped in compartments just below the flight deck.

Commander Van Mater stated that most, if not all, of those on board "did everything possible to save *Suwannee* and to aid their dying and wounded comrades." There is no record of how Royce was involved in these efforts, although Van Mater gave special recognition to "the officers and men of Air Group 60 who were aboard at the time of the attacks and thereafter . . . for their work together in fire-fighting, aiding the wounded, saving of life and helping the medical officers."[243]

Because of the destruction of the bridge and wheelhouse, the *Suwannee* was dead in the water for a while. Power was restored and the ship was again underway when control shifted to the backup command center Batt 2, which had a circuit connection to the Engine Steering Room. The ship could surge through the water and undertake evasive maneuvers, but, pending major repairs, it was no longer an operational aircraft carrier. Adding to the damage from the first kamikaze hit, the forward elevator was demolished, the catapult was destroyed, and 30 percent of the flight deck was charred and distorted. All aircraft on the forward end of the flight deck were, as John Smith put it, "junk," and aircraft "below on the hangar deck couldn't be raised to the flight deck, even if any could be salvaged."[244] Moreover, because of the large number of casualties, the number of men required to carry out flight operations was inadequate.

Official records eventually showed that the kamikaze strikes on October 25 and 26 resulted in 110 fatalities and 160 wounded.[245] In other words, the total number of casualties amounted to about a quarter of the approximately 1,100 personnel aboard. With many men scattered about, having gone over the side and been picked up by destroyers, or having landed on other ships or airstrips, Smith believed that "the number of fully functional personnel aboard the *Suwannee* by the evening of October 26 . . . was well below 50 percent of the allotted complement."[246]

In the combined battles of Leyte Gulf, the second kamikaze hit on the *Suwannee* was the enemy's last gasp. The largest naval battle ever fought—involving 282 ships and nearly 200,000 men, and spanning a geographical area of over 100,000 square miles—was over. From October 23–26, American forces sank 28 enemy ships: four carriers, three battleships, ten cruisers, and eleven destroyers. These losses were the death knell for the Imperial Japanese Navy; except for a disastrous sortie in 1945, the remaining ships were inactive for the rest of the war. The triumph also ensured the liberation of the Philippines, and the loss of the Philippines cut off Japan from vital resources, such as fuel oil, needed to wage war.

The battle (or, more precisely, series of battles) was a tremendous victory for the U.S. by any standard. Yet, controversies arose after the war that dozens of historians have analyzed ever since. One of the most hotly debated issues was the failure to guard the San Bernardino Strait. Americans lost six ships at Leyte Gulf, four of which were sunk when Admiral Kurita surprised Taffy 3 in the Battle off Samar. As Morison recounted, these losses "fell short of a major catastrophe only by the resolute application of air power, aided by the self-sacrificing courage of a few destroyers and destroyer escorts,"[247] and, it should be added, Kurita's decision to pull out of the battle. For this near disaster, some historians fault Admiral Halsey; some argue that Admiral Kincaid shares some of the blame; and some contend that Halsey made the correct decision given "the information available at the time."[248]

Although estimates vary, at least 10,500 Japanese and over 1,500 American sailors and airmen were killed in the Battle of Leyte Gulf. A disproportionate number of these casualties came from Taffy 3 and Taffy 1, where 1,118 ships' crew and 43 aviators were killed and another 913 were wounded. About 200 American and over 300 Japanese aircraft were shot down. The CVE pilots were very busy during the battle. The total number of shootdowns on October 24 and 25 was 341. And though the CVEs had only half as many planes as the Third Fleet, they were credited with 136 kills.

-18-

HOMEWARD BOUND:
October–November 1944

WHILE ROYCE WAS flying sorties over Leyte, Becky was caring for the baby, preparing for his return, and engaging in her usual diversions. An exception to this pattern occurred Friday evening, October 20, when she attended the Classen–Central High School football game. Going to the game was in some ways like reliving her past. She wore her pep uniform, and, as she told Royce, "The score was 6–6 and was really exciting. I was hoarse from yelling so much. Classen got the decision for the conference [title] on penetration." Then she revealed the reason for attending, "I took Dump out and he met his date . . . after the game and then I took them to town. Lila is a really cute girl. She's his latest." Lila was a red skirt pledge, the same pep group that Becky had been in at Central High School. Becky went on to say,

Dump Is growing into quite a nice looking young man and acts and talks more like you every day. Or rather, he acts the way you used to act. You are quite a bit more serious in nature than you were when I first met you, you know. Remember how carefree you were before the war. I remember when I first met you at the Gas Co. when you said, "Oh, girls are all right, but not for me." Now look at you. Do you mind too much, darling? I like you serious.

Two days later, on Sunday, October 22, Becky worked the early afternoon shift at the USO snack bar. That evening, she wrote,

We are keeping up with the Philippine invasion. I suppose you are right in there, too. I hope after this phase of the invasion is over, you'll get to come home. In the last Life Magazine it showed pictures of carrier pilots who came or are on their way home after the first carrier plane attacks on those islands. It said they had been over a year and had started at Tarawa in the Gilberts. That's your record, too, so it certainly looks to me like you and your bunch would be next.

On Wednesday, October 25, she hosted two tables of bridge. Afterward, she again wrote to Royce, mentioning what she had learned about the fighting in the Philippines.

For the past couple of weeks, the news out there has been prominent in all the papers. We have read of the softening up of the Philippines by carrier planes, Luzon and Formosa, etc., and of the successful landing on Leyte Island and today we have listened all day to the reports of the engagement between our fleet and the Jap fleet. They say the Japs have suffered a crushing defeat. We lost our aircraft carrier, The Princeton, and suffered damage to other carriers and destroyers. I hope VF-60 came out ok and that now you can come home. I think you've seen enough action and, darling, I pray you'll get your leave this time. I need you so much. You need a rest, I know, and I want so to do everything I can to make our 30 days together the most wonderful we've ever had and won't forget for a long time to come. I guess I love you more every day and it must stick out all over me. 'Cause today when I got my hair fixed, Ruby said, "You're pretty crazy about that Royce, aren't you?" She didn't even need an answer to that. You are all I talk about, anyway.

In her few remaining letters, Becky never wrote about the Pacific War again. The sinking of the *Princeton* occurred on October 24. After the 25th, the news media may have reported that other ships were hit and sunk; however, it is likely that the names and exact location of some or all these ships were withheld from the media or not divulged at the Navy's request. During World War II, an Office of Censorship created by the U.S. federal government created a voluntary censorship code to guide the nation's newspapers, magazines, and radio stations on what news should not be publicized. Codebooks for American broadcasters and the American press asked them to follow a rule of thumb: "Is this information I would like to have if I were the enemy?" News to avoid included the exact location, movement, and composition of military units and U.S. naval ships. The Navy reported "only those sinkings that it could be sure the enemy knew about, or were apparent because of physical evidence such as wreckage,"[249] which may account for the news about the sinking of the *Princeton*.

For several days, the *Suwannee* crew were unable to send letters out, even if they could the find the time and the necessary paper and envelopes. Even when they could write, they were under strict orders about what they could say. In a message to the crew as the ship began her return to the States, Captain Johnson brought several points to their attention. He emphasized his first point:

As all of you know, we were attacked recently by two Japanese suicide dive bombers. I wish to emphasize and to re-emphasize the importance of forgetting those things right now. Our Navy Department is most concerned over suicide bombers and wish to keep this <u>very secret</u>. They do not wish the Japanese to learn what success they have had. Therefore, do not mention this matter to anyone. Do not whisper to your wife, mother, relatives or acquaintances. <u>THIS IS MOST IMPORTANT</u>.[250]

The Navy did not lift the news blackout on the suicide planes until April 1945, nearly six months after the attacks. Not until then did the American public first learn the word "kamikaze."[251] A wire photo of the *Suwannee* being hit by the first kamikaze pilot was finally released to newspapers on April 5, 1945.[252] Of course, per the usual censorship, the crew could not identify those on board who had been killed or write and post letters of sympathy to their relatives until after the Navy Department had contacted next of kin. So, there wasn't much they could say other than they were ok and were headed home.

The *Suwannee* departed Taffy 1 at 2:05 a.m. on October 27. Earlier that night and the night before they had buried their dead. In a respectful ceremony, each body was wrapped in a canvas bag and weighted with six fire bricks. Crewmen picked up the corners of the bag and slowly marched to a platform on the hangar deck, where a bugler blew Taps and Chaplain Walsh said a prayer. The bag was placed on a long plank and slid down into the dark waters in the navy tradition of burial at sea. The process was repeated many times on those two nights.[253]

The first stop, on October 28, was Kossol Roads in the Palau Islands. After off-loading the most severely wounded onto the hospital ships *Bountiful* and *Mercy*, the *Suwannee* proceeded to Seeadler Harbor, anchoring there on November 4. Enroute, on November 2, services were held aboard ship to honor shipmates lost during the battle.

During the five-day layover, it was quickly determined that the *Suwannee* would have to return to the States for major repairs. To get the ship back in action as soon as possible, the ship's first lieutenant was dispatched to the Bremerton Naval Yard in Puget Sound, Washington, with blueprints from the ship's files, photographs, and detailed descriptions of the damage from the kamikaze attacks. This enabled the yard to start the rebuilding task and prefabricate various replacement components long before the *Suwannee* arrived. The time at Seeadler Harbor also was needed for temporary repairs that would make the ship seaworthy for the long trip home. Finally, many crewmen and airmen who had been displaced during the battle returned to the ship. According to parachute rigger Paul Montgomery, when injured shipmates from the base hospital were told to board the ship, "Ensign Ford, who was also injured, rounded up all the *Suwannee* personnel that could walk. Some of them struggled, but they were determined, and eager to get back aboard their ship. I felt fortunate we were able to ride her back to the States."[254]

Even after picking up their scattered shipmates in the Admiralties, the *Suwannee* still had only about half its regular crew. After the kamikaze attacks, so many key personnel were missing that the operation of the ship depended on everyone working together and doing whatever was needed, regardless of rank. The first attack, for example, nearly wiped out all the cooks and bakers. Their General Quarters stations were on the hangar deck, where the bomb exploded. Only four of 23 survived, and two them were wounded. So a call went out for volunteers who had any previous cooking experience, and together with temporary replacements from other ships, they prepared the meals.

Charles Frederick, an administrative officer in VF-60, who had received prior training in celestial navigation, replaced the ship's navigator, Lieutenant Clarence Premo, who had been killed in the second attack. With their responsibilities previously limited to the air, the pilots took on duties of a ship's officer such as standing bridge watches, monitoring the ship's course and speed, and monitoring boarding and departures from the ship when in port.

Accompanied by a single destroyer escort, the *Suwannee* left Seeadler Harbor on November 9 and set course for Pearl Harbor, arriving on November 19. Medical officer Lieutenant Walter Burwell described a reception at Pearl Harbor that was etched in the memory of everyone onboard:

> As we limped up the channel to the naval base, every Navy ship at anchor or in dock there "manned the rail" in a salute to the *Suwannee*, and our radio received this message: "Welcome to Pearl! Your successful fight against great odds will live as one of the most striking tales of Naval History. The people of our country and those of us in the Naval Service are gratified and proud of your outstanding performance of duty against the best the enemy could offer. As long as our country has men with your heart, courage, skill, and strength she need not fear for her future. To each and every one, a 'Well Done'" – s/ ADM [signed Admiral] Nimitz.[255]

The *Suwannee's* stay at Pearl Harbor was short—just long enough to get supplies for the remainder of the trip and to offload materials usable in the war effort. The next morning the ship sailed for Puget Sound. With minimal chance of encountering a Japanese submarine, they sailed without an escort.

Meanwhile, Becky anxiously awaited word from Royce. When the ship arrived in Seeadler Harbor, he finally was able to mail a brief letter home, which Becky received on November 9. (The copy of this letter is missing.) Until then, she was still in the dark about his return. On November 2, she wrote,

> *I haven't heard anymore from Beedie about coming up here, but I owe her a letter. T-Bone was supposed to call her when he hit the States and I expected her to write when she talked to him, but nary a word from her. They, her family, are pretty upset over her brother. He was badly wounded in France, and they were awaiting news of him when she last wrote.*

I hope this time you won't be disappointed, darling, about coming home. I just don't see how it could happen again. The nine weeks you were talking about will be up the first week in December. I'm counting from the time your last letter was written . . . postmarked the 11th [of October]. Since that letter a lot has happened in the Philippines and I suppose you were in on it; however, I hope now it's over for you. I'm hoping to hear from you in a few days. I've been able to predict fairly accurately when to expect a letter from you by reading the news. I hope you are on your way home by the time we receive another letter. Darling, I miss you so and love you with all my heart. We may have been separated more than a year now, but I feel the same as I did the day you left only more so. You are "all there is" to me and I live only for you and little Royce. Those are time-worn phrases, but they are so true, because even though I don't try to tell you how much I love you in each letter, I want you to know that I love you so much it hurts. There has never in all the months we have been married and separated been anyone else and there never could be. Honey, I'm afraid you've got me for keeps. Mind??

During this period, Becky also wrote about preparing for Royce's return.

I'm fixing up the apartment some. It is very nice, or rather was nice the way it was, but I didn't feel like it was homey enough. So I've been haunting the dime stores and you would be surprised how a few pictures and trinkets have made a difference. I got frames for all six of Royce's large pictures and put them up in the living room. They sure are cute. I got a new lamp shade, some ivy, and a couple of knick-knacks and I like it a lot better. I'm going to get your uniforms fixed right away. . . . I'm going to have your white shirts re-laundered etc. I've already told you, haven't I, that I already have drawer space for you, and I even got something with which to pamper you. I won't tell you what it is either or you would die laughing. Sounds bad, doesn't it, but it isn't really. How would you like having breakfast in bed? Well, that's it – I gave in – I bought a bed-tray that can be propped up after you've eaten so that it holds a newspaper and you can read without any effort. Aren't I crazy? It's fun though!

She also filled Royce in on his son's latest developments.

We don't have a baby anymore – He's a little boy now. Today the doctor told me all the stuff I could feed him now, that I didn't have to boil water and bottles anymore, and she gave him his first whooping cough shot. He didn't feel well at all this afternoon. I don't know when I've seen him lay so still when he wasn't sleeping. He slept quite a bit though and this evening he seemed to have snapped out of it and is sound asleep now. He got over it a lot sooner than most babies. I had better quit talking or I'm likely to find myself up with him half the night. He can eat off the table now – that is, vegetables, except corn, that are finely chopped or mashed. Also, he can have meat now that is ground or chopped up, bacon, beef, chicken, and big-boned fish. I can cut down gradually on the water in his formula until he's getting half and half. Right now he's taking 19 oz. water to 13 oz. milk. Also, I'm to gradually cut out the Karo [syrup used as a sweetener], and I don't have to boil his water anymore. I'm going to continue that, however, cause the city water is terrible. He's getting to be a big boy. He looks more like you, darling. His face is getting leaner and his eyes are so like yours. Sometimes the way he looks at me out of his eyes is so much like you that it is startling. I don't think it's going to be long until he has two upper teeth. You know I just can't believe he's as big as he is and almost seven months old and yet I can't remember what he looked like when he was tiny. Isn't that silly? Time sure gets away from you. Royce weighed 19 lbs. 6 oz. today. I decided the reason I had the cramps this time was carrying him around. You had better get yourself home and take over that job. He's too much for me.

When Becky finally heard from Royce, she began a letter, dated November 9, that she held off sending for a few days.

Know what day this is? We have been married one year and eight months. Doesn't seem that long in a way, does it? I think one reason it doesn't seem like you've been gone so long is because you are so close to me all the time even when you are thousands of miles away. The time we had together is quite dear to me. I can remember it much better than I can this past year, which is more or less blurred. Nothing in particular stands out this past year unless it is little Royce. You are in my thoughts always and have been ever since you left and when I do stop a minute and think of a specific thing about you, it's always something we've done when we were together or plans for when you come home. I never think of loneliness and of what it is without you and when I get to longing for you, I quickly suppress the feeling, because it only makes it harder and is so useless. It isn't that I don't love you or love you less, because I love you more each day, it's just that I'm a sissy, I guess. I don't like thinking of unpleasant things and being away from you is certainly the least desirable thing I can think of. I just kinda leave my mind blank and go along from day to day thinking of you, looking at your picture and your son so much like you, and loving you with all my heart but trying to forget the unhappy part of the story, you out there and me here. Sound funny, doesn't it? You may think I'm getting hard and brittle, but I'm not. I'm quite sure I'll be capable of loving you as much and proving my love and devotion when you come home as I ever was and perhaps even more forcefully.

I received your letter. Was glad to know everything was all right. It had been three weeks since you last wrote. So, you got yourself three

more Japs. Good for you. We decided it was three more besides your
bomber since we already knew about it. That right? Give 'em hell,
honey. If you have to be that close and shooting at the __ __ __ __ __
I hope you blow them all up. Sandy said he didn't say he'd give you $10.00
for each one you shot down, and I told him it was just a code, but that
he ought to give you that and more. You certainly deserve it, darling.

Having been informed that Royce was definitely on his way home and
that the Fleet Post Office would soon cease forwarding mail to the ship,
Becky wrote her last letter.

November 12, 1944

My Darling,

 Am enclosing a letter I wrote a few days ago. I decided against
mailing it the next morning after writing it, but now have changed
my mind again. The first part was written in one of my "moments." I
suppose you are rather familiar with them now. It sounds like something
out of a magazine story, but I've never been good at expressing myself.
I guess I shouldn't try to explain something like that, because after
it's down in black and white, it never quite sounds like you thought
it was going to. I was just trying to tell you how very much I love you,
but as for missing you, even though I did, I did everything I could to
make your being gone easier for myself. It may not have been right to
not let myself think of certain things, to go a lot, and keep busy and
not admit I worried, because I knew that I did worry. It came out
in irritability and quick temperedness, usually when some big battle
was going on over there or when I didn't hear from you. I know that
was wrong, but it is hard for us here and yet not half as hard as it is
for you and so many others to be away from home and fighting. I don't
know exactly why I'm trying to explain all this to you except to try
to make you understand if some of my letters have failed to be what

they should have been. Some of these things may have come out in my letters to you, but, oh, my darling, I do hope they have not fallen too short. I'm selfish, I know, and I let my feelings be of more importance than they should be, but, darling I love you with all my heart and if this darned war will just be over and we can be together gain, I'll do my best to make you the best wife you could want. Will you try me?

Grandma got the Christmas box back that she sent you. She didn't tell us for almost two weeks, but when she heard that we had a letter from you, she told us. We decided that it was because the F.P.O. knows that "60" will be released before Christmas. The Postmaster said the box was all right, but not to try to send it again.

If Royce doesn't say Da-Da when you get home, it won't be my fault. I sit and say Da-da-da-da to him by the hour and he just grins. I'm going to have to braid his hair pretty soon if you don't hurry and get home and take him to the barber. Call 5-7574 (Henry Peterson) first when you hit the states. If no answer, then call Mrs. John Freeman or Major Robert McCormack – 610 NW 20. Mary June Freeman's husband came home this week after 2½ years across.

Love,
Becky and Royce II

The *Suwannee* docked in Seattle in the afternoon on November 26. Within an hour of docking, air group personnel were taken to Sand Point Naval Air Station, where they were quartered for three days while they awaited their new duty assignments. All VF-60 pilots were given stateside duty. Royce got his wish of becoming a flight instructor, as he, Barber, Nesbitt, Shea, La Fargue, and Smith were assigned to the Operational Training Command in Jacksonville, Florida.[256] But first, all members of the air group got a 30-day leave. Royce caught a flight to Oklahoma City. Home for the holidays, this would be Becky and Royce's first Christmas together as a married couple.

EPILOGUE

NATIONWIDE THROUGHOUT THE war, newspapers and magazines featured stories on reunited families. A December 14, 1944, article in the *Oklahoma City Times*, "Battling Hellcat Pilot Comes Home to Meet His Son and Heir," described Royce's homecoming, noting that he had been overseas for 13½ months, and this was his first "vacation" in two years. It included a picture of Becky and Royce holding his son as he reaches for their Christmas tree.

Royce and Becky had all of December to enjoy their reunion. In early January, Royce reported to NAS Daytona Beach, Florida, where he served as a flight instructor. The length of this assignment was indeterminate, as it depended on the course of the war in the Pacific. Becky remained in Oklahoma City, although she and Royce visited one another for a few short periods. Meanwhile, 1945 turned out to be the bloodiest chapter in the history of the Pacific War.

End of the Pacific War

After the decision was made to invade Leyte, the Joint Chiefs continued to debate whether to proceed to Luzon or bypass the rest of the Philippines and take Formosa. In early October, they issued their final strategic directive: MacArthur would invade Luzon on December 20, with the Third Fleet providing cover and support. Thereafter, beginning in January 1945, the Fleet would be detached to support the invasion of two island stepping-stones to Japan: Iwo Jima and Okinawa.[257] All of these targeted dates had to be pushed back, however, because MacArthur's Army encountered strong resistance at Leyte.

With the Imperial Navy no longer an effective fighting force after the Battle of Leyte Gulf, Japan's combat ability was completely dependent on its land and air forces. On land at Leyte, gun emplacements in the rugged mountains provided a formidable line of defense, and reinforcements landing at Ormoc on the northwest coast further strengthened the defense, increasing the number of Japanese troops on the island from 20,000 to 70,000 by the end of November. American forces eventually stopped the influx of Japanese troops at Ormoc. By late December, once they gained control of Leyte and Mindoro, an island just south of Luzon, they were ready to invade Luzon.

From October 25 on, Japan used almost all its planes in kamikaze operations.[258] With a fresh supply of planes flown to the Philippines, the air attacks escalated. At first, the main targets were aircraft carriers, to offset American air power. But after October 26, the second day the *Suwannee* was hit, kamikazes struck both the combat fleet at sea and transports and landing craft, which brought reinforcements and supplies to the invading troops. Kamikaze strikes continued in the Philippines until mid-January 1945, halted not by a shortage of volunteers but by the loss of available aircraft. They were a constant threat, sinking 20 ships and damaging numerous others.[259]

U.S. Army forces under MacArthur's command landed at Lingayen Gulf in northern Luzon on January 9. On February 3, they arrived on the outskirts of Manila, the Philippines capital. One month later, they had recaptured the city, albeit at tremendous cost. Fierce street-to-street fighting and American artillery resulted in the death of an estimated 100,000 Filipino civilians, many massacred by Japanese forces, and the destruction of the city known before the war as the Pearl of the Orient. MacArthur, intent on liberating the entire archipelago, remained in the Philippines until the end of the war, carrying out numerous mopping up operations on Luzon and islands south of Luzon.[260]

Even before the fighting in Manila ended, the rest of U.S. forces in the Pacific were preparing to invade Iwo Jima and Okinawa. By this time, Japanese military leaders no longer believed that the war could be won. On both islands, they therefore prepared for a prolonged battle of attrition, creating fortresses that could withstand air and naval bombardment and exact a heavy price on the invading troops. The objectives were to "seriously delay the final assault on Japan" and to "undermine enemy morale" in hopes of gaining a negotiated peace and preserving national honor.[261]

Iwo Jima, a dot of an island only five miles long with a total area of eight square miles, was chosen as the first operation. It was in the Bonins, a chain of 30 volcanic islands aligned north/south midway between Tokyo and the Marianas. Given its location and topography, Iwo Jima was believed to have great strategic value. It was 750 miles from the Japanese coast. A volcanic crater, Mount Suribachi, rested at its southern tip, but the Japanese had built airfields on the plateau north of the crater. The new long-range B-29 Superfortresses had begun bombing Japan from the Marianas in late November. Securing Iwo would clear the path to the Japanese homeland, provide emergency landings for the B-29s, and place fighter planes in range of Japan so they could escort bombing raids.

After months of sustained bombardment, the Marines landed on Iwo Jima on February 19. They expected to secure the island within a week; however, they fought "for it bitterly almost yard by yard" for 36 days.[262] Patterned after Peleliu, the Japanese had produced a defense in depth, away from the coast. Above ground were camouflaged tanks, blockhouses, and pillboxes, which provided interlocking fields of fire. Below ground was everything else—troops, barracks, weapons, command posts—in caves connected by 11 miles of tunnels at varying levels, most more than 30 feet underground and immune to bombardment.[263]

The Marines landed on the southeastern coast, northeast of Mount Suribachi.[264] As they moved north on the island, they outnumbered the Japanese more than three to one. By virtue of their numerical advantage, the support of naval and aerial strikes, and their courage and determination against a relentless enemy, the Marines prevailed. But the costs were staggering. More than 20,000 Japanese troops, nearly the entire garrison, were killed. And for the only time in the Pacific War, the U.S. had more casualties—25,851 wounded and dead—than the Japanese.[265] An even bloodier slaughter lay ahead at Okinawa.

Outside the Philippines, Okinawa was far larger than any other island objective in the Pacific War—65 miles long and an average of seven miles wide. It also was the most densely populated with about 460,000 Okinawans. Located in the Ryukyus, an island chain extending from the southernmost Japanese island of Kyushu to Taiwan, it was only 350 miles from Kyushu. The purpose of securing it was to develop an air and naval base that would serve as a staging area for an invasion of the Japanese home islands.

The invasion of Okinawa began on Easter Sunday, April 1, 1945. Japanese fortifications were similar to those at Iwo Jima, consisting of a system of natural and manmade defenses of caves, tunnels, and gun positions within three ridges that crisscrossed the southern third of the island.[266] But they assembled more troops, about 110,000, including 20,000 Okinawan conscripts. In addition, while kamikazes had made only a brief appearance at Iwo Jima, the Japanese launched an all-out air attack on ships surrounding Okinawa that would feature more than 4,000 planes.[267]

In the U.S. forces' first major ground campaign on Kakazu Ridge, four miles north of the main defensive line, the fighting was so savage that one Army division took "seven days and over eleven hundred casualties to advance six thousand yards."[268] Such brutal combat would continue for over two months. At the same time, kamikazes made almost daily attacks of one to twenty planes as well as ten mass raids—most with 100–200 planes—about once a week. By the final raid, on June 21–22, organized ground resistance ceased, and Okinawa was officially declared secured on June 21.

In the end on Okinawa, well over 120,000 enemy troops were killed in action, sealed in caves, or buried by the Japanese.[269] Okinawan civilians got the worst of it, with estimates upwards of 150,000 killed in the crossfire.[270] American casualties totaled 12,520 dead and 36,631 wounded in action. The campaign was especially costly for the U.S. Navy: 38 ships were sunk and another 364 were damaged; and Navy casualties included over 4,900 killed or drowned and 4,800 wounded, the heaviest losses of any naval campaign in the war.[271]

Before the Okinawa campaign ended, the Joint Chiefs had made plans to invade the Japanese home islands on November 1, 1945.[272] However, the casualties at Iwo Jima and Okinawa, which "exceeded those suffered during the previous three years of the Pacific war,"[273] made an invasion of Japan unthinkable to many military leaders. The Japanese government had never surrendered, nor had any Japanese military unit surrendered during the war,[274] and a conquest of Japan might "cost a million American casualties and twenty million Japanese."[275] Swayed by such casualty estimates, on July 26 Allied leaders issued a declaration calling for Japan's unconditional surrender. When the Japanese Premier denounced the declaration, President Harry Truman, who had taken office when Roosevelt died in April 1945, issued orders to drop the atom bomb, which had already been delivered to the U.S. air base on Tinian Island.

The targets selected for the atom bomb were Hiroshima and Nagasaki, both large industrial centers with military bases. The first bomb was dropped on Hiroshima on August 6; three days later, another bomb exploded over Nagasaki. The results were horrifying. The military estimated that 110,000 people were initially killed by the two blasts, although many more succumbed later to burns and radiation poisoning.[276] In Hiroshima, structures within 4.4 square miles of ground zero were almost completely destroyed.

Even outlying areas of the two cities suffered damage normally associated with a bomb's direct hit.[277] Influenced by such awesome destructive power, the emperor announced Japan's surrender on August 15, 1945. The war thus came to a sudden end, and the planned Allied invasion never took place.[278]

Royce and Becky

A month after the war ended, Royce was discharged from active duty. Like nearly all World War II veterans, he returned home to civilian life. He expected to follow his father in becoming a lawyer, and he worked out a plan with Oklahoma Natural Gas that would enable him to attend law school at Oklahoma City University while working at ONG, then join the ONG legal department when he finished his degree.

Royce must have been ambivalent about these plans, however, for in February 1946, while in his first semester of law school, he applied for transfer from the Navy Reserve to the Regular Navy. Nearly all Navy personnel who served during the war, including all the pilots in VF-60 except the executive officer and flight surgeon, were in the Navy Reserve. Reservists were civilians who volunteered for or were called to active duty during the war; the Navy was the career of those in the Regular Navy. In August 1946, Royce was given a permanent appointment as a commissioned officer in the Regular Navy; in October, he reported to active duty.

Becky and Royce's second child, Ted Robert, was born in April 1946, and it is possible that Royce's decision to apply for a regular commission was influenced by the financial burden of his expanding family. But a likely motivation was his love of flying. Long after he retired from the Navy, Royce conveyed the exhilaration of flying when discussing career choices with his nephew Tim Singleton. He told Tim that accounting was an honorable profession; so was teaching. "But you can't turn your desk upside down at 10,000 feet." Other pilots have expressed similar views. Astronaut and Senator John Glenn, a Marine corps pilot during World War II, said that love of flying led him to apply for a regular commission and stay in the

Marines. "The danger of combat flying," Glenn said, enhanced his "love of flying in general . . . This was flying with a purpose. We had no air-to-air combat, which is what every fighter pilot wants to do. But bombing runs into antiaircraft fire were a test of skill, nerve, preparation, and focus that I relished."[279] In 1950–51, Royce and Glenn served together at the Naval Air Training Center at Corpus Christi.

Royce's first stop after re-enlisting was the Operations School at NAS Jacksonville, Florida. He then received orders to Long Beach, California, where he was assigned to the USS *Helena*, a heavy cruiser. For a little over two years, beginning in February 1947, Royce flew the Curtis Seahawk, a seaplane that could be fitted with either wheeled or float landing gear. The *Helena* conducted training operations in California waters before departing for Shanghai, China, on April 3, 1948.[280] Throughout the summer and fall, the ship operated primarily in Chinese waters, returning to Long Beach in December. Royce and Becky's third child, Virginia Ruth, was born October 10; so, once again Royce was at sea when Becky gave birth. During this tour he asked the Navy to consider him for postgraduate training in law. For whatever reasons, that assignment never came to pass. In 1956, he finally finished his undergraduate degree, in history, by taking night courses at the University of Maryland while he was stationed at the Pentagon.

Royce had a distinguished 30-year career in the Navy, rising to the rank of Captain. Among his duty assignments were service in the Korean War, commanding officer of two squadrons (VF-94 and VA-152), navigator of the USS *Shangri-La*, and commanding officer of NAS, Agana, Guam, during the Vietnam War. As a pilot in the transitional period from propellor to jet-propelled aircraft, he flew over 40 different Navy aircraft, from the F6F Hellcat and F4U Corsair to the F11F Tiger and F8U Crusader. His numerous decorations included the Bronze Star with "V", Distinguished Flying Cross with two stars, and Air Medal with 11 stars.

Royce's Navy résumé shows broad and diversified assignments. He always said that one thing he liked about being a Naval officer was that you were required to be "a jack of all trades." To prepare to perform various jobs, officers undergo continuous training and education. For Royce, that included attendance at the Naval War College, Armed Forces Staff College, and Jet Transitional Training Unit. It is not surprising, therefore, that after turning in his wings, Royce went back to school, obtained a Master of Accountancy degree from the University of Oklahoma, and ended up teaching at his alma mater, the University of Central Oklahoma.

We do not know how Becky felt about Royce's re-enlistment; her letters during the war suggest that she was ready to follow Royce wherever he was stationed, and she was not opposed to leaving Oklahoma. Still, she may not have realized that being in the Regular Navy would result in her being separated from Royce for nearly six years in the first 20 years of their married life. They ended up having six children, with 14½ years between the first and the last. Royce was home for the births of only two of them. From their first transfer from Jacksonville to Long Beach until Royce's retirement in 1971, the family moved 12 times and lived in 15 different homes.

In many ways, Becky was typical of mothers in the late 1940s and 1950s. She did not work outside the home, and she dedicated her life to her husband and children. Given the family size and Royce's frequent absences, caring for children and performing household tasks consumed almost all her waking hours. For 20 years, there was always a baby or toddler or preschooler who had to be cared for; the family rarely ate out at a restaurant; a load of clothes almost always needed washing; and outside help was rarely hired to clean the house.

Unlike the war years, the family never lived near next of kin, as Royce was usually stationed on one coast or the other. At times, when Royce was away, Becky's mother Beulah came to help; otherwise, she lacked the family support she had gotten during the war. Neighbors and wives of squadron members provided some social support, but for the most part, she was on her own. Under these circumstances, and given how often Royce was away from home, it is a marvel how well Becky managed the household and cared for all the children. A letter written to Royce during the week that their last child, Jeff, was born in October 1958, shows how she was nonpareil at performing diverse tasks throughout each day. Becky picked up her mother at the airport on Monday; hosted a birthday lunch for two women from the neighborhood on Wednesday; then, on Thursday, went to the commissary in the morning, took youngest child Chuck to the doctor in the afternoon, and attended a coffee, which turned out to be a surprise baby shower for her, in the evening. Moreover, she described all this in a lengthy letter written after she got home from the shower. The next day, Friday, October 10, she continued the letter as follows:

> *I went to sleep again. And the unbelievable happened at 5:00 AM this morning. My water broke and I am now in the hospital (5:00 PM) and doing absolutely nothing. I called Shirley B [wife of a squadron member] and she took me to the doctor's at 10:00 AM. I had her drive the Packard so I could fill it with gas and I got a prescription filled for Mother and bought a birthday cake for Virginia [Friday was her daughter's birthday]. The doctor told me to come into the hospital so I had Shirley take me home to get things squared away.*

Becky went on to say that she had been given a shot to induce labor and would "write again when this is over." Jeff was born on Saturday at 2:00 AM.

Family responsibilities forced Becky to be very pragmatic and resourceful. She needed to get things done quickly and efficiently just to keep up with the demands. Although the family was not poor by any measure, money was a constant issue. As Royce told Royce Jr. long after he retired, "when you were growing up, we never had enough money; now we have more than we need." It often was up to Becky to make ends meet. She paid the bills, and there were times when she delayed payment on one item to make payment on something else. She constantly looked for bargains. And, though it is hard to imagine how she found the time, she occasionally sewed outfits to save money on clothes.

Becky's life after the war was in some ways an extension of her experiences during the war. Family disruptions compelled her to become even more independent and more skilled in finances. She also would continue to suffer pangs of separation as well as anxious concerns over Royce's fate when he was away. She no longer had to deal with rationing and other wartime issues, but she now had the added stress of frequently moving, and she could no longer readily call upon her extended family for help.

Others

Royce's brother Bob returned from the Pacific in January 1945 and remained stateside until the war ended and he was released from active duty. Like Royce, he returned to Oklahoma City and went back to school. After graduating from law school in 1950, he and his father Sandy opened a law practice. But when they had trouble attracting clients, Bob left the practice and became an insurance agent. He and Kathleen never had children. Royce's other siblings, Mina and Dump, each were married after the war—Dump to Lila, the girl he took to the football game, as Becky described in her October letter to Royce. Both Mina and Dump named their first child after their father Sandy. All three families settled in Oklahoma City.

When Virginia's husband Bob Parnell returned to the European theater in fall 1944, he ended up at the Battle of the Bulge. Considered the deadliest battle fought by U.S. forces in World War II, this battle took place in the Ardennes Forest of Belgium and Luxembourg in December and January. Parnell assumed command of his company when the commander was killed on January 10. The following day, he volunteered for a hazardous patrol into enemy territory. He and his men not only conducted a thorough reconnaissance of the area, but also established two roadblocks that led to the ultimate victory of his outfit. One day later he was killed at Les Tailles. For his actions, Parnell posthumously received the Silver Star, the third highest combat decoration of the Armed Services. He is buried at Arlington National Cemetery.

Virginia, newly widowed, returned to Oklahoma A&M in the spring of 1945. She met her second husband, Theron Robinson, there. They lived in Oklahoma City for more than a decade before moving permanently to Kansas City. They named their second child Rebecca.

Among the pilots in VF-60, Ed Dashiell and flight surgeon Phil Phillips, both USN before the war, remained in the Navy, and John (Rabbi) Shea, Royce's roommate for much of the tour, applied for a regular commission and pursued a Naval career. In every Statement of Personal History that Royce submitted while in the Navy, Dashiell and Shea are listed as his first two character references. Shea eventually was grounded by a Navy flight surgeon because of aftereffects of his crash landing on the *Suwannee*. Nonetheless, he stayed in the Navy and got in on the ground floor of the Navy's use of computers. Shea's duty assignments included commanding officer of a destroyer (USS *English*), executive officer of a heavy cruiser (USS *Northampton*), and commanding officer of Key West Naval Base. When he retired, his first position was manager of the City of Jacksonville's mainframe computer system. His last job was professor of computer science at Flagler College in St. Augustine, Florida.

Other pilots of VF-60 and nearly all the rest of the air group returned to civilian life. Several went back to school. Paul (Eggbert) Barber, who flew in Royce's division throughout their time at sea, obtained a law degree from the University of Texas. John Smith completed his undergraduate degree at the University of Missouri, Kansas City, obtained a PhD at Iowa State University, and joined the faculty in the Materials Science Department and Ames Laboratory at Iowa State. He had a distinguished career as a metallurgist, authoring over 180 technical papers and serving as editor of professional journals.

Based on an informal survey of the post-war activities of the air group, John Smith found that they chose a diversity of occupations. Several of them became farmers, harvesting peanuts in Louisiana, rice in Arkansas, and corn in Missouri. Illustrative of their diverse endeavors, Hubert Cornwell ended up in men's haberdashery; Glenn (Red) Rynearson became an aeronautical engineer; Edwin Fischer worked in finance and securities; Roy (Tex) Garner ran an insurance business; Ira Pitcher was a banker.[281]

Many members of the air group retained their interest in flying in one form or another. Clarence J. Delk, a pilot in VT-60, flew for Eastern Air Lines. Roy Garner kept a plane and flew an occasional charter flight. Many, including Cornwell, Pitcher, Garner, Smith, and Ralph Kalal, continued to fly through their association with the Naval Air Reserve. For Smith, aviation was a lifelong passion. He retired from his reserve unit as a commander, having logged close to 5,000 hours in well over 100 different types of aircraft.[282] Others obtained civilian pilot's licenses and flew privately. After he retired, John Shea purchased a Cessna Cardinal RG and still had it when he passed away. According to his son John III, his dad "absolutely LOVED flying!"

The husbands of Becky's friends Verla (McDonald) Wilson and Margaret (Gafford) Winner returned home safely. Verla's husband Dee, who was on the casualty list in November 1944, was discharged in July 1945. Margaret's husband Erman, who served with the Marines in World War II, fought in the Army during the Korean War after joining the Oklahoma 45th Infantry Division. He then was associated with the Oklahoma Military Department and National Guard for the next 25 years. Both Verla and Margaret's families resided in Oklahoma City for their entire lives. Becky had very little contact with Verla, Margaret, or Mary after leaving Oklahoma City when Royce re-joined the Navy.

Mary Edith (M.E.) Simpson returned to her home in West Virginia and remarried after the war. Green Peyton Wertenbaker and his wife Barclay lived in San Antonio before and after the war. He is known today for science fiction that he wrote in the 1920s and 1930s. In the 1950s, Wertenbaker became involved in the aerospace industry. He wrote scripts for the television series *Doctors in Space*, which explored human problems of space flight, and he became a speechwriter for NASA.

Impact of the War on Royce and Becky

As Royce and Becky got on with their lives, very few people outside their Navy contacts knew anything about the sacrifices they made during the war. Like most veterans, Royce did not call attention to his service or accomplishments. His war letters indicate that he was duly proud of the awards he received as a combat pilot, but he did not seek fame or recognition. He volunteered to serve because it was the right thing to do. So it was with the Greatest Generation.

It was not apparent to Royce's children whether he suffered ill effects from his wartime experience. So far as we know, he never talked about the war, except perhaps with fellow pilots and shipmates. We do know, however, that he witnessed violent deaths and injury and inflicted violence on the enemy, which were likely to be unsettling. At the least, observing the kamikaze attacks on the *Suwannee* must have been traumatic. Not talking about these experiences, as it was for many other veterans, may have been Royce's way of containing them and not reliving them.

Recent research has shown that negative experiences or trauma also can have long-term positive effects, such as increasing one's appreciation for life.[283] This may apply to Royce. His zest for life was reflected in the way he savored ordinary activities, such as cooking breakfast for the family on a Sunday morning (pecan waffles were a specialty), making homemade ice cream, reading a good book, watching OU football, or playing a round of golf. You could see it when he met someone new or heartily greeted old friends. It also came through in his generally cheerful countenance, sense of humor, and self-deprecating wit, which he often used to show affection for Becky and the children. He surely would have agreed with *Suwannee* shipmate Paul Montgomery's sentiments expressed nearly 50 years after the war: "Sometimes it seems like yesterday, another time it seems like a dream, or that it never happened. But most of all, I think of the wonderful shipmates that didn't make it. I feel fortunate to be alive and I wish they were too."[284]

It is hard to gauge the effects of the war on Becky, especially given Royce's re-enlistment. Historians have debated the impact of the war on long-term changes in gender roles. On the one hand, several scholars have "suggested that continuity rather than change characterized women's lives after the war."[285] While married women entered the labor force in unprecedented numbers during the war, the expectation was that moms would return full-time to the home as soon as the war was over. After the war, as before, traditional family roles, with women supporting their husband's careers, were emphasized. On the other hand, historian D'Ann Campbell contends that servicemen's wives like Becky, whose family lives were disrupted, were "the first group to reflect the future trend toward more equalitarian marriages."[286] "Separation forced both husbands and wives to become more mature, independent, and self-reliant." The loneliness of separation also taught them "how central companionship was to their marriage." "The way they balanced their new strengths with their heightened realization of the importance of companionate marriage was to seek and accept more sharing of power and responsibility within the family." These changes, Campbell believes, reflected "what was happening to American families in general but more slowly."[287]

In the end, the war appears to have had a lasting effect on Becky and Royce's relationship. My siblings and I were in awe of the special relationship they had. We always knew they loved one another deeply and passionately. The uncertainty and stress of the war, with the prospect of death, heightened the emotional power of their letters, and affections regularly expressed in those letters forged their feelings toward one another for the rest of their lives.

Acknowledgments

Reading my parents' letters inspired me to write about their wartime experience. I owe the opportunity to read those letters, first, to my parents. Starting with World War II, Becky saved all the letters that she and Royce wrote to one another. For 50 years, often crisscrossing the country while moving from one residence to another, she stored the accumulating letters in a Chinese trunk. I also could not have read the letters if not for my brother Jeff, who had the foresight to make PDF copies of all of them, store them on a CD, and send copies of the CD to his siblings. Jeff still has the originals.

Although I have written many academic publications, writing my first trade book was a challenge. Fortunately, several people provided the encouragement I needed to allay my doubts that I could write something of general interest. Jan and Ken Kerber kept me going at the beginning of the project, and Ken continued to read and provide valuable feedback on drafts of early chapters. My sister Kat and brother Jeff read every word of the manuscript. They were especially helpful in confirming observations that were inferred from or transcended our parents' letters. Two of my faculty colleagues at the College of the Holy Cross, Vicki Swigert and Susan Rodgers, not only read and made insightful comments on multiple revisions, which resulted in numerous emendations, but also were enthusiastic believers in the project. Knowing that they looked forward to reading each installment was crucial in overcoming the discouraging judgments of publishers who kept telling me that the market for the book was not large enough to justify publication.

Despite rejections from several traditional publishers, preparing and submitting book proposals helped me frame the contribution of the book and broaden its appeal. In learning about the publishing world outside academia, I was aided by information from Holy Cross Professor of Creative Writing Leah Hager Cohen, literary agent Susan Rabiner, and the late Judy Barrett Litoff, historian and author of multiple books based on World War II letters. As I prepared my first proposal, I had several helpful conversations with Jerry Rogers, author of *So Long for Now: A Sailor's Letters from the USS Franklin.* Brian Murphy, President of the Brian Murphy Group, provided further guidance and encouragement throughout the submission process. Likewise, Holy Cross grad ('67) and Navy veteran Jim Delehaunty was helpful during this process and beyond. Based on his recommendation, I asked two career Naval aviators, retired Captain Brendan O'Donnell and retired Rear Admiral Bill McCarthy, to read the manuscript, and both provided testimonials.

Nephew Jonathan Szarzynski sent me a copy of Royce's Flight Log. Al Dipinto loaned me books from his library of books about military aviation. Letitia (Tish) Harder, daughter of VF-60 pilot John Smith, gave me her father's copy of *As We Lived It*, an oral history of the *Suwannee* air groups that turned out to be an important resource. Tish and John D. Shea III, son of VF-60 pilot John (Rabbi) Shea, also provided information about their fathers' post-war lives that I included in the Epilogue. Besides reading portions of the manuscript, Ken Kerber produced preliminary png files of several photographs that are included in the book.

Editor Elsa Peterson was especially helpful in identifying places in the manuscript that needed clarification, amplifying the text where necessary, and abridging an overly long introduction. While we initially did not see eye to eye about my coverage of the Pacific War, she showed great patience as I struggled to determine how best she could help me.

Finally, I drew upon the considerable skills of my immediate family. I pride myself in my ability to write grammatically correct prose. Still, my son Rob showed his editorial prowess in identifying errors in a penultimate draft of the manuscript. Daughter Kate Blehar, a graphic designer and art teacher, designed the book cover, created two maps, and prepared digital files of all the images and photographs that appear in the book. I could not have completed this book without the love and support of my wife, Nancy. She was a constant sounding board, patiently listening to me fret about the project almost daily. A librarian and avid reader, she has an excellent ear for good (and poor) writing. She was the first to read or listen to me read almost every word I wrote. Countless times, I was heartened when she said, "sounds good." When she pointed out clumsy or questionable wording, I usually changed it. Nancy also came up with the main title of the book (and Susan Rodgers the subtitle).

My name alone is identified as the author of this book, but it is clearly the product of my parents and many others. I am deeply indebted to them all.

NOTES

1. Evan Thomas, *Sea of Thunder: Four Commanders and the Last Great Naval Campaign 1941–1945* (New York: Simon and Schuster, 2006), 4.

2. Samuel Eliot Morison, *History of United States Naval Operations in World War II, Volume 12: Leyte, June 1944–January 1945* (Boston: Little, Brown, 1958), 242.

3. Established in 1894, the UDC memorialized confederate soldiers, most notably by funding the erection of hundreds of monuments to generals and local heroes at courthouses and town squares throughout the South. In this and other ways, the UDC was instrumental in creating and sustaining the Lost Cause myth: that secession based on states' rights, not slavery, caused the Civil War; African Americans were contented slaves, loyal to their paternalistic masters; and confederate soldiers were heroic in fighting a battle against a Union vastly superior in men and resources. While distorting history, the myth reinforced a southern ideology that supported white supremacy and racial segregation. For a history of the UDC and its role in the propagation of the myth of the Lost Cause, see Karen L. Cox, *Dixie's Daughters: The United Daughter of the Confederacy and the Preservation of Confederate Culture* (Gainesville, FL: University of Florida Press, 2004).

Gatherings of the Oklahoma City chapter often consisted of luncheons or teas, with programs that honored Confederate veterans, celebrated Robert E. Lee Day, or promoted historical memory of antebellum southern culture through dress, talks, dramatic readings, and songs. In Beulah's day, in Oklahoma, such activities were regularly covered in the city newspaper and two events were held at the Governor's mansion. Today, the movement to remove symbols of white supremacy from public places has made the UDC as unacceptable as confederate war flags and monuments.

4. In the mid-1930s, when Royce and Becky finished grade school, only about 25 percent of the U.S. adult population had finished high school, less than 10 percent had completed 1–3 years of college, and less than 5 percent had obtained a college degree. Extrapolated from U.S. Census Bureau, CPS Historical Time Series Tables. Table A-1. Years of School Completed by People 25 Years and Over, by Age and Sex:

Selected Years 1940 to 2019. URL: https://www.census.gov/data/tables/time-series/demo/educational-attainment/cps-historical-time-series.html. Accessed April 9, 2020.

5. Royce had the second highest grade in the senior class at Duncan High School on the college entrance exam, and he finished second in English Grammar in a statewide contest. See "Norman Gains Edge in Study Group Tests," *The Daily Oklahoman*, April 29, 1938, 22.

6. George Gallup, *The Gallup Poll: Public Opinion, 1935–1971* (Bloomington, IN: Indiana University Press, 1972).

7. When first enacted, the draft was limited to men between the ages of 21 and 36, who were required to serve at least one year. After war was declared, the upper age limit was raised and then the age range was lowered to 18–37. In addition, draft terms were extended through the duration of the war.

8. Barrett Tillman, "'Go West Young Man': The War in the Pacific," *The History of US Naval Air Power*, ed. Robert L. Lawson (New York: The Military Press, 1985), 59–101.

9. Aviation History Unit OP-519B, *The Navy's Air War* (New York: Harper and Brothers, 1946), Chapter 28, Training Naval Aviation's Manpower, URL: https://penelope.uchicago.edu/Thayer/E/Gazetteer/Places/America/United_States/_Topics/history/_Texts/AHUNAW/28*.html. Accessed October 14, 2023.

10. Tillman, "Go West Young Man"

11. "Singleton-Sims Wedding is January Event," *The Daily Oklahoman*, February 7, 1943, 44.

12. See Kristin Celello, *Making Marriage Work: A History of Marriage and Divorce in the Twentieth-Century United States* (Chapel Hill, NC: University of North Carolina Press, 2009), Chapter 2. For a lengthy list of articles in the popular press, see Judy Barrett Litoff, David C. Smith, Barbara Wooddall Taylor, and Charles E. Taylor, *Miss You: The World War II Letters of Barbara Wooddall Taylor and Charles E. Taylor* (Athens, GA: University of Georgia Press, 1990), 317, footnote 13.

13. Cellelo, *Making Marriage Work*, 49.

14. *Ibid.*, 51.

15. See Emily Yellin, *Our Mother's War: American Women at Home and at the Front During World War II* (New York: Free Press, 2004), 5.

16. "Home in Seattle Established by Officer and Bride," *The Daily Oklahoman*, March 21, 1943, 36.

17. "The Saga of Air Group 60," in *Air Group Sixty, 1943–1944*, a yearbook.

18. Paul Popenoe, "If You're a War Bride," *Ladies Home Journal*, September 1942, 24.

19. John F. Smith, *Hellcats over the Philippine Deep* (Manhattan, KS: Sunflower University Press, 1995), 10.

20. Green Peyton, *5,000 Miles towards Tokyo* (Norman, OK: University of Oklahoma Press, 1945), 17.

21. Thomas, *Sea of Thunder*, 12.

22. Smith, *Hellcats*, 10. For a description of these accidents, see Peyton, *5,000 Miles*, 20–22.

23. Robert Blanchard, "Sobering Stats: 15,000 U.S. Airmen Killed in Training in WWII," RealClear History. URL: https://www.realclearhistory.com/articles/2019/02/12/staggering_statistics_15000_us_airmen_killed_in_training_in_ww_ii_412.html. Accessed January 10, 2020.

24. "Aviation Personnel Fatalities in World War II," Naval History and Heritage Command, Navy Department, Bureau of Naval Personnel, Washington, D.C. URL: https://www.history.navy.mil/research/library/online-reading-room/title-list-alphabetically/a/aviation-personnel-fatalities-in-world-war-ii.html. Accessed January 10, 2020.

25. Smith, *Hellcats*, 10.

26. Wertenbaker was an author and editor. Before joining the Navy, he had written two novels, served on the editorial board of *Fortune* magazine, and was a contributing editor to *Time Magazine*. His preferred byline was Green Peyton, his given names.

27. Peyton, *5,000 Miles*, 100.

28. Samuel Eliot Morison, *The Two-Ocean War: A Short History of the United States Navy in the Second World War* (Boston: Little, Brown, 1963), 42.

29. Chief of Naval Operations, Office of, "U. S. Naval Aviation in the Pacific," Naval History and Heritage Command, United States Navy, 1947, 21. URL: https://www.google.com/url?sa=t&rct=j&q=&esrc=s&source=web&cd=&ved=2ahUKEwiuoZPP_cP_AhWYlmoFHcwXDyQQFnoECCEQAQ&url=https%3A%2F%2Fwww.history.navy.mil%2Fresearch%2Fpublications%2Fpublications-by-subject%2Fnaval-aviation-pacific.html&usg=AOvVaw0OuMk9V1qsviCAY9L7LQsH. Accessed June 14, 2023.

30. Jeffrey Record, "Japan's Decision for War in 1941: Some Enduring Lessons," Carlisle, PA: Strategic Studies Institute, U.S. Army War College, February 2009, 27. URL: https://www.hsdl.org/?view&did=38470. Accessed April 30, 2020.

31. John W. Masland, "American Attitudes Toward Japan," *The Annals of the American Academy of Political and Social Science*, Vol. 215, America and Japan (May, 1941), 165.

32. Lydia Saad, "Gallup Vault: A Country Unified After Pearl Harbor," Gallup Vault, December 5, 2016. URL: https://news.gallup.com/vault/199049/gallup-vault-country-unified-pearl-harbor.aspx. Accessed May 1, 2020.

33. Nathan Miller, *War at Sea: A Naval History of World War II* (New York: Oxford University Press, 1995), 207.

34. One crew member died when bailing out and two others drowned. Of eight men captured after landing in Japanese-held territory, three were executed and one died in captivity; the other four were repatriated after the war.

35. The raid also had a deadly impact on the Chinese. To retaliate for the Chinese helping the American flyers elude capture and guiding them to safety, the Japanese

undertook a brutal reprisal, laying waste to 25 villages and towns and taking an estimated quarter-million lives. See James M. Scott, *Target Tokyo: Jimmy Doolittle and the Raid That Avenged Pearl Harbor* (New York: W.W. Norton, 2015).

36. Data from various sources on the Battle of Midway are inconsistent. These data are taken from History.com Editors, "The Battle of Midway Ends," A&E Television Networks. URL: https://www.history.com/this-day-in-history/battle-of-midway-ends. Accessed May 18, 2020.

37. Barrett Tillman, "The Battle of Midway," *Air Force Magazine* 94, no. 2 (February 2011): 90–93.

38. Ernest Joseph King and Walter Muir Whitehill, *Fleet Admiral King* (New York: Norton, 1952), 381.

39. Morison, *The Two-Ocean War*, 42.

40. Samuel Eliot Morison, *History of United States Naval Operations in World War II, Volume 5: The Struggle for Guadalcanal, August 1942–February 1943* (Boston: Little, Brown, 1951), 372. These figures do not include US Navy losses, which were never compiled and "certainly in excess of" the number of Army and Marine Corps troops that were lost. Nor do they include the unknown but equally large number of Japanese sailors who were lost.

41. Chief of Naval Operations, "U. S. Naval Aviation in the Pacific," 27.

42. *Ibid.*, 29.

43. Mark Stille, *US Navy Escort Carriers: 1942–1945* (New York: Osprey Publishing, 2017).

44. William T. Y'Blood, *The Little Giants: U.S. Escort Carriers Against Japan* (Annapolis, MD: Naval Institute Press, 1987), 43.

45. Peyton, *5,000 Miles*, 11, 13, 14.

46. John W. Jeffries, *Wartime America: The World War II Home Front* (Chicago: Ivan R. Dee, 1996), 94–95. See also Karen Anderson, *Wartime Women: Sex Roles, Family Relations, and the Status of Women During World War II* (Westport, CT: Greenwood Press, 1981), 4.

47. John B. Goodman, "Dilbert, USN," *Flying* 35, no. 2 (August 1944): 55. URL: https://books.google.com/books?id=IObo37IFIXUC&pg=PA132#v=onepage&q&f=false. Accessed April 11, 2023.

48. Since 1979, the Gilbert Islands exist as two independent nations: Kribati and Tuvalu.

49. Peyton, *5,000 Miles*, 27, 34–35.

50. Chief of Naval Operations, "U. S. Naval Aviation in the Pacific," 1.

51. Samuel Eliot Morison, *History of United States Naval Operations in World War II, Volume 7: Aleutians, Gilberts, and Marshalls, June 1942–April 1944* (Boston: Little, Brown, 1951), 100.

52. *Ibid.*, 102.

53. *Ibid.*, 107.

54. *Ibid.*, Numbers drawn from Appendix II, 336–42.

55. *Ibid.*, 99.

56. W. R. Dacus and E. Kitzmann, *As We Lived It: U.S.S. Suwannee Air Groups 27, 60, and 40* (U.S.S. *Suwannee* Reunion Association, 1992), 39.

57. From "The War," "At Home," "Family," directed and produced by Ken Burns and Lynn Novak. WETA, Washington DC and American Lives II Film Project, 2007. URL: https://www.pbs.org/kenburns/the-war/family. Accessed October 9, 2023.

58. See, for example, "Using Distraction to Treat Anxiety," eNetMD. URL: https://www.enetmd.com/content/using-distraction-treat-anxiety. Accessed March 11, 2020.

59. Miller, *War at Sea*, 395.

60. Morison, *History of United States Naval Operations, Vol. 7*, 156–58. No two of the several accounts of the complex operation at Tarawa are exactly the same. When in doubt, I relied on Samuel Eliot Morison's history, regarded by many as one of the most authoritative accounts of the war. For a thorough eyewitness account of the battle from the perspective of the Marines, see Robert Sherrod's *Tarawa: The Story of a Battle*. A very good relatively brief account is "Chapter George: Les Braves Gens" from William Manchester's *Goodbye Darkness: A Memoir of the Pacific War* (Boston: Little-Brown, 1980). Manchester was a marine at Tarawa.

61. Peyton, *5,000 Miles*, 40.

62. U.S.S. *Suwannee*, Serial 0107, Fightron Sixty Aircraft Action Report #2, 11/20/1943.

63. Morison, *History of United States Naval Operations, Vol. 7*, 158.

64. *Ibid.*, 168.

65. U.S.S. *Suwannee*, Serial 0107, Fightron Sixty Aircraft Action Report #3, 11/21/1943.

66. Morison, *History of United States Naval Operations, Vol. 7*, 170.

67. *Ibid.*, 173. Robert Sherrod, *Tarawa: The Story of a Battle* (New York: Duell, Sloan, and Pearce, 1944), 101.

68. Peyton, *5,000 Miles*, 49–50.

69. Morison, *History of United States Naval Operations, Vol. 7*, 133.

70. Sherrod, *Tarawa*, 147, 148, 149. Also see Ray E. Boomhower, "The Reporter Who Helped Persuade FDR to Tell the Truth About War," *Smithsonian Magazine*, January 11, 2018. URL: https://www.smithsonianmag.com/history/reporter-who-helped-persuade-fdr-tell-truth-about-war-180967787/. Accessed March 16, 2020.

71. See, for example, Miller, *War at Sea*, 395–96.

72. Morison, *History of United States Naval Operations, Vol. 7*, 184.

73. Y'Blood, *The Little Giants*, 40.

74. U.S.S. *Suwannee*, Serial 018(L), ComFightRon 60 Aircraft Action Report #1, 2/21/1944.

75. Morison, *History of United States Naval Operations, Vol. 7*, 161.

76. Cortni E. Molnar, "'Has the Millenium Yet Dawned?': A History of Attitudes Toward Pregnant Workers in America," *Michigan Journal of Gender and Law* 12, no. 1 (2005): 170. In the United States today, it is common for pregnant women to work outside the home, and workplace discrimination against pregnant women is prohibited by federal and state law. See, for example, American College of Obstetricians and Gynecologists, Committee Opinion, "Employment Considerations During Pregnancy and the Postpartum Period," No. 73, April 2018. URL: https://www.acog.org/clinical/clinical-guidance/committee-opinion/articles/2018/04/employment-considerations-during-pregnancy-and-the-postpartum-period. Accessed January 31, 2023.

77. Institute of Medicine, US Committee on Nutritional Status During Pregnancy and Lactation, *Nutrition During Pregnancy, Part I Weight Gain* (Washington, DC: National Academies Press, 1990).

78. Peyton, *5,000 Miles*, 51.

79. *Ibid.*, 54.

80. Smith, *Hellcats*, 25–26.

81. Peyton, *5,000 Miles*, 63.

82. Y'Blood, *The Little Giants*, 48.

83. Peyton, *5,000 Miles*, 67.

84. Michelle Pautz, "The Decline in Average Weekly Cinema Attendance: 1930–2000," *Issues in Political Economy* 11 (July 2002). URL: https://blogs.elon.edu/ipe/files/2021/02/v11-pautz2.pdf. Accessed September 15, 2023.

85. *Ibid.*

86. Tracy Waldon and James Lande, *Reference Book of Rates, Price Indices, and Household Expenditures for Telephone Service* (Washington, DC: Industry Analysis Division, Common Carrier Bureau, Federal Communications Commission, March 1997). Interpolated from Table 13, AT&T Interstate Residential Tariff Rates for 10-minute Calls, 62. URL: https://transition.fcc.gov/Bureaus/Common_Carrier/Reports/FCC-State_Link/IAD/ref97.pdf. Accessed March 25, 2020.

87. Morison, *History of United States Naval Operations, Vol. 7*, 202–207.

88. Peyton, *5,000 Miles*, 72.

89. See Philip A. Crowl and Edmund G. Love, *The War in the Pacific: Seizure of the Gilberts and Marshalls* (Washington, DC: Center of Military History, United States Army, 1993), 157–65.

90. Morison, *History of United States Naval Operations, Vol. 7*, 218.

91. *Ibid.*, 243.

92. The southern offensive took longer for several reasons. Kwajalein was the largest island in the Atoll and separated from Ebeye by 4.5 miles; more of the surrounding islets were occupied by enemy forces; the garrison was larger than at Roi-Namur; and Japanese resistance, with nightly counterattacks, was intense.

93. *Ibid.*, 278.

94. Peyton, *5,000 Miles*, 75.

95. *Ibid.*, 77.

96. *Ibid.*, 79–80.

97. Morison, *History of United States Naval Operations, Vol. 7*, 329–31.

98. U.S.S. *Suwannee*, Serial 018(L), ComFightRon 60 Aircraft Action Report #1, 2/21/1944. Also see Peyton, *5,000 Miles*, 85.

99. Peyton, *5,000 Miles*, 86.

100. This is how Green Peyton accounted for the decision to replace the bombers with Hellcats (Peyton, *5,000 Miles*, 87–88); however, John Smith contended that when the VF-60 commanding officer "learned that the command at Pearl Harbor was considering replacing the ship's F6Fs with FM2 Wildcats," he convinced the "powers that be" that the F6F could carry out the dive bombing role as effectively as the SBD Dauntless (Smith, *Hellcats*, 47).

101. Smith, *Hellcats*, 47.

102. See "Finger-four," Wikipedia. URL: https://en.wikipedia.org/wiki/Finger-four. Accessed: April 18, 2020.

103. Frank Newport, "Slight Preference for Having Boy Children Persists in U.S.," Gallup News, Social and Policy Issues, July 5, 2018. URL: https://news.gallup.com/poll/236513/slight-preference-having-boy-children-persists.aspx. Accessed July 10, 2020.

104. Samuel Eliot Morison, *History of United States Naval Operations in World War II, Volume 8: New Guinea and the Marianas, March 1944–August 1944* (Boston: Little, Brown, 1953), 5–6.

105. *Ibid*, 6–7.

106. Smith, *Hellcats*, 52.

107. *Ibid.*

108. *Ibid.*

109. As described in *U.S.S. Suwannee CVE 27 Newsletter*, Summer 2006. URL: https://www.usssuwannee.org/2006summer.pdf. Accessed April 24, 2020.

110. Morison, *History of United States Naval Operations, Vol. 8*, 32–33. Morison does not report the total number of planes destroyed; he does state that the number of planes shot down was "not 'over 90' as the pilots claimed." According to Chief of Naval Operations, "U. S. Naval Aviation in the Pacific" (32), "150 aircraft were destroyed."

111. Smith, *Hellcats*, 50.

112. Yellen, *Our Mothers' War*, 22.

113. Laura Schumm, "America's Patriotic Victory Gardens," History Stories, History Channel, August 31, 2018. URL: https://www.history.com/news/americas-patriotic-victory-gardens. Accessed August 5, 2020.

114. George Q. Flynn, *The Draft, 1940–1973* (Lawrence, KS: University Press of Kansas, 1993), 58–59.

115. Albert A. Blum, *Drafted or Deferred: Practices Past and Present* (Ann Arbor, MI: University of Michigan Press, 1967), 44.

116. Peyton, *5,000 Miles*, 95.

117. Smith, *Hellcats*, 56–66.

118. Dacus and Kitzmann, *As We Lived It*, 56; *Air Group Sixty, 1943–1944*, 37.

119. See Elizabeth Temkin, "Driving Through: Postpartum Care During World War II," *American Journal of Public Health* 89, no. 4 (April 1999): 588, and Louise K. Martell, "The Hospital and the Postpartum Experience: A Historical Analysis," *Journal of Obstetric, Gynecologic, & Neonatal Nursing (JOGNN)* 29, no. 1 (January 2000): 65–72. URL: https://www.jognn.org/article/S0884-2175(15)33798-9/fulltext. Accessed February 8, 2021.

120. Martell, "The Hospital and the Postpartum Experience."

121. This trend continued, declining to a low of 1.1 days in 1995, when the medical profession pointed out potentially harmful effects of early postpartum discharges. (See, for example, Rawad Farhat and Mariam Rajab, "Length of Postnatal Hospital Stay in Healthy Newborns and Re-Hospitalization Following Discharge," *North American Journal of Medical Sciences* 3, no. 3, [March 2011]: 146–51.) This ultimately led to the passage of a federal law that mandated insurance companies to cover a hospital stay of at least 48 hours for a mother and newborn following a vaginal birth. At least 24 hours after birth is recommended by the World Health Organization, because the first 24 hours are critical for monitoring the baby's and the mother's health.

122. For example, M. H. Klaus et al., "Maternal Attachment: Importance of the First Post-partum Days," *New England Journal of Medicine* 286, no. 9 (March 1972): 460–3.

123. Martell, "The Hospital and the Postpartum Experience."

124. Smith, *Hellcats*, 64–65.

125. Peyton, *5,000 Miles*, 101.

126. Smith, *Hellcats*, 71.

127. *Ibid.*, 71–72.

128. *Ibid.*, 71.

129. Morison, *History of United States Naval Operations, Vol. 8*, 162.

130. *Ibid.*, 160.

131. Robert Lee Sherrod, *On to Westward: The Battles of Saipan and Iwo Jima* (Baltimore, MD: Nautical and Aviation Publication Company of America, 1990), 33.

132. Morison, *History of United States Naval Operations, Vol. 8*, 166.

133. *Ibid.*, 197.

134. *Ibid.*, 194.

135. The Japanese had reason to believe that they could prevail, although crucial facts only became known long after the battle. They counted on using airbases at Guam and Rota for additional support and refueling. In addition, their lighter planes had a greater range, so that they could attack from a farther distance, taking off "while their carriers were still between 400 and 700 miles away from" the American fleet. "Then they would take advantage of their island bases to land and refuel on Guam and nearby Rota. By the time the task force could close within range to strike back at them, their planes would

be back aboard the carriers." Unfortunately for the Japanese, U.S. aircraft had damaged Marianas airfields and all but eliminated Japanese air strength on Guam before the Battle of the Philippine Sea began. (Peyton, *5,000 Miles*, 110.)

136. Morison, *History of United States Naval Operations, Vol. 8*, 318.

137. U.S.S. *Suwannee*, Aircraft Action Report 4-44, 6/16/1944.

138. U.S.S. *Suwannee*, Report of Anti-Submarine Action by Aircraft, 6/19/1944.

139. Smith, *Hellcats*, 80.

140. Michael J. Davidson, "Friendly Fire and the Limits of the Military Justice System," *Naval War College Review* 64, no. 1 (Winter 2011): 125.

141. Charles R. Shrader, "Friendly Fire," in *The Oxford Companion to American Military History*, ed. John Whiteclay Chambers II (New York: Oxford University Press, 1999), 284.

142. Shrader, "Friendly Fire."

143. Peyton, *5,000 Miles*, 108.

144. Smith, *Hellcats*, 81.

145. Dacus and Kitzmann, *As We Lived It*, 64; U.S.S. *Suwannee*, Serial 069, Action Report, Marianas Operation, 10/2/1944; U.S.S. *Suwannee*, Aircraft Action Report No. 13-44, 6/25/1944.

146. Peyton, *5,000 Miles*, 113.

147. Morison, *History of United States Naval Operations, Vol. 8*, 336.

148. *Ibid.*, 339.

149. Samuel A. Stouffer et al., *The American Soldier: Adjustment During Army Life*, Vol. 1 (Princeton, NJ: Princeton University Press, 1949), 448.

150. *Ibid.*, 449, 451.

151. Smith, *Hellcats*, 76.

152. Thomas D. Morgan, "The Industrial Mobilization of World War II: America Goes to War," *Army History* 30 (Spring 1994): 33.

153. See "Paternity," by William Rose Benet, in *The Lyric Year: One Hundred Poems*, ed. Ferdinand Earle (New York: Mitchell Kennerley, 1912), 11–12.

154. An excellent account of the initial stages of the Battle of Tinian is John Bishop, "The Trick That Won a Steppingstone to Japan," *Saturday Evening Post*, December 23, 1944, 64–66.

155. Morison, *History of United States Naval Operations, Vol. 8*, 369.

156. *Ibid.*, 374.

157. "Some Records Aboard Ship," in *Air Group Sixty, 1943–1944*, 41.

158. Smith, *Hellcats*, 90–91.

159. *Ibid.*, 91–92.

160. *Ibid.*, 92.

161. Robert J. Rielly, "Confronting the Tiger: Small Unit Cohesion in Battle," *Military Review* 80, no. 6 (November-December 2000): 61–65. URL: https://usacac.

army.mil/sites/default/files/documents/cace/DCL/DCL_SmallUnitCohesion.pdf. Accessed July 18, 2021.

162. Smith, *Hellcats*, 92.

163. Morison, *History of United States Naval Operations, Vol. 8*, 400.

164. *Ibid.*, 339.

165. David Owen, "Turning Tricks: The Rise and Fall of Contract Bridge," *The New Yorker*, September 17, 2007. URL: https://www.newyorker.com/magazine/2007/09/17/turning-tricks. Accessed: June 22, 2021.

166. Smith, *Hellcats*, 100.

167. Peyton, *5,000 Miles*, 118.

168. *Ibid.*, 121.

169. Smith, *Hellcats*, 102.

170. *Ibid.*, 101.

171. As provided under the Philippine Independence Act, the Philippines became a Commonwealth government in 1935 in preparation for its independence from the United States.

172. Walter R. Borneman, *MacArthur at War: World War II in the Pacific* (New York: Little Brown, 2016), 60.

173. *Ibid.*, 158.

174. Carsten Fries, "Operation Stalemate II: The Battle of Peleliu, 15 September–27 November 1944," Naval History and Heritage Command. URL: https://www.history. navy.mil/browse-by-topic/wars-conflicts-and-operations/world-war-ii/1944/peleliu. html. Accessed April 14, 2023.

175. Morison, *History of United States Naval Operations, Vol. 12*, 19–20.

176. Robert Ross Smith, *The Approach to the Philippines (U.S. Army in World War II, The War in the Pacific)* (Washington, D.C.: Office of the Chief of Military History, Department of the Army, 1953), 480.

177. This account of the air–sea rescue draws on several sources: Morison, *History of United States Naval Operations, Vol. 12*, 26–27; U.S.S. *Suwannee*, Serial 073, Action Report, Morotai Operation, 10/02/1944; Peyton, *5,000 Miles*, 123–26; and Y'Blood, *The Little Giants*, 103–106.

178. Y'Blood, *The Little Giants*, 105–106.

179. Smith, *Hellcats*, 107.

180. Y'Blood, *The Little Giants*, 105.

181. R. R. Smith, *The Approach to the Philippines*, 491–92.

182. This is a version of a poem entitled "Love," by Mary Carolyn Davies. When it first appeared in a 1936 poetry anthology it was misattributed to the pseudonym "Roy Croft."

183. Smith, *Hellcats*, 114.

184. Quoted in Y'Blood, *The Little Giants*, 90.

185. Y'Blood, *The Little Giants*, 116.

186. Smith, *Hellcats*, 115.

187. *Ibid.*

188. Dacus and Kitzmann, *As We Lived It*, 86.

189. Smith, *Hellcats*, 117.

190. *Ibid.*

191. Matthew A. Baum and Samuel Kernell, "Economic Class and Popular Support for Franklin Roosevelt in War and Peace," *Public Opinion Quarterly* 65, no. 2 (June 2001): 198–229.

192. Thomas J. Cutler, *The Battle of Leyte Gulf: 23–26 October 1944* (New York: HarperCollins, 1994), xiii.

193. Smith, *Hellcats*, 118.

194. Borneman, *MacArthur at War*, 426.

195. Y'Blood, *The Little Giants*, 123.

196. *Ibid.*, 128.

197. Borneman, *MacArthur at War*, 428.

198. Peyton, *5,000 Miles*, 158.

199. Y'Blood, *The Little Giants*, 137.

200. Morison, *History of United States Naval Operations, Vol. 12*, 72.

201. *Ibid.*, 175.

202. *Ibid.*, 186; Cutler, *The Battle of Leyte Gulf*, 147.

203. Mark E. Stille, *Leyte Gulf: A New History of the World's Largest Sea Battle* (Oxford, UK: Osprey, 2023), 136.

204. Morison, *History of United States Naval Operations, Vol. 12*, 58.

205. Cutler, *The Battle of Leyte Gulf*, 162–63.

206. Morison, *History of United States Naval Operations, Vol. 12*, 194.

207. Cutler, *The Battle of Leyte Gulf*, 209.

208. Y'Blood, *The Little Giants*, 205.

209. Miller, *War at Sea*, 469.

210. Thomas, *Sea of Thunder*, 285.

211. Stille, *Leyte Gulf*, 194–95.

212. Cutler, *The Battle of Leyte Gulf*, 235.

213. *Ibid.*, 261.

214. Thomas, *Sea of Thunder*, 295.

215. Cutler, *The Battle of Leyte Gulf*, 116.

216. Dacus and Kitzmann, *As We Lived It*, 96.

217. Smith, *Hellcats*, 124.

218. Y'Blood, *The Little Giants*, 143.

219. *Ibid.*, 117.

220. Bernard Millot, *Divine Thunder: The Life and Death of the Kamikazes*, trans. Lowell Blair (New York: McCall, 1970), 5.

221. Cutler, *The Battle of Leyte Gulf*, 267.

222. Millot, *Divine Thunder*, 39.

223. "Moment of Impact–The Story of the USS *Suwannee*," YouTube video. URL: https://www.youtube.com/watch?v=3X2gFKF5r40&t=2059s. Accessed: August 5, 2022.

224. Smith, *Hellcats*, 145.

225. USS *Suwannee* War Diary, 10/1–30/44, National Archives, Record Group 38: Records of the Chief of Naval Operations, 11–13. URL: https://catalog.archives. gov/id/139867144. Accessed: September 14, 2023.

226. Dacus and Kitzmann, *As We Lived It*, 112.

227. *Ibid.*, 118.

228. *Ibid.*, 115.

229. *Ibid.*, 116.

230. *Ibid.*, 118.

231. Smith, *Hellcats*, 143.

232. Dacus and Kitzmann, *As We Lived It*, 113.

233. Cutler, *The Battle of Leyte Gulf*, 272; Thomas, *Sea of Thunder*, 303.

234. Y'Blood, *The Little Giants*, 235.

235. For example, neither Cutler, *The Battle of Leyte Gulf*, nor Thomas, *Sea of Thunder*, makes any reference to the second kamikaze attack on the *Suwannee*. In *Afternoon of the Rising Sun: The Battle of Leyte Gulf* (Novata, Calif.: Presidio Press, 2001), Kenneth I. Friedman does not cover any of the kamikaze attacks, perhaps because, as he states, "naval historians and analysts . . . [assert] "that the Kamikaze Corps's attacks had no major effect on the Leyte Gulf naval battles" (p. 28).

236. Smith, *Hellcats*, 150.

237. U.S.S. *Suwannee*, Serial 008, Action Report, Leyte Operation, Enclosure F: Executive Officer's Report, 11/6/1944.

238. *Ibid.*, 2–3.

239. *Ibid.*, 5.

240. *Ibid.*, 2.

241. Interview with John DiGiovine, "Moment of Impact."

242. Dacus and Kitzmann, *As We Lived It*, 127, 129.

243. U.S.S. *Suwannee*, Serial 008, Executive Officer's Report, 1.

244. Smith, *Hellcats*, 158.

245. USS *Suwannee* War Diary, 11–17.

246. Smith, *Hellcats*, 158.

247. Morison, *History of United States Naval Operations, Vol. 12*, 337.

248. See Alan Rems, "Seven Decades of Debate," *Naval History Magazine* 31, no. 5 (October 2017): 20–25; Stille, *Leyte Gulf*, 261–63.

249. Michael S. Sweeney, *Secrets of Victory: The Office of Censorship and the American Press and Radio in World War II* (Chapel Hill, NC: University of North Carolina Press, 2001), 85.

250. "Captain's Memo Following Leyte," Suwannee Links, U.S.S. *Suwannee* (CVE 27) website. URL: http://www.usssuwannee.org/images/Cpt.%20Johnson%20Memo. pdf. Accessed August 10, 2022.

251. Bill Gordon, "Kamikaze Images: American Views," December 15, 2004. URL: https://www.kamikazeimages.net/american/index.htm. Accessed August 10, 2022.

252. "U.S. Carrier Hit in Leyte Battle," *Oklahoma City Times,* April 5, 1945, 1.

253. Virtually all the men lost aboard the Suwannee were buried at sea. They were, however, memorialized at the Manila American Cemetery.

254. Dacus and Kitzmann, *As We Lived It*, 127, 136.

255. Walter B. Burwell, "Oral Histories–Battle of Leyte Gulf, 23–35, October 1945" (adapted from "The First Kamikaze," *Navy Medicine* 85, no. 5 (Sep.-Oct. 1994): 6–11, Naval History and Heritage Command. URL: https://www.history.navy.mil/ research/library/oral-histories/wwii/battle-of-leyte-gulf-lt-burwell.html. Accessed August 10, 2022.

256. Smith, *Hellcats*, 167.

257. Samuel Eliot Morison, *History of United States Naval Operations in World War II, Volume 13: The Liberation of the Philippines, Luzon, Mindanao, the Visayas, 1944–1945* (Boston: Little, Brown, 1959), 5.

258. Millot, *Divine Thunder*, 55–56.

259. Sources differ on the number of U.S. ships sunk by kamikazes. Bill Gordon analyzed two oft-cited sources to arrive at these estimates. See Bill Gordon, "Kamikaze Images: 47 Ships Sunk by Kamikaze Aircraft," July 10, 2010. URL: https://www. kamikazeimages.net/background/ships-sunk/index.htm. Accessed February 18, 2023.

260. Morison, *History of United States Naval Operations, Vol. 13*, 213–17.

261. Samuel Eliot Morison, *History of United States Naval Operations in World War II, Volume 14: Victory in the Pacific, 1945* (Boston: Little, Brown, 1960), 92; James H. Belote and William M Belote, *Typhoon of Steel: The Battle for Okinawa* (New York: Harper and Row, 1970), 31.

262. Morison, *History of United States Naval Operations, Vol. 14*, 13.

263. *Ibid.*, 16.

264. Four days after the landing, Marines raised the stars and stripes atop Mount Suribachi. An Associated Press photographer got a picture of the six Marines raising the flag. Two days later it appeared in Sunday papers across the nation, and it became an iconic image of the Battle of Iwo Jima and the Pacific War.

265. Bill D. Ross, *Iwo Jima: Legacy of Valor* (New York: Vanguard, 1985), viii.

266. Bill Sloan, *The Ultimate Battle: Okinawa 1945—The Last Epic Struggle of World War II* (New York: Simon and Schuster, 2007), 14–15; Morison, *History of United States Naval Operations, Vol. 14*, 102.

267. Belote and Belote, *Typhoon of Steel*, 31–32.

268. George Feifer, *Tennozan: The Battle of Okinawa and the Atomic Bomb* (New York: Ticknor and Fields, 1992), 236.

269. Sloan, *The Ultimate Battle*, 327.

270. Feifer, *Tennozan*, 533.

271. Morison, *History of United States Naval Operations, Vol. 14*, 282.

272. There was disagreement, however, about the necessity of an invasion to force Japan to surrender. Admiral King, who had reluctantly supported the JCS decision, believed that a continuing campaign of blockade and bombardment could bring an end to the war. By late summer, a U.S. blockade had brought Japanese shipping within and outside the islands to near collapse. And beginning on the night of March 9–10, Major General Curtis Lemay, commander of the B29 Superfortresses, instituted a ruthless strategy of mass incendiary attacks on Japanese cities. In the first raid, on Tokyo, B-29s dropped 1,600 tons of napalm that incinerated 15.8 square miles of the city, destroyed over 250,000 homes, and killed as many as 100,000 people. By August, the bombers had torched another 60 cities. See Richard B. Frank, "Ending the Pacific War, No alternative to annihilation," in *The Pacific War Companion: From Pearl Harbor to Hiroshima*, ed. Daniel Marston (Oxford, UK: Osprey, 2005), 229; Alvin D. Coox, "Strategic Bombing in the Pacific, 1942–1945," in *Case Studies in Strategic Bombardment*, ed. R. Cargill Hall (Washington, DC: Air Force history and Museums Program, 1998), 253–382. URL: https://media.defense.gov/2010/Oct/12/2001330115/-1/-1/0/AFD-101012-036.pdf. Accessed May 5, 2023.

273. Miller, *War at Sea*, 529.

274. Frank, "Ending the Pacific War," 231.

275. Belote and Belote, *Typhoon of Steel*, 324.

276. Estimates of the number of people who died from the atomic bombing of Hiroshima and Nagasaki vary. Alex Weinstein suggests that the best way of reporting estimates is to make authorship claims more explicit. For example, "The United States estimated that around 70,000 people died at Hiroshima, though later independent estimates argued that the actual number was 140,000 dead." Comparable figures for Nagasaki were 40,000 and 70,000, respectively. Alex Wellerstein, "Counting the Dead at Hiroshima and Nagasaki," *Bulletin of the Atomic Scientists*, August 4, 2020. URL: https://thebulletin.org/2020/08/counting-the-dead-at-hiroshima-and-nagasaki/. Accessed May 5, 2023.

277. "The Effects of Atomic Bombs on Hiroshima and Nagasaki," Atomic Archive. URL: https://www.atomicarchive.com/resources/documents/bombing-survey/section_I.html. Accessed May 5, 2023.

278. At the time, the consensus was that the use of atomic weapons was justified because it brought a swift end to the conflict and saved lives by avoiding an invasion. The final battles and Japanese preparation for an invasion indicated that those in command were not close to capitulating. Even after the atom bombs were dropped, Japanese militarists strongly opposed surrender. Still, the decision to use the atom bomb was

controversial and its military and ethical justification have been debated extensively. See, for example, Frank, "Ending the Pacific War"; Robert P. Newman, *Enola Gay and the Court of History* (New York: Peter Lang, 2004); and Elbridge Colby, "Terrible but Justified: The U.S. A-bomb Attacks on Hiroshima and Nagasaki," Center for a New American Security, September 29, 2015. (URL: https://www.cnas.org/publications/commentary/terrible-but-justified-the-u-s-a-bomb-attacks-on-hiroshima-and-nagasaki. Accessed May 5, 2023.

279. John Glenn with Nick Taylor, *John Glenn: A Memoir* (New York: Bantam Books, 1999), 95.

280. From 1945 to 1949, Navy and Marine forces were deployed in China to support Chiang Kai-shek's Nationalist forces, which was involved in a civil war against Mao Tse-tung's communists. U.S. foreign policy walked a tightrope in supporting Chiang while trying to stay clear of the internal Chinese conflict. See Edward J. Marolda, "Asian Warm-up to the Cold War," *Naval History Magazine* 25, no. 5 (October 2011): 26–32. URL: https://www.usni.org/magazines/naval-history-magazine/2011/october/asian-warm-cold-war. Accessed March 21, 2023.

281. Jack Smith, "What Did They Do After the *Suwannee* (Continued)," *U.S.S. Suwannee CVE 27 Newsletter*, Winter 2008. URL: https://www.usssuwannee.org/2008winter.pdf. Accessed May 5, 2023.

282. *Ibid.*

283. Richard G. Tedeschi, Jane Shakespeare-Finch, Kanako Taku, and Lawrence G. Calhoun, *Posttraumatic Growth: Theory, Research, and Applications* (New York: Routledge, 2018).

284. Dacus and Kitzmann, *As We Lived It*, B1.

285. Sherna Berger Gluck, *Rosie the Riveter Revisited: Women, the War, and Social Change* (New York: Meridian [Penguin], 1987), 259.

286. D'Ann Campbell, *Women at War with America: Private Lives in a Patriotic Era* (Cambridge, MA: Harvard University Press, 1984), 210.

287. *Ibid.,* 211–12.

SELECTED BIBLIOGRAPHY

Anderson, Karen. *Wartime Women: Sex Roles, Family Relations, and the Status of Women During World War II.* Westport, CT: Greenwood Press, 1981.

Belote, James H., and William M Belote. *Typhoon of Steel: The Battle for Okinawa.* New York: Harper and Row, 1970.

Blum, Albert A. *Drafted or Deferred: Practices Past and Present.* Ann Arbor, MI: University of Michigan Press, 1967.

Borneman, Walter R. *MacArthur at War: World War II in the Pacific.* New York: Little Brown, 2016.

Bradley, James, with Ron Powers. *Flags of Our Fathers: Heroes of Iwo Jima.* New York: Bantam Books, 2000.

Campbell, D'Ann. *Women at War with America: Private Lives in a Patriotic Era.* Cambridge, MA: Harvard University, 1984.

Chief of Naval Operations, Office of. "U. S. Naval Aviation in the Pacific." Naval History and Heritage Command. United States Navy, 1947. Accessed January 1, 2023. https://www.history.navy.mil/content/dam/nhhc/research/histories/naval-aviation/ USNavalAviationInthePacific/pacific.pdf

Crowl, Philip A., and Edmund G. Love. *The War in the Pacific: Seizure of the Gilberts and Marshalls.* Washington, DC: Center of Military History, United States Army, 1993.

Cutler, Thomas J. *The Battle of Leyte Gulf: 23–26 October 1944.* New York: HarperCollins, 1994.

Dacus, W. R., and E. Kitzmann. *As We Lived It: U.S.S. Suwannee Air Groups 27, 60, and 40.* U.S.S. *Suwannee* Reunion Association, 1992.

Feifer, George. *Tennozan: The Battle of Okinawa and the Atomic Bomb.* New York: Ticknor and Fields, 1992.

Flynn, George Q. *The Draft, 1940–1973.* Lawrence, KS: University Press of Kansas, 1993.

Frank, Richard B. "Ending the Pacific War, No alternative to annihilation." In *The Pacific War Companion: From Pearl Harbor to Hiroshima,* edited by Daniel Marston, 227–45. Oxford, UK: Osprey, 2005.

Gallup, George. *The Gallup Poll: Public Opinion, 1935–1971*. Bloomington, IN: Indiana University Press, 1972.

Gladwell, Malcolm. *The Bomber Mafia: A Dream, a Temptation, and The Longest Night of the Second World War*. New York: Little, Brown, 2021.

Glenn, John, with Nick Taylor. *John Glenn: A Memoir*. New York: Bantam Books, 1999.

Gluck, Sherna Berger. *Rosie the Riveter Revisited: Women, the War, and Social Change*. New York: Meridian [Penguin], 1987.

Jeffries, John W. *Wartime America: The World War II Home Front*. Chicago: Ivan R. Dee, 1996.

King, Ernest Joseph, and Walter Muir Whitehill. *Fleet Admiral King*. New York: Norton, 1952.

Litoff, Judy Barrett, David C. Smith, Barbara Wooddall Taylor, and Charles E. Taylor. *Miss You: The World War II Letters of Barbara Wooddall Taylor and Charles E. Taylor*. Athens, GA: University of Georgia, 1990.

Manchester William. *Goodbye Darkness: A Memoir of the Pacific War*. Boston: Little-Brown, 1980.

Miller, Nathan. *War at Sea: A Naval History of World War II*. New York: Oxford University Press, 1995.

Millot, Bernard. *Divine Thunder: The Life and Death of the Kamikazes*. Translated by Lowell Bair. New York: McCall, 1970.

Morison, Samuel Eliot. *History of United States Naval Operations in World War II, Volume 5: The Struggle for Guadalcanal, August 1942–February 1943*. Boston: Little, Brown, 1951.

———. *History of United States Naval Operations in World War II, Volume 7: Aleutians, Gilberts, and Marshalls, June 1942–April 1944*. Boston: Little, Brown, 1951.

———. *History of United States Naval Operations in World War II, Volume 8: New Guinea and the Marianas, March 1944–August 1944*. Boston: Little, Brown, 1953.

———. *History of United States Naval Operations in World War II, Volume 12: Leyte, June 1944–January 1945*. Boston: Little, Brown, 1958.

———. *History of United States Naval Operations in World War II, Volume 13: The Liberation of the Philippines, Luzon, Mindanao, the Visayas, 1944–1945*. Boston: Little, Brown, 1959.

———. *History of United States Naval Operations in World War II, Volume 14: Victory in the Pacific, 1945*. Boston: Little, Brown, 1960.

———. *The Two-Ocean War: A Short History of the United States Navy in the Second World War*. Boston: Little, Brown, 1963.

Peyton, Green. *5,000 Miles towards Tokyo*. Norman, OK: University of Oklahoma Press, 1945.

Ross, Bill D. *Iwo Jima: Legacy of Valor*. New York: Vanguard, 1985.

Scott, James M. *Target Tokyo: Jimmy Doolittle and the Raid That Avenged Pearl Harbor.* New York: W.W. Norton, 2015.

Sherrod, Robert Lee. *On to Westward: The Battles of Saipan and Iwo Jima.* Baltimore, MD: Nautical and Aviation Publication Company of America, 1990.

———. *Tarawa: The Story of a Battle.* New York: Duell, Sloan, and Pearce, 1944.

Shrader, Charles R. "Friendly Fire." In *The Oxford Companion to American Military History,* edited by John Whiteclay Chambers II, 284. New York: Oxford University Press, 1999.

Sloan, Bill. *The Ultimate Battle: Okinawa 1945—The Last Epic Struggle of World War II.* New York: Simon and Schuster, 2007.

Smith, John F. *Hellcats over the Philippine Deep.* Manhattan, KS: Sunflower University Press, 1995.

Smith, Robert Ross. *The Approach to the Philippines.* Washington, D.C.: Office of the Chief of Military History, Department of the Army, 1953.

Stille, Mark E. *Leyte Gulf: A New History of the World's Largest Sea Battle.* Oxford, UK: Osprey, 2023.

———. *US Navy Escort Carriers: 1942–1945.* New York: Osprey, 2017.

Stouffer, Samuel A. et al. *The American Soldier: Adjustment During Army Life,* Vol. 1. Princeton, NJ: Princeton University Press, 1949.

Sweeney, Michael S. *Secrets of Victory: The Office of Censorship and the American Press and Radio in World War II.* Chapel Hill, NC: University of North Carolina Press, 2001.

Tedeschi, Richard G., Jane Shakespeare-Finch, Kanako Taku, and Lawrence G. Calhoun. *Posttraumatic Growth: Theory, Research, and Applications.* New York: Routledge, 2018.

Thomas, Evan. *Sea of Thunder: Four Commanders and the Last Great Naval Campaign 1941–1945.* New York: Simon and Schuster, 2006.

Tillman, Barrett. "'Go West Young Man': The War in the Pacific." In *The History of US Naval Air Power,* edited by Robert L. Lawson, 59–101. New York: The Military Press, 1985.

Y'Blood, William T. *The Little Giants: U.S. Escort Carriers Against Japan.* Annapolis, MD: Naval Institute Press, 1987.

Yellin, Emily. *Our Mother's War: American Women at Home and at the Front During World War II.* New York: Free Press, 2004.

INDEX

ABOUT THE AUTHOR

Royce A. Singleton, Jr. is a sociologist specializing in social psychology and research methodology. Now retired, he held teaching positions at the University of California, Riverside (1972-1977) and the College of the Holy Cross (1977-2009). He is the co-author of *Oppression: A Socio-History of Black-White Relations in America* (Nelson-Hall, 1984) and two text-books on methods of social research published by Oxford University Press: *Approaches to Social Research* (Sixth Edition, 2018) and *The Process of Social Research* (Third Edition, 2023). He lives in Holden, Massachusetts, with his wife, Nancy.

Made in United States
North Haven, CT
09 March 2024

49774670R00207